PEARSON EDEXCEL INTERNATIONAL
GCSE (9–1)

ENGLISH AS A SECOND LANGUAGE

Student Book

Nicky Winder
Laurence Gardner

Published by Pearson Education Limited, 80 Strand, London, WC2R 0RL.

www.pearsonglobalschools.com

Copies of official specifications for all Pearson qualifications may be found on the website: https://qualifications.pearson.com

Text © Pearson Education Limited 2017
Edited by Lauren Bickley
Development edited by Bridget Kelly and Andy Pozzoni
Designed by Cobalt id
Typeset by Tech-Set Ltd, Gateshead, UK
Cover design by Pearson Education Limited
Picture research by Louise Edgeworth
Cover photo © Getty Images: Laurie Campbell/Nature Picture Library

The rights of Nicky Winder and Laurence Gardner to be identified as authors of this work have been asserted by them in accordance with the Copyright, Designs and Patents Act 1988.

First published 2017

21

10 9 8 7

British Library Cataloguing in Publication Data
A catalogue record for this book is available from the British Library

ISBN 978 0 435 18894 8

Printed in Slovakia by Neografia

Acknowledgements
The author and publisher would like to thank the following individuals and organisations for permission to reproduce photographs:

(Key: b-bottom; c-centre; l-left; r-right; t-top)

123RF.com: 21, 78 (e), 78 (h), 97 (c), 143b, Alexander Atkishkin 214 (d), alicephoto 162, Antonio Guillem 184, anyka 84 (c), dolgachov 181, feverpitched 62, filiz kavasoglu gureke 236 (f), georgejmclittle 163, Irina Burakova 204br, Katarzyna Białasiewicz 241, marigranula 78 (b), mexitographer 80, Nikolay Neveshkin 87t, Sergejs Rahunoks 204tc, Songquan Deng 122b, tarzhanova 98, tnn103eda 52t, Tomas Marek 87 (b), veryolivephotography 78 (f), Vladislav Zhukov 194 (d), vvoennyy 210, Александр Ермолаев 84 (b); **Alamy Stock Photo**: 87 (e), Adwo 169, Aflo Col, Ltd 199, Amanda Cotton 229, Ben Nicholson 239, Cosmin-Constantin Sava 84 (d), Craig McAteer 97t, Dinodia Photos 104, H. Mark Weidman Photography 52b, Hero Images Inc. 94, Image Source Salsa 93, INTERFOTO 87 (c), James Armstrong 6, Jeff Rotman 228, Julio Bulnes 99, Kevin Wheal 194 (c), Lev Dolgachov 76, Nik Taylor Wildlife 84 (a), Paul Hakimata 201, PhotoAlto 212, The Print Collector 27, Tim Graham 101, UrbanImages 97 (a), Vladimir Nenezic 156t, Wavebreakmedia Ltd PH23L 109 (a), Zoonar GmbH 87 (f); **Getty Images:** Alija / E+ 106, 120, 160, 192, Arctic-Images / DigitalVision 234, mbbirdy / E+ 68, Michael H / Stone 36, Opla / E+ 2; **Pearson Education Ltd:** Tudor Photography 214 (b), Sozaijiten 78 (a); PhotoDisc: Photolink 87 (d); **Shutterstock.com:** 1653286 204tr, aceshot1 236 (a), Africa Studio 43b, 56, 142b, 178, Alexander Image 116/3, 176, Alhovik 214 (c), Alones 142t, Alsu 214 (a), Amnarj Tanongrattana 130, Andrey N Bannov 17b, angellodeco 13, Angelo Ferraris 128, Arch MerciGod 87 (a), arek_malang 58t, aroonrojkul 174, Bikeworldtravel 97 (b), Caron Badkin 5, CCParis 242, Chaikovskiy Igor 122t, Cocos.Bounty 236 (d), Costazzurra 143t, Dan Breckwoldt 146/4, David Ionut 146/6, De Repente 109 (c), Denis Dryashkin 155, Ditty_about_summer 194 (e), Dustin Dennis 38b, Elena Larina 15t, Erik Lam 78 (c), etraveler 97 (d), Fabrik Bilder 4t, Fotochip 4b, g-stockstudio 38t, 109 (d), Galyna Andrushko 42, Gelpi 58b, goodluz 116/1, Happy Together 202, Herschel Hoffmeyer 29, hlphoto 179, I T A L O 194 (f), Iakov Kalinin 131b, Igor Plotnikov 146/5, IgorSolovey 26, Ilona Ignatova 146/2, Ilya Andriyanov 34l, InnerVisionPRO 116/4, Janis Smits 236 (e), juefraphoto 204tl, KAZLOVA IRYNA 236 (c), Keith Levit 204bl, KieferPix 173, Kjersti Joergensen 60, ksb 209, Lonely 147, Lukas Gojda 48, Izf 194 (a), margouillat photo 188, Martin Mecnarowski 224, Mazzzur 146/1, mbonaparte 156b, Mike Mareen 50, mjurik 219, Monika Wisniewska 214 (f), Monkey Business Images 70r, 166, Mooshny 168, New Mindflow 236 (b), Nonchanon 146/3, Odua Images 66, 75, Okssi 43t, Oleksiy Rezin 194 (b), Olena Yakobchuk 17t, paleontologist natural 33, Pan Xunbin 172, PCHT 34r, pics721 223, Pikoso.kz 23, Pressmaster 70l, 182, Rawpixel.com 164, Rex Wholster 131t, Rob Marmion 72, Rohappy 116/2, Ronnachai Palas 78t, salajandani 109 (b), Sean Pavone 170, Smileus 15b, stable 109 (f), svry 44, Sytilin Pavel 146l, Tatyana Vyc 41, Tawee wongdee 190, Thomas Duerrenberger 232, Tim Jenner 63, tinyowl7 84 (e), Tithi Luadthong 133, TunedIn by Westend61 109 (e), Vangert 78 (g), VICTOR TORRES 12, Vinicius Tupinamba 204bc, wavebreakmedia 22, XiXinXing 116/5, xpixel 78 (d), zhangyang13576997233 214 (e)

Inside front cover: **Shutterstock.com:** Dmitry Lobanov

All other images © Pearson Education

We are grateful to the following for permission to reproduce copyright material:

Text
Article on pages 135-6 from 'Driverless cars are going to save the world and I can't wait' The Telegraph, 16/05/2016 (Alex Proud), © Telegraph Media Group Limited 2016; Exercise on pages 148-9 from www.ancientegypt.co.uk/pyramids, © The Trustees of the British Museum, 2017

Endorsement statement
In order to ensure that this resource offers high-quality support for the associated Pearson qualification, it has been through a review process by the awarding body. This process confirms that this resource fully covers the teaching and learning content of the specification or part of a specification at which it is aimed. It also confirms that it demonstrates an appropriate balance between the development of subject skills, knowledge and understanding, in addition to preparation for assessment.

Endorsement does not cover any guidance on assessment activities or processes (e.g. practice questions or advice on how to answer assessment questions), included in the resource nor does it prescribe any particular approach to the teaching or delivery of a related course.

While the publishers have made every attempt to ensure that advice on the qualification and its assessment is accurate, the official specification and associated assessment guidance materials are the only authoritative source of information and should always be referred to for definitive guidance.

Pearson examiners have not contributed to any sections in this resource relevant to examination papers for which they have responsibility.

Examiners will not use endorsed resources as a source of material for any assessment set by Pearson. Endorsement of a resource does not mean that the resource is required to achieve this Pearson qualification, nor does it mean that it is the only suitable material available to support the qualification, and any resource lists produced by the awarding body shall include this and other appropriate resources.

UNIT	FOCUS	THEME	AOs	GRAMMAR
Reading Preparation	Reading Part 1 (p. 4)	Places to visit	1A	Countable and uncountable nouns Articles *some* and *any*
	Reading Part 2 (p. 15)	Celebrities, fame and entertainment	1B, 1C, 1D	Present simple Present continuous Present simple and present continuous
	Reading Part 3 (p. 27)	History and time	1B, 1C, 1D	Adjectives Comparative and superlative adjectives
Writing Preparation	Writing Part 4 (p. 38)	Food and drink	2A, 2B, 2C	Present perfect
	Writing Part 5 (p. 48)	Colours	2A, 2B, 2C	Past simple Past simple and present perfect
	Writing Part 6 (p. 58)	Speech and communication	2A, 2B, 2C, 2D	Past continuous and past simple *would* and *used to*
Listening Preparation	Listening Part 1 (p. 70)	The world of work	3A, 3B	*Wh-* questions and question tags Inversion
	Listening Part 2 (p. 78)	Pets	3B, 3D	*Wh-* questions and question tags Inversion
	Listening Part 3 (p. 87)	Games	3C, 3D	Adverbs of frequency Intensifiers
	Listening Part 4 (p. 97)	Shopping	3B, 3D	Passive
Speaking Preparation	Speaking (p. 108)	Fashion	4A, 4B, 4C	Past perfect Past tenses
Reading Practice	Reading Part 1 (p. 122)	Travel and hospitality	1A	Modal verbs (obligation, advice and permission)
	Reading Part 2 (p. 133)	Technology and the future	1B, 1C, 1D	*will* or *going to* Future simple and future continuous Future perfect Other ways to talk about the future
	Reading Part 3 (p. 146)	Buildings	1B, 1C, 1D	Conditionals (zero, first, second, third)
Writing Practice	Writing Part 4 (p. 162)	Work and jobs	2A, 2B, 2C	Perfect continuous tenses
	Writing Part 5 (p. 172)	Transport	2A, 2B, 2C	Possessives
	Writing Part 6 (p. 181)	Mind and body	2A, 2B, 2C, 2D	Linking words and phrases Discourse markers
Listening Practice	Listening Part 1 (p. 194)	Sport and fitness	3A, 3B	Modals in the past tense Modals of speculation and deduction
	Listening Part 2 (p. 204)	Science	3B, 3D	Gerunds and infinitives
	Listening Part 3 (p. 214)	People and language	3C, 3D	Relative pronouns and relative clauses Defining and non-defining relative clauses Reported speech
	Listening Part 4 (p. 223)	The environment	3B, 3D	*make* and *do*
Speaking Practice	Speaking (p. 236)	The home	4A, 4B, 4C	Tense review

VOCABULARY	EXAM SKILLS	PRACTICE TIME
Adjectives	Skimming and scanning Lexical words Sorting information	Tourist leaflet: 'Honeycomb Hives: the ultimate bee experience!'
Nouns (celebrities and fame)	Selection Identifying synonyms	Newspaper article: 'The shadow side of celebrity'
Phrasal verbs	Verifying information (true, false or not given) Identifying facts, ideas and opinions	Newspaper article: 'Amazing discovery of the Biggest Dinosaur Ever'
Collocations (food and drink)	Understanding register Relevance and word limit	Informal email: cooking a birthday meal
Idioms (colours)	Considering context and purpose Considering audience	Formal letter: school sports day
Verbs (communication)	Finding equivalent expressions Paraphrasing and summarising	Summary (Scientific journal: 'How babies talk')
Nouns (the world of work)	Listening for the overall message Listening for detail	Extracts: restaurants
Collocations (health and training)	Identifying detail Identifying viewpoints (stated and implied)	Dog-training advice
Adjectives and adverbs	Considering statements and implications Identifying facts and opinions	Interview with a writer
Verbs and expressions (shopping) Phrasal verbs (separable and non-separable)	Identifying important information and details	Changes in shopping patterns
Adjectives (fashion)	Speaking skills Pronunciation skills Intonation and stress	Fashion
Compound adjectives	Reflect and evaluate: Reading exam skills	Tourist brochure: 'London with Lonsdale Tours' Holiday leaflet: 'Halliday's Holidays'
Phrasal verbs	Reflect and evaluate: Reading exam skills	Newspaper articles: 'Driverless cars are going to save the world'; 'The Teaching Assistants of the Future?'
Nouns and verbs (buildings)	Reflect and evaluate: Reading exam skills	Website: 'Pyramids' Magazine article: 'Learning about the Leaning Tower!'
Phrasal verbs (work)	Reflect and evaluate: Writing exam skills	Informal emails: part-time jobs
Idioms and expressions (travel)	Reflect and evaluate: Writing exam skills	Report: transport Article: 'My favourite journey'
Collocations (mind and body)	Reflect and evaluate: Writing exam skills	Summaries (Journals: 'Adolescence – a time of challenges'; 'Maintaining emotional health')
Phrasal verbs (sport and fitness)	Reflect and evaluate: Listening exam skills	Extracts: sports venues Extracts: extreme sports
Phrasal verbs (separable and non-separable)	Reflect and evaluate: Listening exam skills	Lecture: moles Class talk: gemstones
Suffixes	Reflect and evaluate: Listening exam skills	Interview with a linguist Dialogue between teachers
Prefixes	Reflect and evaluate: Listening exam skills	Podcast: the wandering albatross School talk: the deep sea
Adjectives (the home)	Reflect and evaluate: Speaking exam skills	The home

ABOUT THIS BOOK

This book is written for students following the Pearson Edexcel International GCSE (9–1) English as a Second Language specification. It can be used for a two-year course, and can also be used flexibly to suit different classroom requirements.

English as a Second Language is a course which supports teachers and learners through cumulative language acquisition and practice, and encourages inter- and intra-personal as well as cognitive skills. The course promotes learner autonomy, for example, through the Writing and Grammar Reference materials included.

Learning objectives
Units and sections are carefully tailored to address key assessment objectives of language building and exam performance, central to the course.

The **Assessment Objectives** listed refer to the skills tested in this part of the exam.

Preparing the Way
The initial parts of the chapters are divided into **Preparing the Way**, where learners practice relevant language and contextualise, and **Focusing on the Exam / Exam Refreshers** which provide detailed guidance as to what to expect, and how to prepare for the exam throughout.

Grammar checkpoint / Vocabulary focus
A range of fun activities, including grammar games, provide practice for language points which are carefully picked to be suitable to the theme. An emphasis is placed on word building skills.

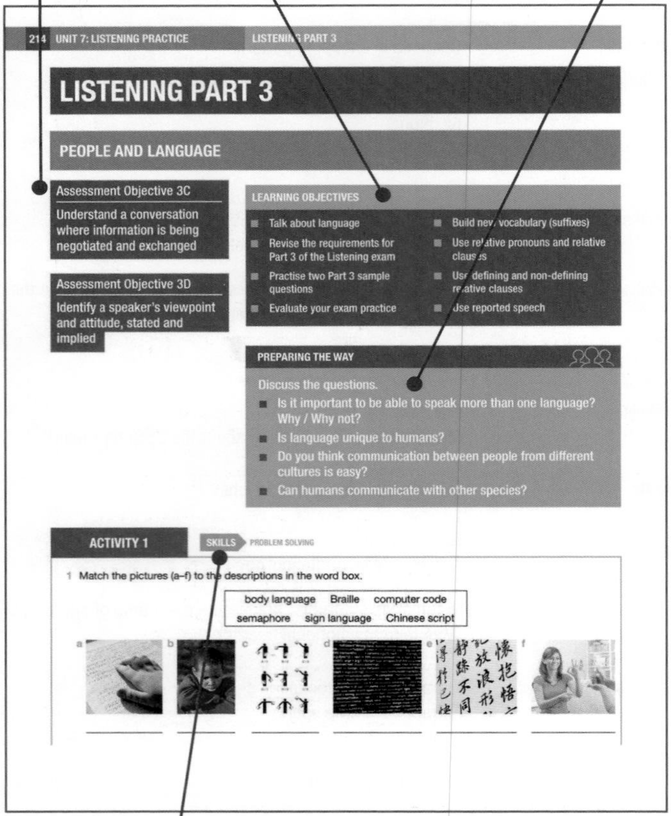
214 UNIT 7: LISTENING PRACTICE

LISTENING PART 3

PEOPLE AND LANGUAGE

Assessment Objective 3C
Understand a conversation where information is being negotiated and exchanged

Assessment Objective 3D
Identify a speaker's viewpoint and attitude, stated and implied

LEARNING OBJECTIVES
- Talk about language
- Revise the requirements for Part 3 of the Listening exam
- Practise two Part 3 sample questions
- Evaluate your exam practice
- Build new vocabulary (suffixes)
- Use relative pronouns and relative clauses
- Use defining and non-defining relative clauses
- Use reported speech

PREPARING THE WAY
Discuss the questions.
- Is it important to be able to speak more than one language? Why / Why not?
- Is language unique to humans?
- Do you think communication between people from different cultures is easy?
- Can humans communicate with other species?

ACTIVITY 1 SKILLS PROBLEM SOLVING

1 Match the pictures (a–f) to the descriptions in the word box.

body language Braille computer code
semaphore sign language Chinese script

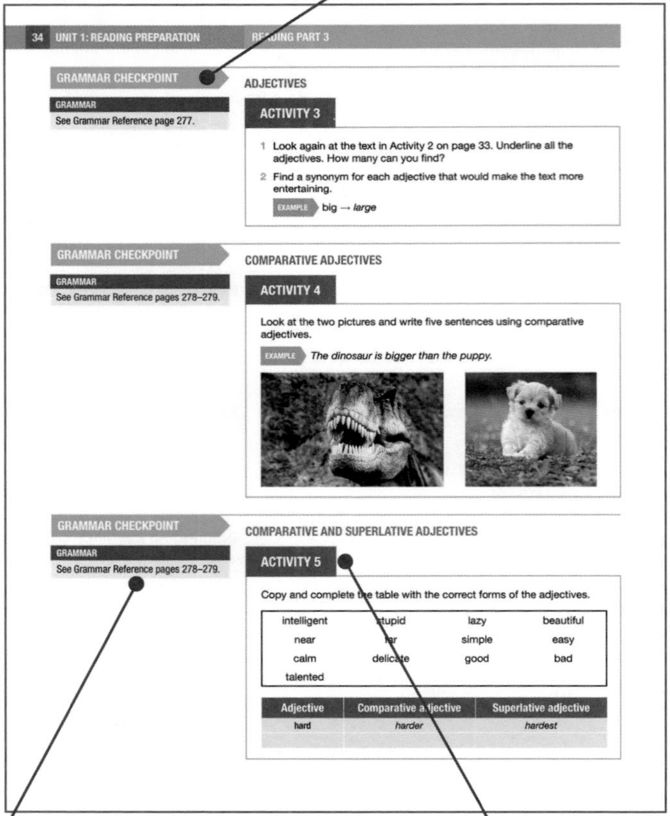
34 UNIT 1: READING PREPARATION

GRAMMAR CHECKPOINT
GRAMMAR
See Grammar Reference page 277.

ADJECTIVES

ACTIVITY 3
1 Look again at the text in Activity 2 on page 33. Underline all the adjectives. How many can you find?
2 Find a synonym for each adjective that would make the text more entertaining.
EXAMPLE big → *large*

GRAMMAR CHECKPOINT
GRAMMAR
See Grammar Reference pages 278–279.

COMPARATIVE ADJECTIVES

ACTIVITY 4
Look at the two pictures and write five sentences using comparative adjectives.
EXAMPLE *The dinosaur is bigger than the puppy.*

GRAMMAR CHECKPOINT
GRAMMAR
See Grammar Reference pages 278–279.

COMPARATIVE AND SUPERLATIVE ADJECTIVES

ACTIVITY 5
Copy and complete the table with the correct forms of the adjectives.

intelligent stupid lazy beautiful
near far simple easy
calm delicate good bad
talented

Adjective	Comparative adjective	Superlative adjective
hard	*harder*	*hardest*

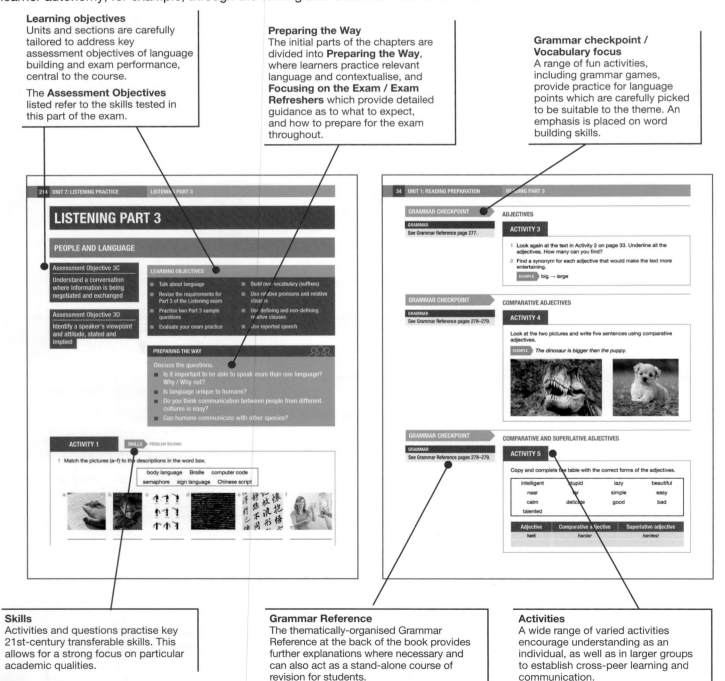

Skills
Activities and questions practise key 21st-century transferable skills. This allows for a strong focus on particular academic qualities.

Grammar Reference
The thematically-organised Grammar Reference at the back of the book provides further explanations where necessary and can also act as a stand-alone course of revision for students.

Activities
A wide range of varied activities encourage understanding as an individual, as well as in larger groups to establish cross-peer learning and communication.

The course is structured around the different parts of the examination. Each chapter is built around practice of one part of the examination paper. The course is divided into units: Reading, Writing, Listening and Speaking. The sections in one unit cover all the parts included in the exam – i.e. three parts each for Reading and Writing and four parts for Listening. The Speaking units have one section only.

The course is divided into two 'cycles': preparation and practice. In the first cycle, emphasis is placed on familiarising students with exam requirements and exam skills learning and practice. In the second cycle, extra guided exam practice is provided and students are given tips on monitoring and improving their performance.

Audio recordings and extra audioscripts are provided online and in the Teacher Resource Pack. This Student Book is supported by a Teacher's Book.

Exam Skills
Skills needed in the examination are presented and practised.

Glossary
Difficult terminology and useful words and phrases are colour coded within the main text. Concise and simple definitions are provided in the glossary at the back of the book, to support understanding of key subject terms.

Practice Time
The first part of each chapter prepares students to practise one part of the exam paper.

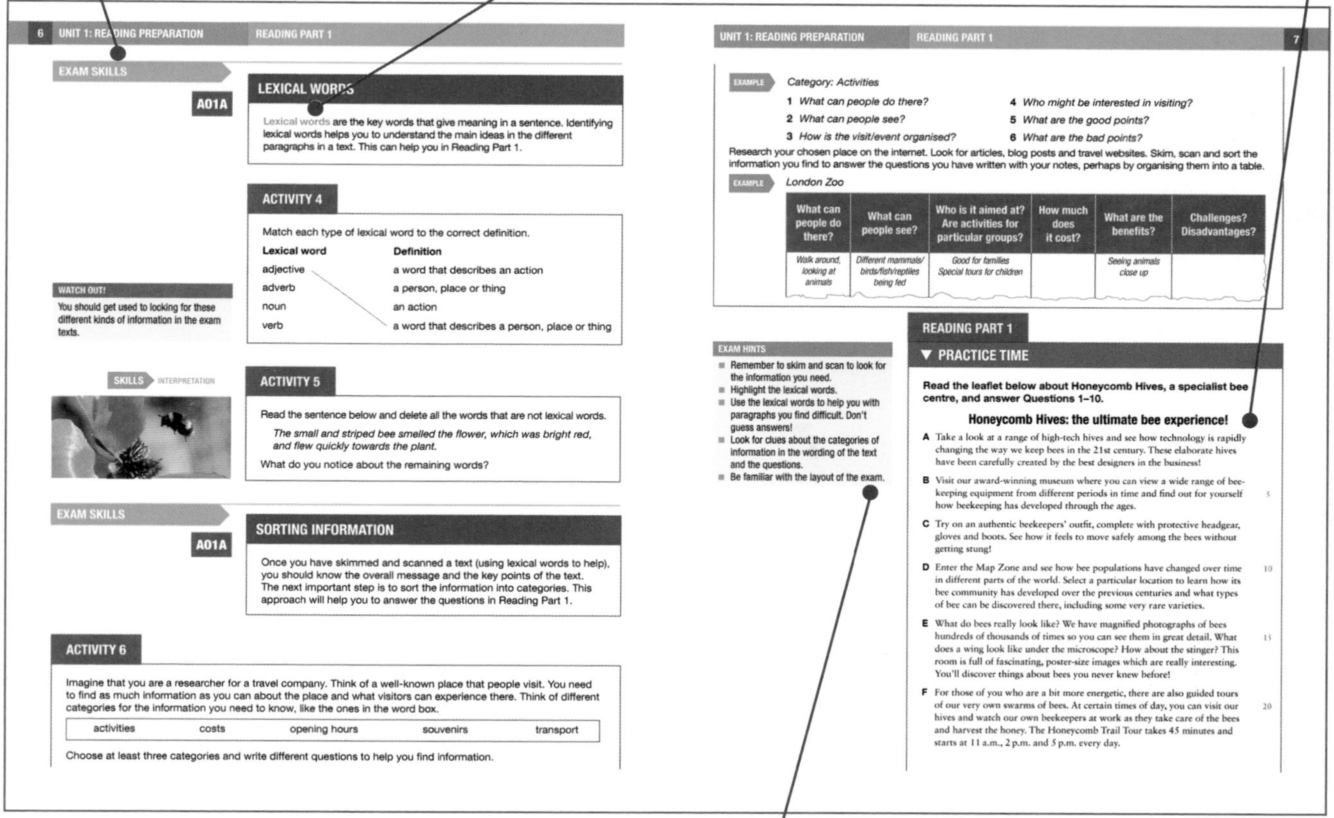

6 UNIT 1: READING PREPARATION READING PART 1

EXAM SKILLS

A01A

LEXICAL WORDS

Lexical words are the key words that give meaning in a sentence. Identifying lexical words helps you to understand the main ideas in the different paragraphs in a text. This can help you in Reading Part 1.

ACTIVITY 4

Match each type of lexical word to the correct definition.

Lexical word	Definition
adjective	a word that describes an action
adverb	a person, place or thing
noun	an action
verb	a word that describes a person, place or thing

WATCH OUT!
You should get used to looking for these different kinds of information in the exam texts.

SKILLS INTERPRETATION

ACTIVITY 5

Read the sentence below and delete all the words that are not lexical words.

The small and striped bee smelled the flower, which was bright red, and flew quickly towards the plant.

What do you notice about the remaining words?

EXAM SKILLS

A01A

SORTING INFORMATION

Once you have skimmed and scanned a text (using lexical words to help), you should know the overall message and the key points of the text. The next important step is to sort the information into categories. This approach will help you to answer the questions in Reading Part 1.

ACTIVITY 6

Imagine that you are a researcher for a travel company. Think of a well-known place that people visit. You need to find as much information as you can about the place and what visitors can experience there. Think of different categories for the information you need to know, like the ones in the word box.

activities costs opening hours souvenirs transport

Choose at least three categories and write different questions to help you find information.

UNIT 1: READING PREPARATION READING PART 1 7

EXAMPLE *Category: Activities*

1 *What can people do there?*
2 *What can people see?*
3 *How is the visit/event organised?*
4 *Who might be interested in visiting?*
5 *What are the good points?*
6 *What are the bad points?*

Research your chosen place on the internet. Look for articles, blog posts and travel websites. Skim, scan and sort the information you find to answer the questions you have written with your notes, perhaps by organising them into a table.

EXAMPLE *London Zoo*

What can people do there?	What can people see?	Who is it aimed at? Are activities for particular groups?	How much does it cost?	What are the benefits?	Challenges? Disadvantages?
Walk around, looking at animals	*Different mammals/birds/fish/reptiles being fed*	*Good for families Special tours for children*		*Seeing animals close up*	

EXAM HINTS
- Remember to skim and scan to look for the information you need.
- Highlight the lexical words.
- Use the lexical words to help you with paragraphs you find difficult. Don't guess answers!
- Look for clues about the categories of information in the wording of the text and the questions.
- Be familiar with the layout of the exam.

READING PART 1

▼ PRACTICE TIME

Read the leaflet below about Honeycomb Hives, a specialist bee centre, and answer Questions 1–10.

Honeycomb Hives: the ultimate bee experience!

A Take a look at a range of high-tech hives and see how technology is rapidly changing the way we keep bees in the 21st century. These elaborate hives have been carefully created by the best designers in the business!

B Visit our award-winning museum where you can view a wide range of bee-keeping equipment from different periods in time and find out for yourself how beekeeping has developed through the ages.

C Try on an authentic beekeepers' outfit, complete with protective headgear, gloves and boots. See how it feels to move safely among the bees without getting stung!

D Enter the Map Zone and see how bee populations have changed over time in different parts of the world. Select a particular location to learn how its bee community has developed over the previous centuries and what types of bee can be discovered there, including some very rare varieties.

E What do bees really look like? We have magnified photographs of bees hundreds of thousands of times so you can see them in great detail. What does a wing look like under the microscope? How about the stinger? This room is full of fascinating, poster-size images which are really interesting. You'll discover things about bees you never knew before!

F For those of you who are a bit more energetic, there are also guided tours of our very own swarms of bees. At certain times of day, you can visit our hives and watch our own beekeepers at work as they take care of the bees and harvest the honey. The Honeycomb Trail Tour takes 45 minutes and starts at 11 a.m., 2 p.m. and 5 p.m. every day.

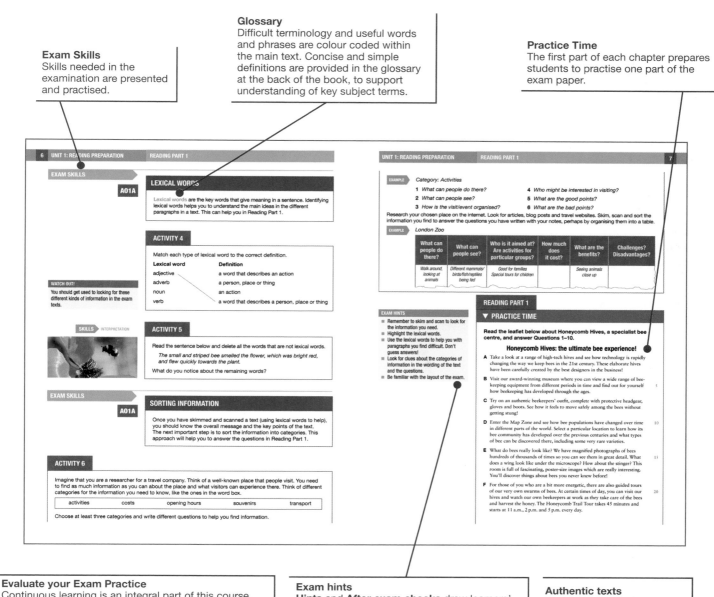

Evaluate your Exam Practice
Continuous learning is an integral part of this course. Students are encouraged to reflect on performance, techniques and challenges, both in the Practice Time tests and in their language learning development. For example, in the end-of-chapter **Self-evaluation** boxes.

Exam hints
Hints and **After exam checks** draw learners' attention to potential problems or common pitfalls in the exam, give practical hints about answering questions in the correct format and provide guidance in checking work.

Authentic texts
Reading and listening activities, and Practice Time texts, expose students to a variety of real-life texts.

ASSESSMENT OVERVIEW

The following tables give an overview of the assessment for this course. You should study this information closely to help ensure that you are fully prepared for this course and know exactly what to expect in each part of the assessment.

PAPER 1	PERCENTAGE	MARKS	TIME	AVAILABILITY
READING AND WRITING Written exam paper Paper code 4ES1/01 Externally set and assessed by Pearson Edexcel Single tier of entry	$62\frac{2}{3}\%$	100	2 hours	January and June exam series First assessment June 2019
PAPER 2	**PERCENTAGE**	**MARKS**	**TIME**	**AVAILABILITY**
LISTENING Written exam paper Paper code 4ES1/02 Externally set and assessed by Pearson Edexcel Single tier of entry	$33\frac{1}{3}\%$	40	50 minutes	January and June exam series First assessment June 2019
PAPER 3	**PERCENTAGE**	**MARKS**	**TIME**	**AVAILABILITY**
SPEAKING (OPTIONAL) Exam paper code 4ES1/03 Externally assessed and endorsed separately Single tier of entry	–	40	9–12 minutes	January and June exam series First assessment June 2019

ASSESSMENT OBJECTIVES AND WEIGHTINGS

SECTION	ASSESSMENT OBJECTIVE	DESCRIPTION	% IN INTERNATIONAL GCSE
READING	A01	**Understand and respond in writing to a range of English texts**	$33\frac{1}{3}$%
		AO1A Understand the overall message of a text	
		AO1B Understand in detail a range of texts, identifying finer points of detail	
		AO1C Distinguish between facts, ideas and opinions	
		AO1D Identify a writer's viewpoint and attitude, stated and implied	
WRITING	A02	**Write clear, relevant texts in English on a range of subjects**	$33\frac{1}{3}$%
		AO2A Demonstrate appropriate use of paragraphing, punctuation and spelling	
		AO2B Write in a range of registers to fit the context and the audience	
		AO2C Demonstrate a control of a range of vocabulary and a variety of grammatical structures	
		AO2D Summarise information provided in text form for a given purpose and audience	
LISTENING	A03	**Understand a wide range of recorded material spoken at normal speed**	$33\frac{1}{3}$%
		AO3A Understand the overall message of a spoken passage	
		AO3B Identify essential and finer points of detail in spoken material	
		AO3C Understand a conversation where information is being negotiated and exchanged	
		AO3D Identify a speaker's viewpoint and attitude, stated and implied	
SPEAKING	A04	**Communicate in speech comprehensibly and fluently**	Endorsed separately
		AO4A Give information and express opinions on a range of topics at different levels of complexity	
		AO4B Respond to a range of questions on a variety of topics	
		AO4C Use a range of vocabulary, grammar and structures appropriately	

RELATIONSHIP OF ASSESSMENT OBJECTIVES TO UNITS

UNIT NUMBER	ASSESSMENT OBJECTIVE			
	A01	A02	A03	A04
PAPER 1	$33\frac{1}{3}$%	$33\frac{1}{3}$%	0%	–
PAPER 2	0%	0%	$33\frac{1}{3}$%	–
PAPER 3	–	–	–	Endorsed separately
TOTAL FOR INTERNATIONAL GCSE	**$33\frac{1}{3}$%**	**$33\frac{1}{3}$%**	**$33\frac{1}{3}$%**	Endorsed separately

UNIT 1 READING PREPARATION

Assessment Objective 1A

Understand the overall message of a text

Assessment Objective 1B

Understand in detail a range of texts, identifying finer points of detail

Assessment Objective 1C

Distinguish between facts, ideas and opinions

Assessment Objective 1D

Identify a writer's viewpoint and attitude, stated and implied

This unit prepares you for the Reading section of Paper 1 Reading and Writing. In these parts of the exam, you need to show that you can understand and respond to a range of texts in English.

The unit contains three parts, which correspond to the three parts of the Reading section. You will need to use different types of reading skill in the different parts:

- Part 1: skimming and scanning skills
- Part 2: read for both gist and detail
- Part 3: read for both gist and detail, follow a line of argument or discussion and identify attitudes and opinions in the text.

Texts in the Reading section of the exam will be taken from a variety of sources, including fiction, and may include factual information, explanation, opinions and biographical writing.

In Parts 1–3 of the exam, you need to meet the Assessment Objectives AO1A, AO1B, AO1C and AO1D. The AOs that will be tested in the exam are indicated at the beginning of the corresponding part of this unit. Note you can also gain marks for Reading in Part 6 of the Writing section of the exam.

The unit focuses on the core reading skills that you need. Working through these lessons and activities will help you develop these skills.

READING PART 1

PLACES TO VISIT

Assessment Objective 1A

Understand the overall message of a text

LEARNING OBJECTIVES

- Talk about learning languages
- Prepare for Part 1 of the Reading and Writing exam
- Skim and scan for information
- Recognise lexical words
- Sort information
- Build new vocabulary (adjectives)
- Use articles
- Use countable and uncountable nouns, and *some* and *any*

DO YOU AGREE?

1 Disagree strongly
2 Disagree a little
3 Agree a little
4 Agree strongly

PREPARING THE WAY

Working in pairs, rank the statements from 1 to 4 based on how much you agree with them. You must both agree on the numbers!

- English is an easy language to learn.
- The best way to learn a language is to travel to a country where people speak it.
- It is easier to read in another language than to speak it.
- People today can learn languages extremely easily because of the internet.

SKILLS PROBLEM SOLVING

ACTIVITY 1

1 Look at the picture on the left. Write three sentences using numbers to describe what you can see.

2 Show your sentences to your partner. Together, write three more sentences, this time commenting on shape and colour.

FOCUSING ON THE EXAM

- Part 1 (Reading and Writing) is worth 10 marks.
- It is based on a collection of short texts, e.g. an advert, timetable or leaflet.
- You need to select and/or match information.

EXAM SKILLS

A01A

SKIMMING AND SCANNING

Two important skills for Reading Part 1 are **skimming** and **scanning**. Skimming means reading a text quickly to find the key points and overall message. Scanning means reading a text quickly to find specific details.

ACTIVITY 2

1 Skim the leaflet and note down the overall topic.

2 Scan the leaflet and note down details about people, dates and times.

HONEYCOMB HIVES

An un-bee-lievable success story

Popular specialist bee centre Honeycomb Hives celebrates its first anniversary today. The centre opened on 1 June last year and has received over 10 000 visitors. Dave Chandler, one of the centre's tour guides, told us, 'Honeycomb Hives is a great place to work. It has a fantastic atmosphere. The place is always buzzing!'

Honeycomb Hives is the most popular tourist attraction in the region. It is open all year round from 10 a.m. until 5 p.m. and many visitors return for a repeat visit.

One reason for the centre's popularity is the range of activities on offer. Manager Scott Sterling said, 'People love Honeycomb Hives. The bees are very interesting and there is a lot to learn. We have activities for people of all ages. There really is something for everyone.'

ACTIVITY 3

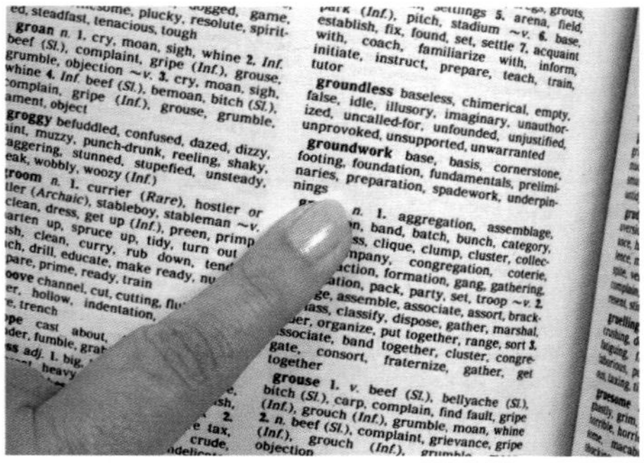

1 What is the difference between skimming and scanning? Discuss in pairs.

2 Which of the following are examples of skimming, and which are examples of scanning?

a Flicking through a catalogue to get ideas for a friend's birthday present Skimming

b Looking up a word in a thesaurus Scanning

c Looking at a section of an instruction booklet to see how to do something

d Checking the time of a TV show you want to watch Skimming

e Reading a film review to decide whether to watch the film Scanning

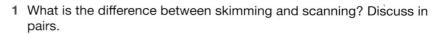

f Picking the website you want from internet search options both

EXAM SKILLS

A01A

LEXICAL WORDS

Lexical words are the key words that give meaning in a sentence. Identifying lexical words helps you to understand the main ideas in the different paragraphs in a text. This can help you in Reading Part 1.

ACTIVITY 4

Match each type of lexical word to the correct definition.

Lexical word	Definition
adjective	a word that describes an action
adverb	a person, place or thing
noun	an action
verb	a word that describes a person, place or thing

WATCH OUT!

You should get used to looking for these different kinds of information in the exam texts.

SKILLS INTERPRETATION

ACTIVITY 5

Read the sentence below and delete all the words that are not lexical words.

The small and striped bee smelled the flower, which was bright red, and flew quickly towards the plant.

What do you notice about the remaining words?

EXAM SKILLS

A01A

SORTING INFORMATION

Once you have skimmed and scanned a text (using lexical words to help), you should know the overall message and the key points of the text. The next important step is to sort the information into categories. This approach will help you to answer the questions in Reading Part 1.

ACTIVITY 6

Imagine that you are a researcher for a travel company. Think of a well-known place that people visit. You need to find as much information as you can about the place and what visitors can experience there. Think of different categories for the information you need to know, like the ones in the word box.

activities	costs	opening hours	souvenirs	transport

Choose at least three categories and write different questions to help you find information.

EXAMPLE *Category: Activities*

1 *What can people do there?*
2 *What can people see?*
3 *How is the visit/event organised?*
4 *Who might be interested in visiting?*
5 *What are the good points?*
6 *What are the bad points?*

Research your chosen place on the internet. Look for articles, blog posts and travel websites. Skim, scan and sort the information you find to answer the questions you have written with your notes, perhaps by organising them into a table.

EXAMPLE *London Zoo*

What can people do there?	What can people see?	Who is it aimed at? Are activities for particular groups?	How much does it cost?	What are the benefits?	Challenges? Disadvantages?
Walk around, looking at animals	*Different mammals/ birds/fish/reptiles being fed*	*Good for families Special tours for children*		*Seeing animals close up*	

EXAM HINTS

- Remember to skim and scan to look for the information you need.
- Highlight the lexical words.
- Use the lexical words to help you with paragraphs you find difficult. Don't guess answers!
- Look for clues about the categories of information in the wording of the text and the questions.
- Be familiar with the layout of the exam.

READING PART 1

▼ PRACTICE TIME

Read the leaflet below about Honeycomb Hives, a specialist bee centre, and answer Questions 1–10.

Honeycomb Hives: the ultimate bee experience!

A Take a look at a range of high-tech hives and see how technology is rapidly changing the way we keep bees in the 21st century. These elaborate hives have been carefully created by the best designers in the business!

B Visit our award-winning museum where you can view a wide range of bee-keeping equipment from different periods in time and find out for yourself how beekeeping has developed through the ages.

C Try on an authentic beekeepers' outfit, complete with protective headgear, gloves and boots. See how it feels to move safely among the bees without getting stung!

D Enter the Map Zone and see how bee populations have changed over time in different parts of the world. Select a particular location to learn how its bee community has developed over the previous centuries and what types of bee can be discovered there, including some very rare varieties.

E What do bees really look like? We have magnified photographs of bees hundreds of thousands of times so you can see them in great detail. What does a wing look like under the microscope? How about the stinger? This room is full of fascinating, poster-size images which are really interesting. You'll discover things about bees you never knew before!

F For those of you who are a bit more energetic, there are also guided tours of our very own swarms of bees. At certain times of day, you can visit our hives and watch our own beekeepers at work as they take care of the bees and harvest the honey. The Honeycomb Trail Tour takes 45 minutes and starts at 11 a.m., 2 p.m. and 5 p.m. every day.

G Have you ever imagined what it's like to be a bee? Now you don't have to! Enter Bee World, where our specially-designed headset lets you see the world around you from a bee's perspective. Cutting-edge technology makes it possible for you to enter the hive, communicate with other bees and even fly around the garden.

H Although Honeycomb Hives is a great place for adults to visit, we certainly haven't forgotten about the children. Our special Bee Buddies, based in the play area, can keep your children entertained with a whole range of games while you explore the Honeycomb Gift Shop or have a quick coffee in the Tea Room.

I Don't forget to visit the gift shop, where you can buy fun presents for friends or family. What could be a better memento than a pot (or two!) of our delicious honey? We provide gift-wrapping services, perfect for special presents. We even supply hampers complete with ten different kinds of honey, not to mention a wide range of books and other memorabilia. We can also give you advice about other presents available to order online.

J If you are hungry and feel like putting your feet up for a few minutes, you could visit The Honeypot Tea Room. With its cosy furniture, it's the ideal place to pause for some refreshment. Here we serve a wide range of hot and cold drinks and plenty of home-baked bread, spread with – you guessed it! – honey, fresh from the hive.

SKILLS PROBLEM SOLVING

A01A

EXAM HINTS

- If you put two or more answers, make sure you put a line through one of the boxes, as shown in the exam instructions.
- Avoid spending too long on any question you find difficult.

WATCH OUT!

Note that some paragraphs might not be used in the answers and some paragraphs might be used more than once.

Questions 1–10

Identify which paragraphs (A–J) contain information listed in Questions 1–10 by marking a cross for the correct answer ☒. If you change your mind about an answer, put a line through the box ⊠ and then mark your new answer with a cross ☒.

You must choose answers only from the information given in the leaflet.

Paragraphs may be used more than once or not at all.

1 Which paragraph refers to a place where you can buy snacks and drinks?

A ☐ B ☐ C ☐ D ☐ E ☐ F ☐ G ☐ H ☐ I ☐ J ☐ (1)

2 Which paragraph refers to getting a closer view of bees?

A ☐ B ☐ C ☐ D ☐ E ☐ F ☐ G ☐ H ☐ I ☐ J ☐ (1)

3 Which paragraph refers to the numbers of bees globally through the ages?

A ☐ B ☐ C ☐ D ☐ E ☐ F ☐ G ☐ H ☐ I ☐ J ☐ (1)

4 Which paragraph refers to modern hives?

A ☐ B ☐ C ☐ D ☐ E ☐ F ☐ G ☐ H ☐ I ☐ J ☐ (1)

我的梦想是史莱姆大师

5 Which paragraph refers to specially-designed clothing?

A	B	C	D	E	F	G	H	I	J	(1)
☐	☐	☒	☐	☐	☐	☐	☐	☐	☐	

6 Which paragraph refers to Honeycomb Hives' own bees?

A	B	C	D	E	F	G	H	I	J	(1)
☐	☐	☐	☐	☐	☒	☐	☐	☐	☐	

7 Which paragraph refers to purchasing tasty treats?

A	B	C	D	E	F	G	H	I	J	(1)
☐	☐	☐	☐	☐	☐	☐	☒	☒	☒	

8 Which paragraph refers to the world as a bee sees it?

A	B	C	D	E	F	G	H	I	J	(1)
☐	☐	☐	☐	☐	☐	☒	☐	☐	☐	

9 Which paragraph refers to activities for younger visitors?

A	B	C	D	E	F	G	H	I	J	(1)
☐	☐	☐	☐	☐	☐	☐	☒	☐	☐	

10 Which paragraph refers to looking after bees in the past?

A	B	C	D	E	F	G	H	I	J	(1)
☐	☒	☐	☐	☐	☐	☐	☐	☐	☐	

(Total for Questions 1–10 = 10 marks)

(Total for Part 1 = 10 marks)

AFTER EXAM CHECK

- Make sure you double-check your answers to ensure they are in the correct box(es).
- Make sure you have answered all the questions (questions with no answers score zero).
- More than one answer to any question will score zero unless you cross the second answer out.

SKILLS SELF-MONITORING

HOW DID YOU DO?

- Check your score. What went well?
- Could you have done better? If so, how?

VOCABULARY AND GRAMMAR

VOCABULARY FOCUS

ADJECTIVES

猪 onggpig

ACTIVITY 1

Match the adjectives in the Honeycomb Hives leaflet on pages 7–8 to the correct definitions.

EXAMPLE having lots of small parts put together in a complicated way — *elaborate*

1 using the latest technology — high-tech

2 not fake — ~~original~~ authentic

3 intended to prevent harm or danger — safe

4 unusual — rare variety
5 extremely interesting — fascinating
6 active and keen to do things — authentic
7 made for a particular need or situation — specially-designed
8 very modern — cutting edge
9 relaxing and warm — cosy

ACTIVITY 2

Match the adjectives from Activity 1 to the correct **synonyms**. You can use a dictionary to help.

EXAMPLE detailed — *elaborate*

1 genuine — authentic
2 preventative — 3
3 tailored to — specially-designed
4 technologically advanced — 1 high-tech
5 up-to-date — 8 cutting-edge
6 uncommon — 4 rare
7 captivating — ~~cosy~~
8 comfortable — 9 ~~ener~~ cosy
9 dynamic — 6 energetic

ACTIVITY 3

Circle the correct words.

1 These hats are really **cutting edge** / **protective** in design. They use a new **high-tech** / **energetic** fabric invented in Japan.

2 We live in this **cutting edge** / **authentic** fisherman's cottage built in 1850. It was inhabited by fishermen's families until the 1950s. It's not very big or **elaborate** / **protective**, but it's very **cosy** / **fascinating**.

3 Do you know where I can buy a **specially-designed** / **rare** pair of walking boots? My old ones have lost their **protective** / **authentic** layer and my feet get wet every time it rains!

4 Andrea is a police officer and always has a lot of **cosy** / **fascinating** things to say about her job. She has to be so **energetic** / **rare** every day.

GRAMMAR CHECKPOINT

GRAMMAR

See Grammar Reference page 256.

COUNTABLE AND UNCOUNTABLE NOUNS

ACTIVITY 4

Sort the words into the correct columns.

~~gift~~ furniture bread advice hive honey tour shop clothing museum

Countable nouns	Uncountable nouns
gift	

ACTIVITY 5

The letter below contains 12 mistakes (not including the example) with countable and uncountable nouns. Read it and correct the mistakes.

Dear Klaus,

Thank you for your letter asking me about my recent holiday to Penang. The best part was my visit to Penang National Park. The information online ~~aren't~~ *isn't* very reliable, so I will tell you all about it here. Many peoples come to visit the park and there are tour in many languages. Generally, in Malaysia there are many bilingual people compared to other countries. Everyone are also very friendlies!

There are some good advice I can give you if you are planning to go and visit the nature park. I recommend going early in the morning because then there are less crowd. You will see much fine views so remember to take your camera!

There is a tea room and café where you can buy delicious Malaysian snack. There are also an excellent gift shop, if you want to do some shoppings. I bought a really cute poster of a monkey eating some breads.

I hope you found my informations helpful. Come to visit soon!

Best wishes,
Hilda

SKILLS CREATIVITY

ACTIVITY 6

Klaus has written to you asking for advice about visiting your country. Write a reply giving him your opinion about the best places to visit and the best local activities. Use at least five countable nouns and five uncountable nouns in your letter.

GRAMMAR CHECKPOINT

GRAMMAR

See Grammar Reference pages 254–255 (Articles) and 256–257 (Partitives).

ARTICLES

ACTIVITY 7

Tick the correct sentences.

1 a What were you doing the last night?
  b What were you doing last night?

2 a Do you have a umbrella?
  b Do you have an umbrella?

3 a The France is a beautiful country.
  b France is a beautiful country.

4 a I would like to visit the Canary Islands.
  b I would like to visit Canary Islands.

5 a The zoo has two bears: a brown one and a black one.
  b The zoo has two bears: the brown one and the black one.

6 a Do you watch lots of films?
  b Do you watch the lots of films?

7 a Where's the hat I gave you earlier?
  b Where's a hat I gave you earlier?

8 a I play the lot of video games.
  b I play a lot of video games.

9 a I go to a university near here.
  b I go to an university near here.

10 a Bears live in forests.
  b The bears live in the forests.

11 a Next week there is a Honey Festival at Honeycomb Hives.
  b The next week there is a Honey Festival at Honeycomb Hives.

12 a Thanks for the help.
  b Thanks for help.

13 a I need the help.
  b I need help.

14 a I don't like the dogs normally, but this one is nice.
  b I don't like dogs normally, but this one is nice.

15 a This class lasts an hour.
  b This class lasts a hour.

ACTIVITY 8

1 Read the news article extract about an unusual experience. Fill in the gaps using *a*, *an*, *the* or no article (-).

Visitors to [1]________ specialist bee centre, Honeycomb Hives, had [2]________ unusual experience earlier today, when [3]________ bear was seen entering [4]________ centre, perhaps in [5]________ search of [6]________ honey. [7]________ bear was described as 'brown', 'medium-sized' and 'exceptionally hungry'.

2 Read the interview with Honeycomb Hives tour guide, Dave Chandler. Fill in the gaps using *a*, *an*, *the* or no article (-).

Reporter: Please, Mr Chandler, tell us what happened.

Dave: Well, it was [1]________ three o'clock and I was at [2]________ work – I'm [3]________ tour guide at Honeycomb Hives – when suddenly I saw [4]________ bear come in from [5]________ woods opposite [6]________ Honeypot Tea Room and start sniffing [7]________ hives. At first I thought I was crazy. I mean, this is [8]________ England! What's [9]________ wild bear doing here?

Reporter: And why was [10]________ bear there?

Dave: Apparently, it had escaped from [11]________ wildlife park near here. Luckily, [12]________ bear's keepers were able to come and catch it before anyone was hurt.

Reporter: How long did that take?

Dave: About [13]________ hour.

Reporter: So, where is [14]________ bear now?

Dave: Back at [15]________ wildlife park, I hope!

3 Listen to the interview and check your answers.

GRAMMAR CHECKPOINT

GRAMMAR

See Grammar Reference page 256.

SOME AND *ANY*

ACTIVITY 9

Read this conversation between visitors to the Honeycomb Hives gift shop. Fill in the gaps using *some* or *any*.

Ali: I'd like to buy [1]________ honey. These pots will make great presents.

Rebecca: I agree. I'd also like [2]________ of this orange-flavoured one! But I haven't got [3]________ money!

Ali: I don't have [4]________ with me either. Don't you have [5]________ cash?

Rebecca: No. Ah – I do have my card.

Ali: If we buy [6]________ beeswax candles as well, we can probably pay by card.

Rebecca: Great idea. Let's get [7]________ of those too, then!

SELF-EVALUATION

Tick the relevant boxes.

I now feel confident about ...	STRONGLY AGREE	AGREE	DISAGREE	STRONGLY DISAGREE
▶ TALKING ABOUT LEARNING LANGUAGES				
▶ SKIMMING AND SCANNING FOR INFORMATION				
▶ SORTING INFORMATION				
▶ RECOGNISING LEXICAL WORDS				
▶ USING NEW VOCABULARY (ADJECTIVES)				
▶ USING COUNTABLE AND UNCOUNTABLE NOUNS				
▶ USING ARTICLES				

If you ticked ‘disagree’ or ‘strongly disagree’, you need to revise these parts.

READING PART 2

CELEBRITIES, FAME AND ENTERTAINMENT

Assessment Objective 1B

Understand in detail a range of texts, identifying finer points of detail

Assessment Objective 1C

Distinguish between facts, ideas and opinions

Assessment Objective 1D

Identify a writer's viewpoint and attitude, stated and implied

LEARNING OBJECTIVES

- Talk about fame and celebrities
- Prepare for Part 2 of the Reading and Writing exam
- Select relevant detail from the text
- Identify synonyms
- Build new vocabulary (nouns: celebrities and fame)
- Use the present simple
- Use the present continuous

PREPARING THE WAY

Discuss the following questions.

- What are the advantages of being a celebrity? What are the disadvantages?
- Have you ever seen a celebrity?
- Do celebrities deserve privacy?
- Who do you think is the most well-known celebrity of all time?

Imagine you are having a party. Make a list of five celebrities (living or from the past) to invite. Write two sentences explaining your reasons for choosing each celebrity.

SKILLS INTERPRETATION

ACTIVITY 1

Listen to the Ridgefield United Press Conference and answer the questions.

1 Did Ridgefield United win their game? Yes
2 Did the opposition score a goal? No
3 Did Fred Sandilands play today? No
4 Does José want to talk about the present or the future?
5 Why? hes playing another
6 How much money are Ridgefield United offering to pay for a player from another team, according to the reporter? 100 mil

FOCUSING ON THE EXAM

- Part 2 (Reading and Writing) is worth 15 marks.
- It is based on a long text, e.g. extracts from leaflets, adverts or articles.
- You need to complete two or three different tasks. These can be: multiple choice, short-answer questions, true / false / not given, note completion, sentence completion, diagram completion or summary completion.
- You need to distinguish between facts, ideas and opinions.
- You need to identify details in the text(s).
- You need to identify the writer's viewpoint and attitude, stated and implied.

EXAM SKILLS

SELECTION

An important skill for Reading Part 2 is the ability to identify and select information from a range of text types.

You need to identify:

- factual information (facts) about people, places or times
- abstract information, such as feelings or ideas.

There will be clues to help you. The wording of the question will tell you whether to look for facts or ideas. Sometimes, but not always, the wording might include 'opinion' words, e.g. *What does the writer think about …, He thinks …, She felt …, Her hope was …*

A01B

ACTIVITY 2

1 Read the email from the personal assistant of a celebrity, Rachel Ritz, to a music studio manager.

SEND | Save Now | Discard

TO manager@studio.com
Add Cc Add Bcc

SUBJECT Arrangements for Rachel Ritz
Attach a file

Dear Sir or Madam,

I am writing to you because I am Rachel Ritz's personal assistant. Ms Ritz is going to perform at your venue this evening. As you know, Ms Ritz is the most popular and beautiful singer of our generation. There are a number of items which Ms Ritz feels are essential to her comfort and security. I am sure your studio will do everything to make Ms Ritz's stay at the studio as pleasant as possible.

Ms Ritz requires the attention of a personal hair stylist and make-up artist before she appears on stage. They must arrive at least 3 hours before the performance. Ms Ritz also requires three large rooms for her entourage before and after the show. These must be entirely light blue. This is Ms Ritz's favourite colour and it helps her to relax before a show. Please paint the walls, the ceiling and the floor light blue. Please make sure the curtains and all the furniture is light blue too. Please also provide honey-scented candles and a fruit basket with a selection of healthy, fresh fruit in her room. Ms Ritz has radiant skin because of all the fresh fruit she eats. She also needs access to a light blue swimming pool (28°C).

We require at least 25 security guards on duty in the stage area and dressing rooms. This is very important, because Ms Ritz gets headaches when she feels unsafe.

We trust you will make the arrangements and we look forward to seeing you later.

Yours sincerely,

Joe Dimarco

2 Answer the questions and make notes about the different types of information.
- **a** What are the main demands from the celebrity? Highlight the key words.
- **b** What do you think about Rachel Ritz? Are there any phrases or sentences which are about personality, ideas and feelings?

3 Use your notes with the selected information to write a 50-word email from the studio manager to their staff. Explain Rachel's requirements.

EXAM SKILLS

IDENTIFYING SYNONYMS

To help select the right information, you need to think about synonyms when you are reading. Synonyms are words that have the same meaning. Look for words in the text that are synonyms of words in the exam question.

For example:
- the question refers to 'enjoyment'
- the text includes the word 'pleasure'
- the sentence or paragraph containing the word 'pleasure' should help you to answer the question.

ACTIVITY 3

Look again at this paragraph, taken from the text in Activity 2.

I am writing to you because I am Rachel Ritz's personal assistant. As you know, Ms Ritz is going to perform at your venue this evening. As you know, Ms Ritz is the most popular and beautiful singer of our generation. There are a number of items which Ms Ritz feels are essential to her comfort and security. I am sure your studio will do everything to make Ms Ritz's stay at the studio as pleasant as possible.

1 Working in pairs, find synonyms for the underlined words in the text.

2 Answer the questions, using the synonyms to help.
   a What is the name of the celebrity's employee?
   b Where is Ms Ritz going to sing?
   c Why is this email important?

ACTIVITY 4

Make a list of ten lexical words. Working in pairs, find synonyms for each one. You can use a dictionary or thesaurus to help.

EXAM HINTS

- The questions will follow the order of information presented in the texts and all information required in the answers will be found in the text.
- Look for key words and phrases in the text. These help to identify which paragraph contains the information you need for each answer.

READING PART 2

▼ PRACTICE TIME

Read the article on celebrities and answer Questions 11–25.

The shadow side of celebrity

Many people dream of becoming famous actors, singers or athletes. The idea of living a millionaire lifestyle can seem like a dream come true. We imagine stars wearing expensive clothing brands, eating delicious food every day in exclusive restaurants and, best of all, taking luxurious holidays to exotic locations. But celebrities also face many problems that other people don't have – like constant media attention from the paparazzi.

Paparazzi are journalists who follow celebrities around, take photos of them and then sell the photos to newspapers and magazines. Understandably, not everybody enjoys all this attention! Can you imagine being followed everywhere you went with people trying to take your picture – even if you didn't want them to? Elizabeth Olsen, an actress used to media attention from a relatively early age, isn't keen on the idea, saying: 'No, I wouldn't want the paparazzi ever following me in my life.'

Sometimes paparazzi photographs are flattering. However, photographs of celebrities looking unglamorous are often sold for far more money. The paparazzi don't care about privacy for the celebrity. Sometimes they even take photos of people inside their own houses, or hack into their phones to obtain private pictures. Telephoto lenses, which make it possible to take pictures (even close-ups) from a distance, have made the paparazzi's job a lot easier – and celebrities' lives more complicated.

There are many well-documented examples of celebrities attempting to control the paparazzi without success. Popular gossip site Buzzfeed claimed that Beyoncé's publicist emailed them and requested the removal of some unflattering photos of the singer taken during the Super Bowl's half-time show. Buzzfeed did not take the photos down, but posted the email on their website along with the pictures. This article has received well over 2 000 000 views!

Some celebrities develop unusual methods for dealing with the paparazzi. Daniel Radcliffe, star of the Harry Potter films, spends months wearing the same outfit every day – the same jacket and the same hat. This means that the paparazzi photographs always look identical, so the magazines are not interested in publishing the photos. He says that 'There's nothing better than seeing the paparazzi get really frustrated.'

Andrew Garfield and Emma Stone, stars in the film 'The Amazing Spider-Man' (2012), have a different technique for dealing with the paparazzi. If photographers are waiting for you outside a restaurant, write the names of a list of charities on some pieces of card. Then, as you leave the restaurant, hold the cards up in front of your face so that the pictures generate free publicity for the organisations. This certainly puts the media's high level of interest to good use!

While some celebrities work out ways to frustrate the paparazzi, not everyone manages to do so. The so-called 'paps' can be very determined in their pursuit of pictures. Imagine what it must feel like to know that there is someone waiting to take pictures of every 'bad-hair day' and that every terrible photo of you will exist permanently. It's not just the paparazzi, either. Many people now have smartphones, so it's increasingly easy for members of the public to snap unflattering shots of celebrities whenever they're out and about. Such photos are later sold, or simply uploaded to social media sites that make sure they never disappear.

It's easy to imagine the positives of being a celebrity. There is an argument that those who enter the entertainment world nowadays know about the potential difficulties, but perhaps more people should remember that fame is not without its share of problems.

Tom Robbins,
National Report

SKILLS INTERPRETATION

A01B

Questions 11–20

Answer the following questions. For each question write no more than THREE words taken from one point in the text. DO NOT write full sentences.

11 What problem do celebrities have to face that others don't? (1)

constant media attention

12 What did Elizabeth Olsen experience when she was young? (1)

media attention

13 What types of photograph often attract high fees? (1)

unglamorous

14 How do some famous people cope with interest from the media? (1)

....

15 What is a characteristic of photographs of Daniel Radcliffe? (1)

identical

16 Daniel Radcliffe enjoys annoying a certain group. Who? (1)

....

17 When was 'The Amazing Spider-Man' released? (1)

2012

18 How can charities benefit from Andrew Garfield and Emma Stone's method of coping with stardom? (1)

....

19 What do members of the public use to take photos of celebrities? (1)

smart phones

20 What feature of celebrity life is it easy to imagine? (1)

positeves of being a celebrity

(Total for Questions 11–20 = 10 marks)

SKILLS INTERPRETATION

A01D

EXAM HINT

Make sure you only mark a cross in one box for Questions 21–25. If you make a mistake, put a line through the wrong answer as shown in the instructions.

Questions 21–25

Identify which of the options given for Questions 21–25 accurately completes the given statements by marking a cross for the correct answer ☒. If you change your mind about an answer, put a line through the box ☒ and then mark your new answer with a cross ☒.

21 Which of these do people see as the biggest advantage of a millionaire lifestyle, according to the writer? (1)

- ☐ **A** Buying designer clothes
- ☑ **B** Taking holidays in exclusive locations
- ☐ **C** Going to top restaurants
- ☐ **D** Eating delicious food

22 What does the writer think about the paparazzi? (1)

- ☐ **A** They have a difficult job.
- ☐ **B** They have a useful job.
- ☑ **C** They make life difficult for celebrities.
- ☐ **D** They improve the daily life of a celebrity.

WATCH OUT!

Use key words in the questions as well as in the text to help you locate your answers.

23 According to the writer, what is the worst thing about telephoto lenses for celebrities? (1)

- ☐ **A** Paparazzi can use them to take close-ups.
- ☑ **B** Paparazzi can use them to take pictures from a distance.
- ☐ **C** Paparazzi can use them to take photos indoors.
- ☐ **D** Paparazzi can use them to take pictures the celebrities don't want them to take.

24 What did Andrew Garfield and Emma Stone use to help charities? (1)

- ☐ **A** The media's curiosity
- ☐ **B** The media's interest in them
- ☑ **C** The media's desire to help charities
- ☐ **D** Payment from the media

25 How long does the writer say that bad photos will last? **(1)**

- ☐ **A** A few years
- ☐ **B** They disappear if they are not sold
- ☑ **C** Forever
- ☐ **D** Until they're deleted

(Total for Questions 21–25 = 5 marks)
(Total for Part 2 = 15 marks)

AFTER EXAM CHECK

Spelling is not assessed in this part of the exam. However, you are still advised to spell accurately. You can copy the correct spellings from the source text.

SKILLS SELF-MONITORING

HOW DID YOU DO?

- Check your score. What went well?
- Could you have done better? If so, how?

VOCABULARY AND GRAMMAR

VOCABULARY FOCUS

SKILLS CRITICAL THINKING

NOUNS: CELEBRITIES AND FAME

ACTIVITY 1

1 Listen to the celebrity interview and answer the comprehension questions in three words or less.

- a What is the name of the interviewer? Jeremy Miles
- b What does Rachel think of her admirers? annoying
- c How does Rachel describe herself?
- d Where did the interviewer hear about Rachel's new record deal? social media
- e What does Rachel hope to be in her new career?

2 Listen again and circle the ten words or phrases you hear from the list.

round of applause	social media
talent	privacy
paparazzi	TV drama
a piece of gossip	publicity
introvert	incompetence
a fact	extrovert
stardom	reality TV

ACTIVITY 2

1 Match the words from the list in Activity 1 on page 21 to the correct definitions. There are four extra words that have not been defined in the list below.

a The ability to do something well tolent

b Television programmes that feature real people doing real things reality TV

c Photographers who follow famous people to take photographs sold to newspapers paparazzi

d The state of not having your life known about by other people privacy

e A short period of clapping to show enjoyment round of applause

f The state of being famous ______

g An active and confident person who enjoys spending time with other people extrovert

h Ways of sharing information such as opinions, images and videos with friends and fans using the internet social media

i Information that may or may not be true a peace of gossip

j Attention from newspapers and television publicity

2 The four extra words from Activity 1 are all **antonyms** of other words in the list. Can you find them?

ACTIVITY 3

1 Read and fill in the gaps with the correct words or phrases.

a Film stars and musicians often have to help get ______ for their work. For example, they need to appear at events. It's not suitable work for introverts!

b Have you heard that ______ about Peter Purple? He's apparently making a film with Vanessa Roberts.

c I protect my ______ carefully. I never give interviews and I never use ______ to broadcast where I am. That way the ______ can't follow me.

d She started as a waitress, then became assistant chef and was head chef after one year. What a great ______!

e He appeared on a ______ programme about people working in supermarkets. He soon progressed to 'real' acting in the theatre. He says that there's nothing like the sound of ______.

f She loves the attention and publicity of ______ because she's a real ______ at heart.

ACTIVITY 4

Discuss in pairs.

- Would you like to be on reality TV? Why/Why not?
- How important is your privacy to you?
- Do you use social media? What do you use it for?

GRAMMAR CHECKPOINT

PRESENT SIMPLE

GRAMMAR

See Grammar Reference pages 261–262.

ACTIVITY 5

Read the text and fill in the gaps using the present simple.

Celebrities [1]________ (handle) the paparazzi in different ways. Daniel Radcliffe, star of the Harry Potter films, [2]__wears__ (wear) the same outfit every day for months. So, however much the paparazzi [3]________ (take) photographs of him, the pictures [4]__are__ (be) always very similar, so that magazines [5]________ (not want) to publish the photos. He [6]________ (like) causing problems for the paparazzi!

ACTIVITY 6

Read and complete the sentences with the present simple.

EXAMPLE (–, Rachel, want)
Rachel doesn't want the newspaper to publish unflattering photos.

1 (+, we, accept)
____________ full responsibility for the problem.

2 (?, they, know)
____________ what time the show will start?

3 (+, she, do)
____________ yoga with a personal trainer.

4 (+, I, be)
____________ confident that I will achieve stardom.

5 (–, Rachel, regret) (+, she, hope)
____________ the decision at all, but ____________ that it won't change anything.

6 (–,?, you, want)
____________ to go outside?

7 (–,?, it, be)
____________ the right answer?

8 (+, she, carry)
_____________ her mum's shopping home every day.

9 (+, Ricardo, fly)
_____________ to France next week.

SKILLS CREATIVITY

ACTIVITY 7

What do you think that your favourite celebrity does on a typical day? Write a paragraph describing their daily routine using the present simple.

EXAMPLE *Daniel Craig wakes up at 7.15 and has a fruit smoothie.*

GRAMMAR CHECKPOINT

GRAMMAR

See Grammar Reference page 262.

PRESENT CONTINUOUS

ACTIVITY 8

Put the sentences in the correct order using the present continuous. Sometimes, more than one order is possible.

EXAMPLE well / we / moment / the / are / very / playing / at
We are playing very well at the moment.

1 getting / we / the / results / we / deserve / are / that

2 a / talking / are / about / people / transfer

3 as / well / the / is / not / performing / as / we / are / referee

4 playing / he / Lucas / job / is / and / is / a / great / doing

5 true / you / million / that / it / bidding / euros? / is / over / are

GRAMMAR GAME

▼ PICTIONARY

- Take it in turns to draw an action on a piece of paper, e.g. a police officer chasing a dog.
- Members of the group make guesses about your drawing using the present continuous, e.g. *The police officer is chasing the dog.*
- Whoever guesses correctly gets a point and is the next person to draw.
- Whoever has the most points at the end, wins!

GRAMMAR CHECKPOINT

GRAMMAR

See Grammar Reference pages 261–262.

PRESENT SIMPLE AND PRESENT CONTINUOUS

ACTIVITY 9

Read and tick the correct sentences.

1 a Don't Chris and Paul know about the paparazzi?
  b Aren't Chris and Paul knowing about the paparazzi?

2 a This fish stew smells awful.
  b This fish stew is smelling awful.

3 a I'm trying to hear the announcement but it's very unclear.
  b I try to hear the announcement but it's very unclear.

4 a I'll be home soon. I leave work now.
  b I'll be home soon. I'm leaving work now.

5 a What do you do? I'm reading a book.
  b What are you doing? I'm reading a book.

6 a What do you do? I'm a publicist.
  b What are you doing? I'm a publicist.

7 a He seems fun to spend time with.
  b He is seeming fun to spend time with.

ACTIVITY 10

Complete the sentences using the present simple or the present continuous.

EXAMPLE (–, Sally, sing)
Sally isn't singing right now.

1 (?, Rachel, look)
______________ strange to you?

2 (+, Chris, update)
______________ his status on his social media networks every hour. It's ridiculous!

3 (–, I, know)
______________ what's happening in the world of reality TV at the moment.

4 (?, you, think)
You look happy. What ______________ about?

5 (?, you, believe)
______________ the latest piece of gossip?

6 (–, I, have)
__________ any privacy right now and I'm finding it very difficult.

7 (–, ?, everyone, like)
Why __________ Coldplay?

8 (+, he, relax)
In the photo __________ on a deckchair by the pool.

9 (?, you, work)
__________ on the Science project while Daniel is sick?

10 (–, Janet, come)
__________ to the after-show party after all.

SELF-EVALUATION

Tick the relevant boxes.

I now feel confident about ...	STRONGLY AGREE	AGREE	DISAGREE	STRONGLY DISAGREE
▶ TALKING ABOUT FAME AND CELEBRITIES				
▶ SELECTING RELEVANT INFORMATION FROM THE TEXT				
▶ IDENTIFYING SYNONYMS				
▶ USING NEW VOCABULARY (NOUNS: CELEBRITIES AND FAME)				
▶ USING THE PRESENT SIMPLE				
▶ USING THE PRESENT CONTINUOUS				

If you ticked 'disagree' or 'strongly disagree', you need to revise these parts.

READING PART 3

HISTORY AND TIME

Assessment Objective 1B

Understand in detail a range of texts, identifying finer points of detail

Assessment Objective 1C

Distinguish between facts, ideas and opinions

Assessment Objective 1D

Identify a writer's viewpoint and attitude, stated and implied

LEARNING OBJECTIVES

- Talk about history
- Prepare for Part 3 of the Reading and Writing Exam
- Verifying information (true, false or not given)
- Identify different types of information (facts, ideas and opinions)
- Build new vocabulary (phrasal verbs)
- Use comparative and superlative adjectives

PREPARING THE WAY

Discuss the questions.

- Who decides what is recorded as history?
- Can you trust what you learn about the personalities of individuals who lived 1000 years ago? Why / Why not?
- What is the use of learning about history?
- What is the most significant historical event of all time?

SKILLS INTERPRETATION

ACTIVITY 1

Listen to a gallery guide talking about a painting and answer the questions.

1 When did King Canute live? 1000 years ago 995-1035
2 Why is he wearing brightly coloured clothes? Because he was a king
3 Do other paintings of Canute exist? ~~no~~ Yes
4 What is Canute doing in the painting and why? Command the waves.
5 Did this event really happen? ~~NO~~ w~~d~~k
6 Why do people remember stories like this? Humble ruler

Because he showed that even though he's a king he can't change nor controll the nature.

FOCUSING ON THE EXAM

- Part 3 (Reading and Writing) is worth 20 marks.
- It is based on a long text, e.g. a report or article.
- You need to complete two or three different tasks. These can be: multiple choice, short-answer questions, true / false / not given, note completion, sentence completion, diagram completion or summary completion.
- You need to distinguish between facts, ideas and opinions.
- You need to identify the writer's viewpoint and attitude, stated and implied.

EXAM SKILLS

A01C

VERIFYING INFORMATION (TRUE, FALSE OR NOT GIVEN)

One of the possible tasks in Reading Part 3 is to read a text and decide whether statements about the text are true or false. The other option is 'not given'. Choose this option when you cannot determine whether the statement is true or false by reading the text, because the information does not appear in the text.

SKILLS CRITICAL THINKING, SELF-DIRECTION

ACTIVITY 2

1 Work in a group to do some research and fill in the gaps with facts about one of the following dinosaurs.

A Tyrannosaurus Rex **B** Brontosaurus

The ______________ had ________________ as a special feature.

The ______________ ate ________________.

The ______________ weighed ______________.

The ______________ was ______________ tall.

The ______________ lived in ______________.

The ______________ became extinct ______________ years ago.

2 Write five new statements about your chosen dinosaur. Change the facts so that some of them are false.

3 Give your facts to another group. Look at the other group's facts and guess whether they are true or false. Is there any missing information?

4 Check your guesses.

5 Working individually, use your research to write a paragraph about your chosen dinosaur. Include two opinions about it, as well as at least five facts.

EXAM SKILLS

A01C

IDENTIFYING FACTS, IDEAS AND OPINIONS

The texts in Reading Part 3 will contain information that can be fact, ideas or opinions. A useful skill is to be able to identify these different types of information.

ACTIVITY 3

1 Match the sentences to the categories listed in the word box. Discuss in pairs.

facts	ideas	opinions

- Dinosaurs laid eggs.
- Dinosaurs are cute.
- Let's go to the Natural History Museum.

2 Working in pairs, list two more examples for each category.

EXAMPLE

Facts	Ideas	Opinions
There are 100 centimetres in a metre.	*I'm going to build a bridge.*	*I like my neighbour.*

ACTIVITY 4

Look at the picture to the left. Write three factual sentences about it and three sentences based on opinion.

READING PART 3

▼ PRACTICE TIME

Read the article on dinosaurs and answer Questions 26–45.

Amazing discovery of the 'Biggest Dinosaur Ever'

Palaeontologists working in South America have discovered the bones of the world's biggest dinosaur. Dinosaur enthusiasts all over the world are excited by this highly significant find.

Drawing on what is known about the remains that have been dug up so far, it is believed that the newly-unearthed dinosaur weighed approximately 77 tonnes and was 40 metres long. The palaeontologists looking after the site where the bones were first found believe that its height was about 20 metres. These calculations are based on the size of its thigh bones and mean that, when it was alive, this immense creature weighed about the same as 32 rhinos.

One of the reasons why the palaeontologists were particularly excited about this find was that the dinosaur previously known as the biggest, the *Argentinosaurus*, was actually seven tonnes lighter. This meant this new find was the heaviest dinosaur ever discovered!

The interest in the discovery wasn't limited to Argentina, where the bones originally came from. People all over the world find dinosaurs fascinating and events such as this make it easy to see why. Partly it's the fact that dinosaurs look so different from most of the species we're familiar with and partly it's their sheer size – no wonder so many film crews travelled to Argentina to capture the events on camera. For some of the scientists involved, it must have been a life-changing moment when they realised the implications of their discovery.

Perhaps the most extraordinary detail about this incredible find is the way that the events unfolded. The dinosaur bones were not discovered as part of a planned excavation. Instead, as with so many discoveries in the world of science, someone actually came across them by accident. It was not even a scientist who found the bones; they were unearthed by a local farm worker in a desert in Patagonia who wasn't even looking for them!

Once the palaeontologists heard about the find, they hurried to excavate the rest of the skeleton properly, discovering a number of additional bones in the process. Not all of the bones came from the original dinosaur; it is thought that they belonged to a group of about seven. None of the skeletons of these seven dinosaurs was complete, but by assembling the separate bones – over a hundred – that were dug up, the palaeontologists were able to calculate the weight of the dinosaur by drawing on their knowledge of dinosaur anatomy.

The palaeontologists have confirmed that this new species of dinosaur, a herbivore, walked the Earth about 100 million years ago. They have reported that it is an example of a species known as a titanosaur, but have not yet come up with a scientific name.

Of course, plenty of claims for the title of the 'world's biggest dinosaur' have been made before. If you look up earlier finds, you'll discover that the previous title-holder, the *Argentinosaurus*, was a close neighbour of the newly-discovered dinosaur and was also unearthed in Patagonia. It was found by Guillermo Heredia, a rancher, and again the initial find was made by accident.

Heredia thought that he had dug up a huge piece of ancient wood, but a few years later South America's most respected palaeontologist, José F Bonaparte, identified the 'wood' as part of the remains of a new type of herbivore. This huge plant-eating dinosaur was named after the country in which it was found. Although at the time the *Argentinosaurus* was the biggest dinosaur known, it weighed 70 tonnes, so was slightly lighter than its successor.

Unfortunately, establishing a dinosaur's weight is a very complex process and the scientists who attempt to do this are not always in agreement with each other. A major problem is that it is very rare to find a specimen that is completely intact. Originally the *Argentinosaurus*, for example, was estimated to be bigger than it turned out to be. Some researchers even thought it might be as heavy as a 100 tonnes.

With the new species of titanosaur, although the scientists studying it cannot be 100 per cent certain that their calculations are correct, they have a very good sample size: having a large number of bones from the seven dinosaurs, means that their sums are more likely to be accurate. This helps them to be more sure that this is indeed the biggest dinosaur ever.

Some experts remain cautious, though, reflecting on the difficulties of establishing the exact sizes and shapes of these ancient creatures and many admit that there is an element of guesswork. Even so, it seems certain that the new discovery is likely to make its way into the history books. Dinosaurs have fascinated so many people for centuries and discoveries like this make us reflect on the life of these amazing creatures.

SKILLS DECISION MAKING

EXAM HINTS

- If you give more than one answer for Questions 26–30 you will get zero, even if one of your answers was correct.
- Remember to only choose 'not given' when you cannot say if the statement is true or false. Usually it is because the information is not there in the text.

AFTER EXAM CHECK

- Make sure you have not missed any questions.
- Make sure you have not marked a cross in more than one box for each question.

EXAM HINT

When answers have a limit of three words, remember that any numbers or figures are included in this word limit.

WATCH OUT!

For Questions 31–40, make sure you stick to the three-word limit – you will get zero if you write more than is required, even if the right answer is included.

AFTER EXAM CHECK

- Make sure that you have not missed any questions.
- Make sure that you have not used too many words to fill the gaps.

Read the statements below. Decide whether they are TRUE, FALSE or NOT GIVEN according to the text.

Mark a cross ☒ for the correct answer. If you change your mind about an answer, put a line through the box ☒ and then mark your new answer with a cross ☒.

		True	False	Not Given	
26	The palaeontologists measured the bones to calculate the dinosaur's weight.	☒	☐	☐	(1)
27	The remains of the biggest dinosaur were found by a farm worker.	☒	☐	☐	(1)
28	The new dinosaur was a meat eater.	☐	☒	☐	(1)
29	The discovery of a whole dinosaur skeleton is quite unusual.	☒	☐	☒	(1)
30	Calculating dinosaurs' sizes accurately is crucial for scientific advances.	☐	☐	☐	(1)

(Total for Questions 26–30 = 5 marks)

Questions 31–40

Complete the following sentences using no more than THREE words taken from one point in the text.

31 The newly-discovered dinosaur had a weight equivalent to .... (1)

32 Estimates make it .... heavier than *Argentinosaurus*. (1)

33 Many people worldwide think dinosaurs are .... (1)

34 People .... Argentina to film the discovery. (1)

35 The bones were first found in a .... (1)

36 Weight was estimated using information about .... (1)

37 It is a .... of titanosaur. (1)

38 The remains of the *Argentinosaurus* were first thought to be .... (1)

39 Deciding on a dinosaur's .... is not simple. (1)

40 Working out the exact dimensions of a dinosaur involves a .... (1)

(Total for Questions 31–40 = 10 marks)

WATCH OUT!

Some of the words have similar meanings. Make sure you pick the best word to fit the sentence. You may not need to use all the words in the word box.

AFTER EXAM CHECK

Make sure you answer all the questions and that you follow the instructions.

Questions 41–45

Complete the summary of the text using words in the box below. Each word may be used once or not at all.

accuracy	guessed	specimens	maximum	life	examples
gigantic	existence	estimated	fairness		

The remains of a dinosaur believed to be the largest in **(41)** .... were discovered in a desert in Patagonia, in South America. The dinosaur, a **(42)** .... specimen, is thought to have lived in forest regions. Although a complete skeleton has not been uncovered, the bones of seven **(43)** .... have been found so far. This has enabled the palaeontologists working on the excavation to calculate the dinosaur's size with more **(44)** .... than is often the case.

Previously, a dinosaur known as the *Argentinosaurus*, also found in Patagonia, was thought to be the largest. However, the *Argentinosaurus* had an **(45)** .... weight of 70 tonnes. The new dinosaur is believed to have been seven tonnes heavier.

(Total for Questions 41–45 = 5 marks)
(Total for Part 3 = 20 marks)

SKILLS SELF-MONITORING

HOW DID YOU DO?

- Check your score. What went well?
- Could you have done better? If so, how?

VOCABULARY AND GRAMMAR

GRAMMAR CHECKPOINT

GRAMMAR

See Grammar Reference pages 268–269.

PHRASAL VERBS

ACTIVITY 1

1 Look at the phrasal verbs in the word box, then find them in the text 'Amazing discovery of the "Biggest Dinosaur Ever"' on pages 29–30 and underline them.

draw on	look after	come from	come across
look for	look up	turn out	reflect on

2 Match the phrasal verbs to the correct definitions.

Phrasal verbs	**Definition**
draw on	originate
look after	find unexpectedly or without intention
come from	think about
come across	use (especially knowledge or experience)
look for	research, consult other sources
look up	take care of
turn out	happen in a particular way, usually unexpectedly
reflect on	search for

SKILLS ANALYSIS

ACTIVITY 2

Complete the blog post below by using one phrasal verb from Activity 1 to fill each gap.

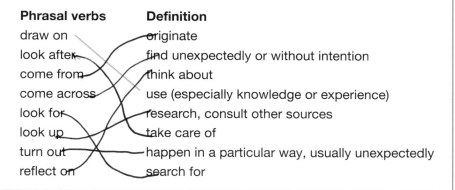

diggerblog.com

MY DAY WITH DINOSAURS

Today, we need to [1] ________ ideas about moving the newly-discovered bones back to the museum. I'm sure that if we talk about it we can agree on something. It may also be helpful to [2] ________ how they've moved big bones like this in the past. It's amazing to think that this time last week we didn't know that such an interesting dinosaur skeleton existed. What a great day for palaeontologists everywhere when that farm worker made his incredible discovery! This new find deepens our research, which is really nice for me.

It is good to think that someone just found these bones, yet they turned out to be so important. Where does luck like this [3] ________? It makes you [4] ________ the role that chance plays in scientific work. We really can [5] ________ a whole new set of data for future research; already it has such important implications and as time goes on we may [6] ________ even more reasons to recognise its significance.

It is a real honour to excavate these remains and I think that in the future they may [7] ________ to be even more important than we now realise. We now just have to make sure we [8] ________ these bones as carefully as we can!

GRAMMAR CHECKPOINT

GRAMMAR

See Grammar Reference page 277.

ADJECTIVES

ACTIVITY 3

1 Look again at the text in Activity 2 on page 33. Underline all the adjectives. How many can you find?

2 Find a synonym for each adjective that would make the text more entertaining.

EXAMPLE big → *large*

GRAMMAR CHECKPOINT

GRAMMAR

See Grammar Reference pages 278–279.

COMPARATIVE ADJECTIVES

ACTIVITY 4

Look at the two pictures and write five sentences using comparative adjectives.

EXAMPLE *The dinosaur is bigger than the puppy.*

GRAMMAR CHECKPOINT

GRAMMAR

See Grammar Reference pages 278–279.

COMPARATIVE AND SUPERLATIVE ADJECTIVES

ACTIVITY 5

Copy and complete the table with the correct forms of the adjectives.

intelligent	stupid	lazy	beautiful
near	far	simple	easy
calm	delicate	good	bad
talented			

Adjective	Comparative adjective	Superlative adjective
hard	*harder*	*hardest*

GRAMMAR GAME

▼ SURVEY TIME

- Working in groups, look at the statements in the survey below. Helen is beautiful ☺!
- Ask your classmates questions to help you complete the statements.
- Answer your classmates' questions.
- Complete the statements as fast as you can. Sometimes the answer will be 'No one'.
- Whoever completes the survey first, wins!

Nathan lives nearer to our school than me.	Trinity lives further from our school than me.
Helen is older than me.	Helen's elder brother is younger than me.
Wendy has more brothers and sisters than me.	Noone has fewer brothers and sisters than me.
Noone has the oldest pet in the class.	Nick has the youngest sibling.
The tallest person in my group is Sissi.	The youngest person in my group is Sissi.

ACTIVITY 6

The form of comparative adjectives depends on the number of syllables in the base adjective. Insert a slash (/) whenever there is a syllable break. Some words have only one syllable.

EXAMPLE dangerous → *dan / ge / rous*

1 ugly
2 fast
3 articulate
4 ridiculous
5 fascinating
6 simple
7 infuriating
8 bored
9 confusing
10 helpful

SELF-EVALUATION

Tick the relevant boxes.

I now feel confident about ...	STRONGLY AGREE	AGREE	DISAGREE	STRONGLY DISAGREE
▶ TALKING ABOUT HISTORY				
▶ VERIFYING INFORMATION (TRUE, FALSE OR NOT GIVEN)				
▶ IDENTIFYING FACTS, IDEAS AND OPINIONS				
▶ USING NEW VOCABULARY (PHRASAL VERBS)				
▶ USING COMPARATIVE ADJECTIVES				
▶ USING SUPERLATIVE ADJECTIVES				

If you ticked 'disagree' or 'strongly disagree', you need to revise these parts.

UNIT 2 WRITING PREPARATION

Assessment Objective 2A

Demonstrate appropriate use of paragraphing, punctuation and spelling

Assessment Objective 2B

Write in a range of registers to fit the context and the audience

Assessment Objective 2C

Demonstrate a control of a range of vocabulary and a variety of grammatical structures

Assessment Objective 2D

Summarise information provided in text form for a given purpose and audience

This unit prepares you for the Writing section of Paper 1 Reading and Writing. In this part of the exam, you need to show that you can write clear, relevant texts in English on a range of subjects.

The unit contains three parts, which correspond to the three parts of the Writing section. You need to write different types of text in the different parts:

- Part 4: a short piece of writing, such as an email, in response to a given situation
- Part 5: a factual piece of writing, such as a report or article, based on your own knowledge and interests
- Part 6: a response to one or two short texts (including some marks gained by using reading skills) and a summary for a given purpose and reader.

In Parts 4–6 of the exam, you need to meet the Assessment Objectives AO2A, AO2B, AO2C and AO2D. The AOs that will be tested in the exam are indicated at the beginning of the corresponding part of this unit.

The unit focuses on the core writing skills that you will need. Working through these lessons and activities will help you develop these skills.

WRITING PART 4

FOOD AND DRINK

Assessment Objective 2A

Demonstrate appropriate use of paragraphing, punctuation and spelling

Assessment Objective 2B

Write in a range of registers to fit the context

Assessment Objective 2C

Demonstrate a control of a range of vocabulary and structures

LEARNING OBJECTIVES

- Talk about food
- Prepare for Part 4 of the Reading and Writing exam
- Identify and use formal and informal register
- Consider relevance and word limits in the exam
- Build new vocabulary (collocations: food and drink)
- Use the present perfect

PREPARING THE WAY

Discuss the questions.

- Should food be both healthy and tasty? Which is more important?
- Should eating always be a social activity?
- Imagine that you can only eat food from one country. Which country would you choose?

ACTIVITY 1

1 Sort the food vocabulary into the correct columns.

delicious tasty honey coffee ~~sliced~~
~~watermelon~~ bread fruit home-baked fresh

Adjectives	Nouns
sliced	*watermelon*

2 Add at least five more food and drink words to each column. Try to think of unusual words. You can use your dictionary to help.

SKILLS ▸ CREATIVITY

3 Choose a category from the word box and create your own menu.

fine dining
space-age food
class picnic

FOCUSING ON THE EXAM

- Part 4 (Reading and Writing) is worth 10 marks.
- You need to write an informal email, letter or postcard, e.g. to a school friend.
- You are given a short description of a situation which sets the context.
- You need to follow the instructions and cover all the points in the question.
- You need to present and ask for specific information.
- You need to write in an appropriate format and style.
- You need to write 75–100 words.

EXAM SKILLS

A02B

REGISTER

An important skill for Writing Part 4 is understanding differences in **register**. In this part of the exam, you are required to write informally (perhaps to a friend or family member), so you need to use words and styles that are appropriate for **informal writing**.

What people say depends on **audience** and **context**.

- An **informal register** is used when talking to friends and family. The tone is warm and more relaxed. The features of informal language normally include:
  - **contractions**
  - simpler vocabulary
  - slightly shorter sentences
  - more reference to personal experience.
- A **formal register** is used in formal situations or when talking to people you do not know very well. The tone is polite and less relaxed.

ACTIVITY 2

1 What are the differences between the two sentences? Which is formal and which is informal?

a It's been great fun and I've loved the whole thing. Informal

b The experience has been delightful and I have thoroughly enjoyed myself. formal

2 Sort the phrases into the correct columns.

I don't like him much.	Why don't you try this?
I need help with this.	The man does not impress me.
I require additional support.	I would suggest this action.

Informal	Formal

ACTIVITY 3

1 (very informal) ⟷ 5 (very formal)

1 Rate the list of written greetings. Give them a number between 1 and 5.

a Hi

b Greetings

c To whom it may concern

d Hello

e Dear

2 Rate the closings.

a Yours sincerely

b Take care

c Yours truly

d See you soon!

e Best wishes

3 Discuss with a partner which greetings and closings would be appropriate to use in Writing Part 4 of the exam.

SKILLS ADAPTIVE FUNCTION

ACTIVITY 4

1 Read the postcard. Underline the phrases that are not suitable for an informal piece of writing.

Warmest greetings Ravi!

How are things? I hope you're exceptionally healthy. I am having an exquisite time here in Italy. It's a beautiful country and the food is yummy. There are also numerous spectacular locations to visit. Have you had any thoughts about what we could do upon my return? I regret that it may be ages until we see each other again.

Lots of love,

Jason

2 Rewrite the phrases you underlined to make them more informal.

EXAM SKILLS

A02B

RELEVANCE AND WORD LIMIT

In Writing Part 4 you will lose marks if you do not cover all of the points in the question. However, anything you write over 100 words will not be marked. You must make sure that what you write is relevant to the question. Do not add extra details that are not asked for.

ACTIVITY 5

Read this sample question for Writing Part 4. Do not answer the question, but note the word count limits and the three points. Then read the two sample answers.

You have decided to take up a new hobby. Write an email to your friend asking for his/her advice about which hobby you should choose.

In your email you **must** write:

- why you want to start a new hobby
- which two hobbies you have considered
- questions to ask for your friend's opinion.

You **must** write between **75 and 100 words only**.

EXAM HINT

You do not need to include any email headings like 'To', 'From' or 'Subject' in the exam. You only need to write the main email text.

WATCH OUT!

Be absolutely sure to cover all the points in the question. Your email may be shorter than one you would usually write to a friend or a family member.

Student A

SEND Save Now Discard

TO Kim@supermail.com
Add Cc Add Bcc

FROM Lea@applecart.com
Attach a file

B I U A

Hello Kim,

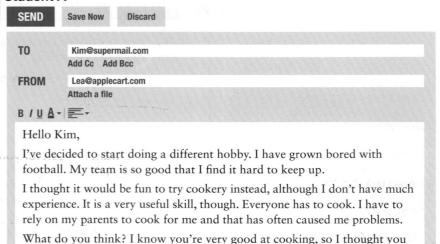

I've decided to start doing a different hobby. I have grown bored with football. My team is so good that I find it hard to keep up.

I thought it would be fun to try cookery instead, although I don't have much experience. It is a very useful skill, though. Everyone has to cook. I have to rely on my parents to cook for me and that has often caused me problems.

What do you think? I know you're very good at cooking, so I thought you could give me some tips.

Talk soon,
Lea

Student B

SEND Save Now Discard

TO Gabriela@supermail.com
Add Cc Add Bcc

FROM Ali@studentzone.com
Attach a file

B I U A

Hi Gabriela,

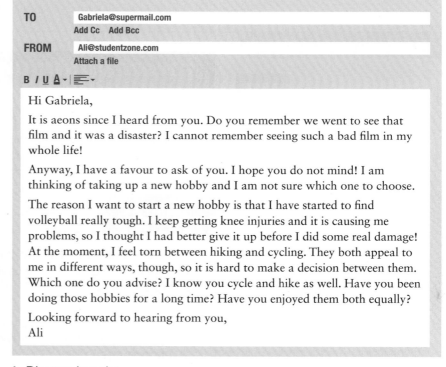

It is aeons since I heard from you. Do you remember we went to see that film and it was a disaster? I cannot remember seeing such a bad film in my whole life!

Anyway, I have a favour to ask of you. I hope you do not mind! I am thinking of taking up a new hobby and I am not sure which one to choose.

The reason I want to start a new hobby is that I have started to find volleyball really tough. I keep getting knee injuries and it is causing me problems, so I thought I had better give it up before I did some real damage! At the moment, I feel torn between hiking and cycling. They both appeal to me in different ways, though, so it is hard to make a decision between them. Which one do you advise? I know you cycle and hike as well. Have you been doing those hobbies for a long time? Have you enjoyed them both equally?

Looking forward to hearing from you,
Ali

1 Discuss in pairs.
- Imagine you are the examiner. Which response would you give the highest marks to? Why?
- Count the number of words in Ali's email. At what point would the examiner stop marking?
- How could Ali start his email to make sure all three points are covered?

2 Write your own response to the Writing Part 4 sample question on page 41.

A02B

SKILLS CREATIVITY, EXECUTIVE FUNCTION

EXAM HINTS

- Don't write a long introduction.
- Make sure that the introduction is relevant, unless it is extremely brief, e.g. *How are you?*
- Keep the register informal for the whole response.
- Make sure you cover each of the three points in enough detail.
- Remember to focus on register, relevance and closings.

WATCH OUT!

Don't let your language become too informal. Avoid text speak.

SKILLS SELF-MONITORING

AFTER EXAM CHECK

- Make sure you didn't write more or less than the word limit.
- Make sure you used the correct register consistently.

WRITING PART 4

▼ PRACTICE TIME

You have decided to cook a birthday meal for your friend. Write an email to this friend, asking for their ideas.

In your email you **must** write:

- why you want to cook for your friend
- which meal you want to make
- questions to ask for your friend's opinion.

You **must** write between **75 and 100 words only**.

(Total for Part 4 = 10 marks)

HOW DID YOU DO?

- Check your score. What went well?
- Could you have done better? If so, how?

VOCABULARY AND GRAMMAR

VOCABULARY FOCUS

COLLOCATIONS: FOOD AND DRINK

ACTIVITY 1

1 Listen to the dialogue and make notes.
- Where are Jane and Hassan? Restaraunt
- What is the problem? Strange taste of fish.
- What solutions do they discuss? Food refund, different course.

2 Try to make collocations using one word from each column.

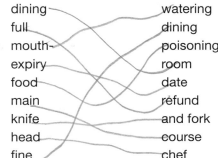

dining	watering
full	dining
mouth-	poisoning
expiry	room
food	date
main	refund
knife	and fork
head	course
fine	chef

3 Listen to the dialogue again and check your collocations.

ACTIVITY 2

Match the collocations from Activity 1 on page 43 to the correct definitions.

1 You get this when you receive all your money back for a service you were not happy with ____________

2 Utensils that can be used for eating ____________

3 When food stops being fresh enough to eat ____________

4 Illness caused by bad food ____________

5 The biggest, most substantial part of a meal ____________

6 Eating high quality food ____________

7 The part of a restaurant where you eat ____________

8 Food that looks extremely tasty ____________

9 The person in charge of food preparation ____________

ACTIVITY 3

Jane writes about the meal on a travel website. Read the review and fill in the gaps using the collocations from Activity 1 on page 43.

Review of The Great Fish Restaurant

My friend Hassan and I have just had a rather unpleasant experience at the Great Fish restaurant. It's a [1]__________ __________ restaurant with an excellent reputation for really delicious seafood dishes. We thought the meal would be [2]__________-__________ but we were really disappointed.

It started off well. We were greeted politely and shown to our seats in the main [3]__________ __________. They have [4]__________ __________. The waiters were very attentive and we were all ready to enjoy our meal.

The starter arrived and was fine, but then the waiter brought us our [5]__________ __________ and that's when the trouble started. Both of us had fish and as soon as we tasted it we realised something was wrong. I've never eaten fish with such a strange taste before. It must have been past its [6]__________ __________. We didn't want to eat any more of it, in case it gave us [7]__________ __________ so we put down our [8]__________ __________ after a few mouthfuls and asked for a [9]__________ __________.

The waiter was very polite about it, but we won't be going back – so much for [10]__________ __________!

GRAMMAR CHECKPOINT

GRAMMAR

See Grammar Reference pages 262–263.

PRESENT PERFECT

ACTIVITY 4

Listen to the first part of the dialogue again and complete the table with the present perfect verbs and the time phrases. One of the verbs has no time phrase.

Verb	Verb form in dialogue	Time phrase
book	*we've booked*	*already*
hear		*several times*
eat		
decorate		
see		

ACTIVITY 5

Complete the sentences correctly using the verbs in the word box in the present perfect.

break	ever be	not complete	~~never taste~~	go	not see

EXAMPLE I *have never tasted* fish like this before.

1 The fish ________ past its expiry date.

2 ________ he ________ here before?

3 I'm sorry, I ________ the exercise.

4 Who ________ the jar of honey?

5 We ________ Paul today.

ACTIVITY 6

Put the present perfect sentences in the correct order. Sometimes more than one order is possible.

EXAMPLE to / decided / hobby / a / I / doing / start / have / different
I have decided to start doing a different hobby.

1 problems / caused / has / it / often

2 have / much / you / money / how / spent?

3 before / had / this / haven't / meal / they

4 eaten / thanks / I've / already / but

5 weeks / I / ill / 've / for / last / been / two / the

ACTIVITY 7

Complete the sentences using the present perfect.

EXAMPLE (+, ?, Jeff, wake up)
Has Jeff woken up yet?

1 (–, ?, Barcelona, lose)
Why __________ yet this year?

2 (+, she, fly)
__________ before.

3 (+, we, do)
__________ the reports.

4 (–, Abed, find)
__________ the answer yet.

5 (?, she, write)
__________ the email to headquarters?

6 (–, ?, they, eat)
Why __________ breakfast?

7 (–, I, try)
__________ that.

8 (?, Britta, have)
__________ lunch yet?

9 (+, we, finish)
__________ the exercise! We can use the present perfect!

SKILLS COMMUNICATION

GRAMMAR GAME

▼ I HAVE NEVER EVER…

- Hold up five fingers.
- Take it in turns to describe something you have never done using the phrase *I have never ever* (for example, *I have never ever visited Paris*). The sentence must be true!
- Anybody who has done the action (*visited Paris*) lowers one of their fingers.
- If no one has done the action, then the speaker lowers one finger.
- Whoever lowers all of their fingers first, loses the game. The person remaining is the winner!

SELF-EVALUATION

Tick the relevant boxes.

I now feel confident about ...	STRONGLY AGREE	AGREE	DISAGREE	STRONGLY DISAGREE
▶ TALKING ABOUT HISTORY				
▶ IDENTIFYING AND USING FORMAL AND INFORMAL REGISTER				
▶ WRITING RELEVANT CONTENT WITHIN A WORD LIMIT				
▶ USING NEW VOCABULARY (COLLOCATIONS: FOOD AND DRINK)				
▶ USING THE PRESENT PERFECT SIMPLE				

If you ticked 'disagree' or 'strongly disagree', you need to revise these parts.

WRITING PART 5

COLOURS

Assessment Objective 2A

Write using correct paragraphing, punctuation and spelling

Assessment Objective 2B

Write in a range of registers to fit the context and the audience

Assessment Objective 2C

Demonstrate a control of a range of vocabulary and a variety of grammatical structures

LEARNING OBJECTIVES

- Talk about colours
- Prepare for Part 5 of the Reading and Writing Exam
- Consider context and purpose when writing
- Consider audience when writing
- Build new vocabulary (idioms: colours)
- Use the past simple

PREPARING THE WAY

Discuss the questions.

- What is your favourite colour? Why?
- Which colour best represents your personality? Why?
- Do different colours have different meanings in different cultures?
- Imagine you can only wear two colours for the rest of your life. Which colours would you choose? Why?
- Do humans and animals see colours in the same way?

indigo	green	orange
red	black	turquoise
white	yellow	brown
blue	violet	grey
cream	pink	purple

ACTIVITY 1

1 Look at the colours. Make a list of all the objects you can see around you that match the colours.

2 Discuss in pairs.

- Seven of these colours are visible in rainbows. Do you know which ones?
- Have you ever seen a rainbow in real life?
- Where or when do rainbows normally appear?

FOCUSING ON THE EXAM

- Part 5 (Reading and Writing) is worth 20 marks.
- You need to write a semi-formal report, article or semi-formal letter, e.g. for a teacher or the school magazine.
- You need to present specific information.
- You need to write in an appropriate format and style.
- You need to follow the instructions and cover all the points in the question.
- There is a very short description of a situation which sets the context and outlines what you should write.
- You need to write 100–150 words.

EXAM SKILLS

A02B

CONTEXT AND PURPOSE

An important skill for Writing Part 5 is matching your writing to the context and **purpose** that you are given. Writing Part 5 is a semi-formal task. You need to think carefully about the type of text that is required and choose the correct words and style for the task.

ACTIVITY 2

1 Working in pairs, make notes about these different text types, considering the questions below. layouts

- Letters name, date, adress.
- Reports Font, chapter, title.
- Articles Intro, body text, conclusion

a What are the features of **layout** of these three **genres**?

b What are the language features used for these three genres?

2 Make a list of different contexts and audiences for these different types of text.

SKILLS DECISION MAKING

ACTIVITY 3

Read Texts A and B and then answer the questions.

Text A

Rainbows are formed when tiny droplets of water are illuminated by sunlight. These droplets then form minute prisms which refract light at different frequencies. These frequencies produce a spectrum of colour known as a rainbow. Isaac Newton identified the colours visible to the human eye as (in sequence): red, orange, yellow, green, blue, indigo and violet.

Text B

I'll never forget the moment I first saw a rainbow. It was a truly breathtaking sight. I was only seven years old. It felt as if my heart had stopped beating for a moment. Time stood still. It was amazing – the colours were gorgeous. It was the most beautiful thing I had ever seen.

Which text is:

	A	B
more factual?	☐	☐
more imaginative?	☐	☐
from a personal account?	☐	☑
from a Science textbook?	☑	☐

SKILLS ANALYSIS

ACTIVITY 4

1 Draw a table like the one below. Find six lexical words from each text and add them to the table.

Text ___ : Personal account	Text ___ : Science textbook
I saw, It felt, breathtaking, my heart, I'll never forget.	identified, illuminated, frequencies, spectrum, prisms, refract.

2 Which list would be better for these purposes?
- creative writing B
- giving information Text A
- giving personal history Text B
- explaining facts A

3 Which list would be the most suitable for a report? A

EXAM SKILLS

CONSIDERING AUDIENCE

Another important skill in Writing Part 5 is identifying and adapting your work for the audience for your text. Your words and expressions must be suitable for the audience.

Imagine your friend asks you what you think of your school meals. You might say:

- *'They're awesome!'*
- *'They're disgusting!'*

However, if the context is a letter or report to your head teacher, your language will be more formal:

- *'They are delicious / extremely tasty.'*
- *'They are disappointing / unpleasant.'*

This is because the context and audience influences the use of language, both when you speak and when you write.

WATCH OUT!

Remember, the examiner will look not just at **what** you write, but also at **how** you write it. Make sure you choose words that are appropriate for the context and the register required.

ACTIVITY 5

Working in pairs, discuss how you would reply to these questions if they were asked by:

a your friend
b an adult interviewing you for a work placement job.

- Did you enjoy your English lessons last week?
- What do you think of the school's sports facilities?
- Can you think of any improvements to the school that would help students?

SKILLS DECISION MAKING

ACTIVITY 6

1 Read Text C on the next page and choose the correct words in the table to describe it.

Text type / genre	Register	Language
report letter article	informal semi-formal formal	informative poetic scientific emotional

WATCH OUT!

Newspaper articles are often laid out in columns, but you do not need to recreate this layout for the exam.

Text C

COME RAIN OR SHINE!

When the Green Road School football team left school this morning, the students who had to stay indoors were green with envy because it was a beautiful day. However, the weather had some surprises in store for the players. First, their game against St Mark's College was interrupted by rain and later a beautiful rainbow appeared directly above the playing fields. By the time the game was in the second half, the atmosphere was extremely tense. The temperature had fallen dramatically during the morning and some of the spectators complained that they were blue with cold! In the first half of the game, the two teams had managed to score one goal each in quick succession. Supporters from both schools were watching the ball intently as players chased it, everyone eager to create a golden opportunity to make the score 2-1. When players had about 20 minutes left, it started raining. The rain soon turned to a very heavy downpour and the referee was forced to stop play. The break only lasted for 10 minutes though. To everyone's surprise, the rain suddenly stopped, the sun broke through the clouds and a double rainbow appeared. Double rainbows happen once in a blue moon. Everyone cheered and then started playing again. This colourful event certainly lifted everyone's spirits – at least for a short time. Later on, though, the losing team, St Mark's College, went home red-faced after Green Road scored two goals in the last five minutes.

▲ Winning goal worth the wait

2 Discuss in pairs.

- What does the title mean? The change in the weather
- Who is the audience for this text? Students
- How and why is the register suitable for the audience?

EXAM HINTS

- Choose the appropriate register for context, purpose and audience.
- Use the appropriate language for the register.
- Choose an appropriate layout for the text.

WRITING PART 5

▼ PRACTICE TIME

You are the representative for the school Sports Club. Sports Day has been cancelled due to bad weather. You need to write a letter to your head teacher to tell him/her about new plans for sports day.

In your letter you **must**:

- explain why the original Sports Day was cancelled
- explain how students felt about the cancellation
- write how this event will be organised (include information about dates, venue and schedules).

You **must** write between **100 and 150 words only**.

(Total for Part 5 = 20 marks)

SKILLS SELF-MONITORING

AFTER EXAM CHECK

- Make sure you wrote 100–150 words.
- Make sure you covered each of the three points in enough detail.

HOW DID YOU DO?

- Check your score. What went well?
- Could you have done better? If so, how?

VOCABULARY FOCUS

VOCABULARY AND GRAMMAR

IDIOMS: COLOURS

ACTIVITY 1

Listen to the extracts from Text C and choose the correct definitions for the colour idioms.

1 green with envy
   a angry and unwell   b very envious   c a bit jealous

2 blue with cold
   a extremely cold   b very ill   c slightly unhappy

3 a golden opportunity
   a a great success   b a lot of money   c a chance that should not be missed

4 once in a blue moon
   a very rarely   b every year   c occasionally

5 red-faced
   a very upset   b furious   c embarrassed

ACTIVITY 2

1 Look at some more colour idioms. Can you work out what they mean? Discuss in pairs and match the idioms to the correct definitions.

Colour idiom	Definition
see red	reveal your real personality and intentions
roll out the red carpet	do exceptionally well in a test or exam
show (your) true colours	make extensive preparations for a visit from someone important
pass with flying colours	feel extremely angry

2 Still working in pairs, write a sentence using each colour idiom.

SKILLS INTERPRETATION

ACTIVITY 3

Read the diary entry and fill in the gaps using each of the idioms from Activities 1 and 2 on page 53 once, written in the correct form.

Date: 1 January

I hope the rest of the year is an improvement on today! It started badly when the central heating broke. I was almost [1] ~~green with envy~~ ________. I called the engineer, who said that the heating was fine; it was the battery in the thermostat that had broken. Talk about feeling [2] ~~[illegible]~~ cold ________! The whole thing was so embarrassing.

Then my friend Lil rang me. She's going to a New Year's concert tonight. I feel a bit jealous, because my favourite band is playing and I can't go. In fact, I'm [3] ~~furious~~ green with envy ________. It's not just that their music is great but that they hardly ever play; they only give concerts [4] once in a blue moon ________. Anyway, before I told Lil that I can't go, she offered me her ticket! I thought that was so generous of her. She really [5] showed true colors ________ when she made that suggestion.

Last time they played here, they invited members of the audience up on stage to sing with them, but I was too scared to volunteer. I'm always missing [6] a golden opportunity ________ like that; it makes my mum [7] extremely angry ________ sometimes.

On the other hand, the reason I can't go to tonight's concert is because I'm going to the family New Year's party. It won't be as exciting as the concert, but I know I'll enjoy it. My aunt is flying in all the way from Australia to see us so we're going to [8] roll out the red carpet ________ for her. She's just qualified as a lawyer! She did really well and [9] ~~pass with flying~~ colors ________

GRAMMAR CHECKPOINT

GRAMMAR

See Grammar Reference pages 263–264.

PAST SIMPLE

ACTIVITY 4

Sort the verbs in the word box into the correct columns, according to their pronunciation in the past simple.

~~want~~	shout	love	wash	retire	try	dance	allow	play
cough	visit	start	beg	relax	direct	close	like	need
	clean	watch	hope	irritate	mend	work		

Verb *-ed* sound	Verb *-t* sound	Verb *-d* sound
wanted	want	retired
shouted	shout	closed
loved		danced
		irritated
		hoped
		need

ACTIVITY 5

Complete the sentences with the past simple.

EXAMPLE (?, Sally, go)
Did Sally go to the beach last weekend?

1 (+, we, meet) we met at Honeycomb Hives yesterday.
2 (+, I, wake up)
I woke up at five this morning so I wouldn't miss my train.
3 (–, we, have) we had breakfast today. There wasn't enough time.
4 (+, the Miami Dolphins, win) (+, the Buffalo Bills, lose)
__________ the game and __________; it's as simple as that.
5 (+, I, lie) I lied to you about the result. I'm sorry.
6 (+, he, lie) he layed on the grass and got stains on his clothes.
7 (+, you, keep up) (+, I, be)
you ~~did~~ kept up keep really well during the race, __________ impressed.
8 (+, we, hold) (–, it, change)
we held a meeting to discuss the problem, but didnt pass anything.
9 (+, I, write) i wrote a ten-page essay about Art History last night.
10 (–, ?, you, paint)
Why didnt you paint the room the colour we wanted?

ACTIVITY 6

Working in pairs, ask each other about your last holiday or trip using the past simple.

- Where did your partner go?
- Did he or she do any enjoyable activities?
- What food did he or she try?
- What was the weather like?

Tell the class about your partner's last holiday using the past simple.

GRAMMAR CHECKPOINT

GRAMMAR

See Grammar Reference pages 262–264.

PAST SIMPLE AND PRESENT PERFECT

ACTIVITY 7

Sort the time expressions below into the correct columns, according to the tense in which they are normally used.

~~yesterday~~ today this week last month 1996 ever this year the 90s

Past simple	Present simple
yesterday	today
last month	this week
1996	this year
the 90s	ever

ACTIVITY 8

Circle the correct sentences.

1 She broke her foot last week. / She has broken her foot last week.
2 He never tried Korean food before. / He has never tried Korean food before.
3 Did you go to the party on Saturday? / Have you gone to the party on Saturday?
4 She never ate at that restaurant. / She has never eaten at that restaurant.
5 Why did you leave France to live here? / Why have you left France to live here?
6 I spent yesterday making the cake. / I have spent yesterday making the cake.
7 What time did you arrive? / What time have you arrived?
8 I slept all afternoon last Tuesday. / I have slept all afternoon last Tuesday.
9 I started the project but I haven't finished. / I've started the project but I haven't finished.
10 I painted the room in 2015. / I have painted the room in 2015.

ACTIVITY 9

Complete the sentences using the past simple or the present perfect.

EXAMPLE (+, Pauline, score)
Pauline scored in the game yesterday.

1 (+, she, eat) she ate three pizzas last week.
2 (+, I, twist) I twisted my ankle, so I can't drive to work.
3 (-, Emi, cook) Emi ~~never~~ cooked Moroccan food before.
4 (?, you, read) Have you read the paper this morning?
5 (+, Ramin, be)
Will Ramin be there since 9 a.m. I don't know what time he'll leave.
6 (+, they, eat)
They ate at that restaurant when they were children.
7 (?, you, live)
How long have you lived here for?
8 (?, you, like) (+, Tim, go)
Do you like the card? Tim went all the way to the museum to buy it.
9 (-, they, watch)
They never watched that programme before.
10 (+, Paul, be) (+, I, arrive)
Paul have been ~~here~~ here ever since I arrived. .

GRAMMAR GAME

▼ TIME EXPRESSIONS

- Working in pairs, write six new irregular verbs onto six cards in the present simple. Then write six time expressions on different cards (you can refer to Activity 8 on page 56 for help).
- Place them face-down on the table in two piles (verbs and time expressions).
- Take it in turns to take two cards, one from each pile. You must then make a sentence, using the verb and the time expression on the cards you selected.
- Check the sentences after you say them. If you were correct, you get a point. The student with the most points at the end of the game, wins!

SELF-EVALUATION

Tick the relevant boxes.

I now feel confident about ...	STRONGLY AGREE	AGREE	DISAGREE	STRONGLY DISAGREE
▶ TALKING ABOUT COLOURS				
▶ CONSIDERING THE FEATURES OF WRITING FOR DIFFERENT CONTEXTS AND PURPOSES				
▶ CONSIDERING THE FEATURES OF WRITING FOR DIFFERENT AUDIENCES				
▶ RECOGNISING WHEN WRITING SHOULD BE FACTUAL RATHER THAN DESCRIPTIVE				
▶ USING NEW VOCABULARY (IDIOMS: COLOUR)				
▶ USING THE PAST SIMPLE AND PRESENT PERFECT				

If you ticked 'disagree' or 'strongly disagree', you need to revise these parts.

WRITING PART 6

SPEECH AND COMMUNICATION

Assessment Objective 2A

Demonstrate appropriate use of paragraphing, punctuation and spelling

Assessment Objective 2B

Write in a range of registers to fit the context and the audience

Assessment Objective 2C

Demonstrate a control of a range of vocabulary and a variety of grammatical structures

Assessment Objective 2D

Summarise information provided in text form for a given purpose and audience

LEARNING OBJECTIVES

- Talk about speech and communication
- Prepare for Part 6 of the Reading and Writing exam
- Find equivalent expressions for given phrases
- Identify and paraphrase relevant information in a text
- Make inferences/predictions about the content of a text
- Summarise information effectively
- Build new vocabulary (verbs: communication)
- Use the past simple and past continuous
- Use *would* and *used to*

PREPARING THE WAY

Discuss the questions.

- What are the differences between virtual interaction (texting, online) and face-to-face interaction?
- What type of communication do you prefer and why?
- How do people in your country normally socialise?
- How long could you survive without social interaction?

ACTIVITY 1

Think back to when you were a small child. Discuss in pairs.

- How old were you when you learned to talk?
- What was your first word?
- Were there any words you found difficult when learning to talk?
- Did you make up any words when you were learning to talk?

ACTIVITY 2

Working in pairs, discuss the qualities in the following list and decide which qualities contribute the most to a good conversation.

- Ability and willingness to listen carefully
- The desire to be very polite
- A wide vocabulary
- A positive attitude
- A sense of humour
- Interest in the person you are speaking to
- Knowledge about current events
- Honesty and sincerity
- Perfect ability to speak the language
- An interest in philosophy and politics
- A friendly and open personality
- Willingness to talk about yourself
- Clear speech with no mumbling
- A wide range of interests
- Familiarity with the latest gossip
- Willingness to compromise

FOCUSING ON THE EXAM

- Part 6 (Reading and Writing) is worth 25 marks (5 marks for extracting the relevant information, 20 marks for putting it into your own words).
- You need to write a summary based on the text provided.
- You will also need to draw inferences and/or make predictions about the content of the text.
- The context is formal or semi-formal, e.g. for your teacher.
- You need to write 100–150 words.

EXAM SKILLS

FINDING EQUIVALENT EXPRESSIONS

An important skill for Writing Part 6 is the ability to present information given in a different way, in a formal or semi-formal context.

ACTIVITY 3

Working in pairs, find different ways to express the following. Use a dictionary or thesaurus if you need.

1 We won't be early.
2 This train is the slowest I've ever travelled on!
3 Come round to mine at seven.
4 The desert has no water.

EXAM HINT

Synonyms and antonyms are very helpful tools for making equivalent expressions. See pages 10, 17, 22 and 34.

EXAM SKILLS

EXAM HINT

In the exam, 5 marks are available for finding the correct information to write your summary. You need to read and extract the relevant information from the text(s) as defined by the guidance given in the question. You can also be awarded up to 20 marks for writing your own summary to satisfy the points in the bullet points of the question.

EXAM HINT

The part of the summary that you write for the third bullet point may be based on **inference** or **prediction**.

SKILLS INTERPRETATION

EXAM HINT

This activity allows you to practise reading and extracting information with a view to then summarising the information.

EXAM HINT

Highlighting the relevant parts of the text for the exam question will save you time. You can then exclude the sections that are not relevant – you will not need to read them again.

PARAPHRASING AND SUMMARISING

Another important skill for Writing Part 6 is the ability to **paraphrase** and **summarise** information given. You need to use your own words as much as possible to answer the questions and address the bullet points in the exam, so try not to rely on the language of the original text.

Although you must put the relevant information into your own words, you can borrow key words from the text if necessary. For example, if the text was about parachutes, you would have to use *parachute* in your summary, as there is no natural-sounding alternative in English.

ACTIVITY 4

Read the extract from an article about dolphin communication and the sample first or second bullet point of a Writing Part 6 sample question below it.

Research on dolphin communication has come up with some very interesting findings. Scientists have announced that their findings confirm what we already thought: dolphins are highly intelligent creatures, able to detect and communicate a wide range of sounds. New technology has recorded them at very close range and, apparently, the dolphins sounded as if they were talking to each other. Some of these sounds, such as clicks, were being used in order to find out about their environment. This is known as 'echolocation' and it works like a form of radar: the dolphin makes a clicking sound which bounces off whatever is in their surroundings, giving the dolphin important information. As well as making clicking noises, amazingly, the dolphins were whistling – again, they were communicating with other dolphins, or so the scientists believe.

You are doing a project on dolphin communication. Read the text and write a summary for your teacher.

In your summary you **must**:

- explain **one** way in which dolphins are able to find out information about their environment.

1 Mark the section of the article where you can find the information asked for. You can use your skimming and scanning skills to help you. Where do the relevant sections of the text start and finish?

2 Re-read the section of the article you have marked and underline the phrases which give the information you need. Pick one and think about how you could paraphrase it. Use the questions below to help you.

> makes a clicking sound which bounces off whatever is in their surroundings

a Can I think of synonyms for any of the verbs or nouns? (e.g. *makes*)

b Can I shorten any of the noun phrases or use different parts of speech, such as nouns/verbs/adjectives, to explain the same idea? (e.g. *a clicking sound*)

c Are there any phrases which could be deleted or changed? (e.g. *whatever is in*)

3 Read this first sentence from a student answer to the sample question on page 60 and answer the questions below.

> Dolphins use a technique called 'echolocation' to get information about their environment.

a Can you explain the technique that the student has used to start the response? Consider the key words and their position in the article text and in the response.

b Can you explain how and whether this technique is helpful for paraphrasing and/or summarising?

ACTIVITY 5

Read the article from Activity 4 and the sample question on page 60 again. Then read the sample student answers.

Student A

Some of these noises, like clicks, are used to find out about their environment. This is called 'echolocation' and it works like radar: the dolphin makes a click sound which bounces off their surroundings. This gives the dolphin important information.

Student B

Dolphins make use of sounds, such as clicks, in order to discover more about the nature of their surroundings. This process is known as 'echolocation' and it works like a type of radar. The sounds strike any object in the vicinity, giving the dolphin vital data.

Discuss in pairs.

- Which response do you think is better? Why?
- Which shows more successful use of the student's own words?
- Compare the student responses with the original text and make a note of the changes. Which response is more like a summary of the original, and which is more like a paraphrasing of the original?

EXAM HINTS

You have to re-write the material that is relevant to the bullet points in *your own words as far as possible.* In order to access the full mark range:

- make sure your writing flows well and is well organised
- communicate facts or ideas clearly
- use vocabulary that is appropriate for the context
- use a range of vocabulary, with correct usage and spelling
- use a range of grammatical structures accurately
- use punctuation correctly.

SKILLS ADAPTIVE LEARNING

EXAM HINT

To summarise a change, you need to summarise the situation before and after the change.

WATCH OUT!

Full summaries generally include an introduction and conclusion. In the exam, however, you should focus **only** on the three bullet points in the question. Do not include extra material about the topic or text, except where you are asked to speculate or make predictions in the last bullet point.

EXAM HINT

Organise your writing clearly, making sure you use a separate paragraph for each separate bullet point in the question.

WRITING PART 6

▼ PRACTICE TIME

You are doing a project on the way that babies and young children learn to talk. Read the text below and write a summary for your teacher.

How babies talk

Did you know that human beings are capable of making thousands of different sounds? And on average, we have learned to recognise 200–300 different words by the time we are just two years old. How do we learn so many words? And how do we actually learn to talk?

It is odd to think that human beings evolve in a relatively short space of time from newborn babies who can only really make involuntary sounds to children who can have sustained conversations about a range of topics.

To begin with, babies make so-called 'vegetative' noises – these are sounds, like crying, that the baby has no conscious control over. Within a few weeks that starts to change and before the age of 18 months, the majority of babies have said their first word(s).

One process that occurs during this period is that the baby becomes increasingly focused on the sounds around it – particularly the speech sounds. Until the age of nine months, babies of all nationalities sound the same, but then the sounds they make start to change. Although they cannot say actual words yet, the noises they produce are recognisably those of the language(s) surrounding them. If you want your child to grow up bilingual, or multilingual, let him/her have exposure to the second or third language before the age of nine months. This will provide a huge advantage in learning that language later on – especially when it comes to pronunciation.

Over the years, many debates have existed about how babies learn to communicate. One psychologist, Burrhus Frederic (B.F.) Skinner, believed that babies learn to talk by copying the speech of those around them, usually their family. He thought that they were 'conditioned' into talking through 'positive reinforcement' of their behaviour. In other words, they were trying to copy others and were praised when they did so successfully.

A linguist called Noam Chomsky rejected Skinner's claims that babies learn language through imitation. He believed that babies were born already 'programmed' to talk – the ability to speak is already present but needs to be activated. He argued that babies often use words in sequences or forms not copied from their parents.

A more recent thinker, Jerome Bruner, emphasised the role of parents and other caregivers in helping babies acquire language. He argued that they were using continuous feedback from their environment in order to develop their own language and that interactions such as telling stories and asking children questions were key to this.

It has generally been accepted now that each of these three explanations contains some truth, but that no single theory in isolation can explain the mystery that is child language development.

On a final note, linguists have found that babies of all nationalities understand many more words than they are able to use. To put it another way, babies' reception of language exceeds their production. In this way, they are similar to students of foreign languages, who often understand significantly more than what they can say.

In your summary you **must**:

- explain **two** ways in which babies' language changes just before and after the age of nine months
- state **three** factors that help babies learn to speak, according to Skinner, Chomsky and Bruner
- give **your predictions** about the future language skills of a child in a bilingual or multilingual family.

You will be awarded up to **5 marks** for using relevant information from the text.

You **must** write between **100 and 150 words only**. You **must** use your own words where possible.

(Total for Part 6 = 25 marks)

AFTER EXAM CHECK

Make sure you have used your own words where possible. Remember to change the sentence structure as far as you can, as well as the vocabulary.

SKILLS SELF-MONITORING

HOW DID YOU DO?

- Check your score. What went well?
- Could you have done better? If so, how?

VOCABULARY AND GRAMMAR

VOCABULARY FOCUS

SKILLS ANALYSIS

VERBS: COMMUNICATION

ACTIVITY 1

1 Find the communication verbs in the word box in the article on page 62.

debate	speak (to)	talk (to)	copy	communicate
praise	emphasise	reject	say	tell

2 Discuss in pairs.

a What does each verb mean?

b *Say*, *speak*, *tell* and *talk* have very similar meanings. What is the difference between them?

ACTIVITY 2

Complete the sentences using *say*, *speak*, *tell* or *talk*.

1 I often ____ Luka to check her spelling using a dictionary.

2 In this lecture, Dr Chan will _____ about how apes communicate with each other.

3 A lot of people are going to ____ about this film when it's released.

4 I always ___ that this is the best restaurant in town.

ACTIVITY 3

Match the correct communication verbs from Activity 1 on page 63 to the correct definitions.

1 To say something in a way that gives it more importance ________

2 To exchange information or conversation with other people, using words, signs or writing ________

3 To refuse to accept, believe in or agree with something ________

4 To purposefully say something or make a sound in exactly the same way as someone else ________

5 To discuss a subject formally when you are trying to make a decision or find a solution ________

6 To say that you admire and approve of someone or something, especially publicly ________

ACTIVITY 4

Circle the correct words.

1 I can't **emphasise** / **debate** enough how dangerous it is to cycle without a helmet.

2 She was **saying** / **talking** to me for hours about that really boring Maths lesson.

3 The difficulty for babies is that they can't **praise** / **communicate** by talking.

4 Always **say** / **copy** your name when you answer the phone at work.

5 We weren't arguing. We were **talking** / **debating** the value of studying Science subjects.

6 Don't **speak** / **communicate** when there's an exam taking place in the next room.

7 She always **rejects** / **emphasises** my ideas before I've had a chance to explain them.

8 She always **debates** / **praises** Tom's ideas even though they aren't very well thought-through.

9 Please **tell** / **say** us a story before bedtime tonight!

10 Parrots are very good at **copying** / **rejecting** sounds, which is why some people think they can talk.

ACTIVITY 5

Fill in the gaps using verbs from Activity 1 on page 63, using the correct form.

1 We always __________ Jan, but she doesn't understand how talented she is.

2 When are you going to ___________ to Hari about how much unhealthy food he eats?

3 Small children like to __________ what their parents say as it makes them feel grown-up.

4 The police officers couldn't agree on who had committed the crime, even though they _______________ it for hours.

5 I'm ready to leave when you are – just ______ the word!

6 The committee have _____________ proposals to build a new hospital in Dakar, on the grounds that it is too expensive.

7 He ___________ me about his childhood last night.

8 Dolphins ___________ with each other by using special whistling sounds.

9 The report will _____________ the need for reforms in the farming industry.

10 She hasn't ____________ to him since the earthquake.

ACTIVITY 6

Sort the words and phrases in the word box into the correct columns, depending on whether they follow *say*, *speak*, *tell* or *talk*. Each one can be used more than once.

to someone	something	someone	about
a story	a fact	an anecdote	me

say	speak	tell	talk

GRAMMAR CHECKPOINT

GRAMMAR

See Grammar Reference page 264.

PAST CONTINUOUS

ACTIVITY 7

Put the past continuous sentences in the correct order. Sometimes more than one order is possible.

1 doing / you / what / Paul / were / called? / when

2 sleeping / while / travelling / were / we / was / I

3 was / work / when / dropped / Sarah / running / for / she / her / phone / late

4 well / dancing / but / band / playing / nobody / were / was / the

GRAMMAR CHECKPOINT

GRAMMAR

See Grammar Reference pages 263–264.

PAST CONTINUOUS AND PAST SIMPLE

ACTIVITY 8

Which tense should you use to talk about the following? Write past continuous or past simple.

1 a completely finished action _____
2 the shorter of two simultaneous actions in the past _____
3 the longer of two simultaneous actions in the past _____
4 a sudden action in a story _____
5 background information in a story _____
6 one of two simultaneous actions in the past of equal length _____

ACTIVITY 9

Complete the sentences using the past continuous or the past simple.

1 (+, she, eat)
_____ lunch at 1 p.m. today.

2 (?, you, chat)
What _____ about when I got here?

3 (–, Rose, do)
_____ anything when I called her.

4 (+, the coffee, taste)
_____ funny to me.

5 (–, I, see) (+, I, go)
_____ anyone when _____ into the room.

6 (+, Femi, break)
_____ the jar last Friday.

7 (?, you, have)
What _____ for breakfast this morning?

8 (+, the doctor, forget) (+, I, have to)
_____ to write me out the prescription, so _____ go back to the clinic.

9 (+, you, be) (+, I, speak)
_____ really peculiar this morning when _____ to you.

10 (+, I, tell)
_____ her about the project this morning.

GRAMMAR CHECKPOINT

WOULD AND *USED TO*

GRAMMAR

See Grammar Reference page 267.

ACTIVITY 10

Read the sentences and correct any mistakes you find.

1. I used to play on the beach with my father.
2. I would play football for hours when I was younger.
3. I didn't used to eat so many vegetables.
4. I would have a dog when I was a child.
5. Did you use to go to this school?
6. I never would play video games before I moved here.
7. Who used to help in the kitchen?
8. He wouldn't always have showers.
9. My friend is used to flying his kite when he was a boy.
10. Jennifer would always ask for extra dessert.

SKILLS EXECUTIVE FUNCTION

GRAMMAR GAME

▼ WHAT WERE YOU DOING …?

Ask and answer questions with your partner using the past continuous and different time expressions like the ones in the word box.

Last Saturday at lunchtime	This day last year
This day 5 years ago	This time last week

- *What were you doing …?*
- *Where were you living …?*

Try to find three times when you were both doing the same thing.

EXAMPLE
A: *What were you doing this time last week?*
B: *I was learning English at school. What were you doing?*

SELF-EVALUATION

Tick the relevant boxes.

I now feel confident about ...	STRONGLY AGREE	AGREE	DISAGREE	STRONGLY DISAGREE
▶ TALKING ABOUT SPEECH AND COMMUNICATION				
▶ PUTTING WORDS AND PHRASES INTO MY OWN WORDS				
▶ IDENTIFYING AND PARAPHRASING RELEVANT INFORMATION IN A TEXT				
▶ FOCUSING ON THE PARTICULAR REQUIREMENTS FOR A SUMMARY IN THE EXAM				
▶ SUMMARISING INFORMATION EFFECTIVELY				
▶ USING NEW VOCABULARY (VERBS: COMMUNICATION)				
▶ USING THE PAST CONTINUOUS				
▶ USING *WOULD* AND *USED TO*				

If you ticked 'disagree' or 'strongly disagree', you need to revise these parts.

UNIT 3
LISTENING PREPARATION

Assessment Objective 3A

Understand the overall message of a spoken passage

Assessment Objective 3B

Identify essential and finer points of detail in spoken material

Assessment Objective 3C

Understand a conversation where information is being negotiated and exchanged

Assessment Objective 3D

Identify a speaker's viewpoint and attitude, stated and implied

This unit prepares you for Paper 2 Listening. In this part of the exam, you need to show that you can understand a wide range of recorded material.

The unit contains four parts, which correspond to the four parts of the Listening exam. You will need to use different types of listening skill in the different parts:

- Part 1: listen for detailed information
- Part 2: follow a discussion or argument, identifying attitude and opinions of speakers and following instructions
- Part 3: listen to a longer recording, e.g. a conversation, and identify a speaker's viewpoint and attitude, stated and implied
- Part 4: listen to a longer recording, identify essential and finer points of detail and identify a speaker's viewpoint and attitude, stated and implied.

In Parts 1–4 of the exam you need to meet the Assessment Objectives AO3A, AO3B, AO3C and AO3D. The AOs that will be tested in the exam are indicated at the beginning of the corresponding part of this unit.

The unit focuses on the core listening skills that you need. Working through these lessons and activities will help you develop these skills.

LISTENING PART 1

THE WORLD OF WORK

Assessment Objective 3A

Understand the overall message of a spoken passage

Assessment Objective 3B

Identify essential and finer points of detail in spoken material

LEARNING OBJECTIVES

- Talk about jobs and work experience
- Prepare for Part 1 of the Listening exam
- Understand the overall message of a spoken text
- Identify details in a spoken text
- Build new vocabulary (nouns: the world of work)
- Use *wh*- questions

PREPARING THE WAY

Discuss the questions.

- What would be your ideal job?
- What makes a job fun?
- What is the purpose of work experience?

ACTIVITY 1

Look at the two pictures below. Answer the questions.

1 What is happening in each picture?

2 How do you think the people are feeling?

3 Have you ever had a job interview? If so, what was it like?

FOCUSING ON THE EXAM

- Part 1 (Listening) is worth 10 marks. It is based on short listening texts.
- You may need to complete one or two tasks, e.g. multiple matching or multiple choice, and short-answer questions.
- If a short-answer question is given, you are usually asked to write no more than two, three or four words for each answer.
- You will need to use different types of listening skill for the Listening exam.

EXAM SKILLS

LISTENING FOR THE OVERALL MESSAGE

Try to get a sense of the topic and content of the passage quickly. Listen for key words and also be aware of verb tenses. Is the speaker describing an event from the past or are they discussing something that is ongoing? What is their relationship to the listener? Are they giving the listener information or advice?

ACTIVITY 2

1 Sometimes we hear what is said to us, but we don't really listen to it. What is the difference in meaning between the verbs *hear* and *listen*? Discuss in pairs. hear is hear but not listen. listen is think and analyze

2 Fill in the gaps using *hear* or *listen* in the correct form.

a We could ___hear___ the cheer from two streets away.

b The receptionist gave directions to the conference suite and Mel ___listen to___ carefully.

c The baby ___hear___ his father and smiled.

d 'Where are you going?' The boy ___hear___ the words and stood still.

e I told Hasani what to do, but he wasn't ___listening___.

f I ________ to the radio in the car this morning so I could find out who had won the election.

3 Do any of the sentences above describe the following skills? Discuss in pairs and choose your answers.

- Listening for details ____________
- Listening for the overall message ____________

SKILLS REASONING, ARGUMENTATION

1. ~~informative~~, text, call, face to face, video call, class time, assembly

ACTIVITY 3

1 Make a list of six different types of speech that you have heard this week, e.g. conversations with friends, phone messages, speeches or radio programmes.

2 Order the items in your list according to how closely you actually listened to them.

3 Compare your list with a partner. Discuss in pairs.
- Are they similar?
- What are the differences?
- Why did you listen to some types of speech more closely than others?

EXAM SKILLS

LISTENING FOR DETAIL

Be alert to specific details, e.g. dates, times, names, places and events. When you read the questions, notice which types of detail will be needed. Listen for them carefully. The questions will usually follow the order of information presented in the texts and all required answers will come from the text. Make sure you are familiar with the correct format for writing detail, e.g. using capitals for names.

ACTIVITY 4

Listen to the people talk about their work and write the correct numbers next to the professions.

designer 5	musician 3	athlete 6
doctor 1	lawyer 4	engineer 2

SKILLS DECISION MAKING

EXAM HINTS
- You will hear each recording twice.
- Skills such as selecting and sorting information are transferable skills that can be used in Paper 2.
- If you give more than one answer for Questions 1–5, you will get zero, even if one of your answers is correct.

LISTENING PART 1

▼ PRACTICE TIME

Section A

In this section, you will hear five short extracts in which people are talking about places to eat.

Read the list of places below, then listen to the extracts.

For each question, 1–5, identify which place (A–H) is being described by each speaker by marking a cross ☒ for the correct answer. If you change your mind about an answer, put a line through the box ☒ and then mark your new answer with a cross ☒.

Not all places are described and each place may be used more than once.

One mark will be awarded for each correct answer.

A motorway restaurant
B vegetarian restaurant
C drive-through fast-food diner
D public barbecue area
E pizza restaurant
F street fruit and vegetable stall
G shopping centre café
H fish and chip shop

1 Speaker 1 (1)

A	B	C	D	E	F	G	H
☐	☐	☐	☐	☐	☐	☒	☐

2 Speaker 2 (1)

A	B	C	D	E	F	G	H
☒	☐	~~☒~~	☐	☐	☐	☐	☐

3 Speaker 3 (1)

A	B	C	D	E	F	G	H
☐	☒	☐	~~☒~~	☐	☐	☐	☐

4 Speaker 4 (1)

A	B	C	D	E	F	G	H
☐	☐	☐	☐	☐	☒	☐	☐

5 Speaker 5 (1)

A	B	C	D	E	F	G	H
☐	☐	☒	☐	☐	☐	☐	☐

EXAM HINT

For Questions 6–10, make sure you keep to the word limit, e.g. two or three words. You will get zero if you write more than is required, even if the right answer is included.

WATCH OUT!

Make sure that the word or words you choose are grammatically correct answers to the question.

AFTER EXAM CHECK

- Make sure you didn't give more than one answer for Questions 1–5.
- Make sure you kept to the specified word limit for Questions 6–10.
- Make sure you have answered all the questions and followed the instructions.
- If you made a mistake, make sure you have put a line through the incorrect answer.

Section B

In this section, you will hear a woman talking to some students who are starting their work experience at her pizza restaurant.

For Questions 6–10, listen and answer the questions below. Write no more than FOUR words for each answer.

One mark will be awarded for each correct answer.

6 How long has Lena owned the restaurant? (1)

over 20 years
....

7 What might Lena offer to good student workers? (1)

Job
....

8 What is the most important thing for the restaurant? (1)

cleanliness ~~Hygiene~~ ~~Excellent food and service~~
....

9 What is Lena's ideal student worker like? (1)

polite and communicative
....

10 What is provided for staff who don't want to eat pizza every day? (1)

salads
....

(Total for Part 1 = 10 marks)

SKILLS SELF-MONITORING

HOW DID YOU DO?

- Check your score. What went well?
- Could you have done better? If so, how?

VOCABULARY AND GRAMMAR

VOCABULARY FOCUS

NOUNS: THE WORLD OF WORK

ACTIVITY 1

Match the words in the word box to the correct definitions.

customer work experience staff trainee
apprenticeship full time part time contract
briefing manager workplace uniform application

1 A short period of unpaid work to learn more about that type of work _work experience_
2 Working for all the hours of a week during which it is usual for people to work or study _full time_
3 A formal request to be considered for a job _application_
4 An official agreement between two or more people stating what each will do in, for example, a job ~~apprenticeship~~ _contract_
5 A generally fixed period of working for an employer to learn a particular skill or job in detail ~~contract~~ _apprenticeship_
6 The people who work for an organisation _staff_
7 A particular type of clothing worn by all the members of a group or organisation _uniform_
8 The room or building where you work _workplace_
9 Information or instructions that you get before you have to do something _briefing_
10 The person responsible for a business or department and the people in it _manager_
11 Someone who is learning how to do a job _trainee_
12 Someone who buys goods or services from a shop or company _customer_
13 Working for only a part of each day or week _part time_

ACTIVITY 2

Fill in the gaps using the words from Activity 1.

1 As a ________, you will learn how to offer great service to customers.

2 Are you free this afternoon to attend the ________ on health and safety in the workplace?

3 Why was that ________ so angry? Weren't you polite to her? She was only here for 5 minutes!

4 Thank you for your well-written ________. We'd like to offer you an interview tomorrow at three o'clock.

5 I would like to apply for that job, but I don't think I have enough ________.

6 Helena thinks that the staff ________ isn't warm enough. She always wears an extra sweater and scarf.

7 Can you work ________? We only need a waitress on Wednesdays and Friday mornings.

8 I was offered the job a month ago, but they still haven't sent me the ________, so I don't know any more details about when I will be working.

9 They want me to work ________ on a three-month contract. That means giving up my studies as I'll no longer be able to fit them in.

10 We will be offering a nine-month ________ to anyone who has just left school and is genuinely keen to learn how to cook in a fine dining establishment.

11 Could you please get your ________? I need to make a complaint.

12 The best thing about this job is the other ________. They are all so friendly and motivated.

13 It is up to members of staff to keep the ________ tidy and organised.

ACTIVITY 3

Discuss in pairs.

- Have you ever done any work experience? If so, what?
- What work experience would you like to get?
- What are the benefits of a full-time job compared to a part-time job?
- Which do you think is more important: happy staff or happy customers? Why?

GRAMMAR CHECKPOINT

GRAMMAR

See Grammar Reference page 272.

At the moment -
When will you eat?
when are you finishing?

This year -
When are you finishing school?
When will you turn 16?

Normally -

Tomorrow -
When will you have a training,
When will you come back from the trip.

WH- QUESTIONS AND QUESTION TAGS

ACTIVITY 4

Match the questions to the correct answers.

Question	Answer
What are you doing later?	At seven.
Where are you eating dinner?	With my family.
Why didn't you eat at home?	Having dinner.
Who did you eat with?	Quite pleasant.
How are you finding the meal?	In town.
When are you eating dinner?	I didn't have any food in the house.

ACTIVITY 5

1 Write two *wh-* questions for each of the following time expressions. Use appropriate tenses.

- At the moment
- Normally
- Yesterday
- This year
- Tomorrow

2 Working in pairs, ask and answer the questions you have written.

yesterday -

ACTIVITY 6

Complete the questions with possible beginnings.

EXAMPLE *You volunteer at the library group*, don't you?

1 ____________, don't you?
2 ____________, do you?
3 ____________, aren't you?
4 ____________, aren't they?
5 ____________, isn't she?
6 ____________, is he?
7 ____________, haven't you?
8 ____________, hasn't he?
9 ____________, have you?
10 ____________, has he?

GRAMMAR CHECKPOINT

GRAMMAR

See Grammar Reference pages 274–275.

HINT

Inversion means changing the normal order of subject and verb.

I had suspected … → *Had I suspected* …

INVERSION

ACTIVITY 7

1 Read the work experience report and circle the seven examples of **inversion**.

Under no circumstances had I suspected how intense my first work experience would be. After I sent the application, I was invited for an interview and they accepted me. I was so happy! Little did I know that it would be one of the most challenging weeks of my life.

No sooner had I arrived than they put me in the kitchen and told me to start arranging the toppings on the pizzas! I don't have any qualifications at all, so I thought they would teach me how to do things on my first day without any pressure, but they just threw me straight in. Not until much later that week did they show me a video about all the correct cooking methods. Nowhere, at any point, was there anything written down to help me.
Anyway, hardly had I started working when they told me that my shift was over! I couldn't believe it. Apparently, I had been working for five hours – it felt like five minutes. Never had the time passed so quickly. So even though it was very challenging, in the end I really enjoyed everything.

2 Circle the negative words and phrases which come before each inversion. Are extra words and phrases also needed after the inversion?

ACTIVITY 8

Using the meaning from the first sentence, make new sentences containing inversion. Use the starting words and phrases given.

EXAMPLE The actor appeared and everyone started to cheer.
No sooner had the actor appeared than everyone started to cheer.

1 I saw Venice and I fell in love with the city.
No sooner ________________________________.

2 I will not talk to him again.
Under no circumstances ________________________________.

3 I did not know what would happen.
Little ________________________________.

4 I did not realise my mistake until later.
Not until later ________________________________.

SELF-EVALUATION

Tick the relevant boxes.

I now feel confident about ...	STRONGLY AGREE	AGREE	DISAGREE	STRONGLY DISAGREE
TALKING ABOUT JOBS AND WORK EXPERIENCE				
UNDERSTANDING THE OVERALL MESSAGE OF A SPOKEN TEXT				
IDENTIFYING DETAILS IN SPOKEN TEXTS				
USING NEW VOCABULARY (NOUNS: THE WORLD OF WORK)				
USING *WH-* QUESTIONS				
USING INVERSION				

If you ticked 'disagree' or 'strongly disagree', you need to revise these parts.

LISTENING PART 2

PETS

Assessment Objective 3B

Identify essential and finer points of detail in spoken material

Assessment Objective 3D

Identify a speaker's viewpoint and attitude, stated and implied

LEARNING OBJECTIVES

- Talk about animals and pets
- Prepare for Part 2 of the Listening exam
- Identify detail in a spoken text
- Identify viewpoints and attitudes in a listening text
- Build new vocabulary (collocations: health and training)
- Use prepositions of time, place and movement

PREPARING THE WAY

Discuss the questions.

- What type of animals make the best pets?
- Do animals have personalities?
- What is it that makes animals different from humans?
- Do you think that animals dream?
- Should laws exist to protect animals?
- If you could be an animal, which one would you be? Why?

ACTIVITY 1

SKILLS DECISION MAKING

Lots of different pets are competing against each other in a pet show. Working in pairs, match the pets (a–h) to the superlatives in the word box to decide which pet wins each category.

a

b

c

d

e

f

g

h

best at swimming	best at talking	fluffiest	most intelligent		
cutest	slowest	cleverest	oldest	loudest	prettiest

FOCUSING ON THE EXAM

- Part 2 (Listening) is worth 10 marks.
- It is based on a longer listening text, e.g. a monologue or radio broadcast.
- You need to complete the tasks given, e.g. multiple choice, note/sentence/chart/table/diagram completion, or short-answer questions.
- You may need to complete sentences in a specified number of words.
- You will hear the text twice and will be given time to read the questions before the recording begins.
- You will be expected to respond to the questions as you listen.
- You need to identify information stated explicitly, as well as implied viewpoints and attitudes.

EXAM SKILLS

IDENTIFYING DETAIL

An important skill for Listening Part 2 is the ability to identify key points and detail. Think about the different kinds of detail that might be included: facts to do with time, colour, size, shape. Listen for key words that help you focus on the right part of the text.

ACTIVITY 2

1 Listen to the four pet show introductions. Identify the four pets.

2 Listen again and choose the correct answers.

1 What details are given about the first pet?
a how long it lives **b** how high it jumps **c** its appearance

2 What details are given about the second pet?
a its age **b** its appearance **c** where it lives

3 How many details are given about the third pet's appearance?
a one **b** three **c** five

4 What is the main detail given about the fourth pet?
a its size **b** its colour **c** its diet

EXAM SKILLS

IDENTIFYING VIEWPOINTS (STATED AND IMPLIED)

A secondary skill for Listening Part 2 is the ability to identify a speaker's views, both **stated** and **implied**. As well as facts, the text may contain different **viewpoints** and attitudes and you will need to identify these. Listen to find out how the speaker feels about the topic discussed in the text and try to work out how they want the listener to feel about it.

SKILLS INTERPRETATION

ACTIVITY 3

1 What is the difference between stated information and implied information? Discuss in pairs.

2 Sort the statements into the correct columns to check your understanding.

- a Pets make your life more rewarding.
- b ~~Goldfish live in water~~.
- c Puppies are cute.
- d Kittens are young cats.

Information is stated	Information is implied
Goldfish live in water.	

ACTIVITY 4

1 Read the sentences in the table. Then listen to a dog trainer talking about caring for your dog and complete the table.

	True or False? (T/F)	Stated ✓ or implied ✗
1 Exercise is good for dogs.		
2 The dog trainer likes long walks.		
3 The dog trainer likes the outdoors.		
4 Young dogs and old dogs have the same requirements.		
5 Dogs are dangerous when they are not on a lead.		

2 Which words or phrases in the recording helped you with your answers? Listen again and make notes to explain your answers.

A03B

SKILLS INTERPRETATION

EXAM HINTS

- Remember that you will hear the text twice and will be given time to read the questions before the recording begins.
- Respond to the questions as you listen.
- Remember that the emphasis in Questions 11–18 is likely to be factual. Questions 19–20 are more likely to be based on feelings or ideas.
- Read the word limit carefully. It may be two, three or four words.

LISTENING PART 2

▼ PRACTICE TIME

In this part, you will hear a man talking about dog training.

For Questions 11–18, listen and complete the notes. Write no more than THREE words for each answer.

One mark will be awarded for each correct answer.

Dog-training advice

Advice on ground rules

Let your dog know who is boss from the **(11)** .... (1)

Keep your dog off the **(12)** .... (1)

Stick to regular **(13)** .... (1)

Advice on training

To train your dog successfully, you will need
(14) ......to be friend...... and ......consistent...... (1)

Praise your dog when he or she obeys your **(15)** ......tike sit commands...... (1)

After basic training, most dogs will sit, stay and come to
(16) ......the will...... (1)

Advice on agility training

Particular breeds, such as collies and Alsatians, are associated with agility training because they have intelligence and **(17)** .... (1)

Ask a **(18)** .... before arranging any training for your dog. (1)

WATCH OUT!

Correct spelling is not a requirement for this part of the exam, but your answer must be comprehensible (i.e. capable of being understood) to gain marks.

AO3B

SKILLS INTERPRETATION

EXAM HINT

Don't mark a cross in more than one box for Questions 19–20. If you make a mistake, correct it by putting a line through your cross (as shown on the exam paper) otherwise your answer will not count.

Questions 19 and 20 must be answered with a cross in a box ☒. If you change your mind about an answer, put a line through the box ☒ and then mark your new answer with a cross ☒.

19 What does the speaker think of the relationship between dog and owner? (1)

- ☐ **A** It will improve the dog's performance.
- ☐ **B** It isn't very significant.
- ☒ **C** It takes time to develop.
- ☐ **D** It's more important for young dogs.

20 What does the speaker admire about his own dog? (1)

- ☐ **A** His fitness
- ☒ **B** His intelligence
- ☐ **C** His personality
- ☐ **D** His obedience

(Total for Part 2 = 10 marks)

AFTER EXAM CHECK

Make sure you didn't write more than the specified number of words for any of your answers for Questions 11–18.

SKILLS SELF-MONITORING

HOW DID YOU DO?

- Check your score. What went well?
- Could you have done better? If so, how?

VOCABULARY AND GRAMMAR

VOCABULARY FOCUS

COLLOCATIONS: HEALTH AND TRAINING

ACTIVITY 1

1 Match the extracts (a–j) from the dog-training advice in Practice Time to the sentences (i–x) with a similar meaning.

a For example, once he or she develops **bad habits**, it can be very difficult to break them.

b Remember that dogs learn through **positive reinforcement**.

c It's a pleasure to watch a happy, healthy dog, especially one that has come from a **rescue centre**.

d … they tend to be very clever and to have high **energy levels** …

e There has to be **mutual trust**.

f I would say, don't expect to get **instant results**.

g Check with your dog's vet before starting your dog on any kind of **training programme.**

h He was a rescue dog and wasn't in the best **state of health**.

i … his life on the streets meant that before that he was **severely underweight**.

j … that made him an **ideal candidate** for agility work.

i It's great to see a dog in a good state, particularly one that comes from a refuge for animals.

ii Praising a dog is a really good way to help it progress.

iii The dog's lifestyle had caused him to be extremely thin.

iv It's hard to change a dog that displays negative behavioural patterns.

v He is very well-suited to training in quick movements and jumps.

vi Clever dogs with lots of physical power and enthusiasm will be very good at learning how to move.

vii Success doesn't always come immediately.

viii It's important that both the dog and trainer have confidence in each other.

ix You should make sure your dog is healthy before embarking on any teaching of new skills.

x The dog's physical condition was poor.

2 Look at the words in bold in sentences (a–j) and underline the parts of the extracts (i–x) that are similar.

EXAMPLE a For example, once he or she develops **bad habits**, it can be very difficult to break them.

iv It's hard to change a dog that displays <u>negative behavioural patterns</u>.

ACTIVITY 2

Fill in the gaps using the **bold** collocations from Activity 1.

1 Shaan always expects ______________ after doing something for a short time. She needs to understand that practice makes perfect.

2 30 per cent of the population is now ______________ as a result of the extreme food shortages.

3 I've looked through all the applications and I think I've found our ______________! I'll invite her for an interview next week.

4 My doctor told me that eating too much sugar is a ________________ which I need to change.

5 If there isn't ______________ between the horse and the horse rider, things can quickly go wrong.

6 My ____________ have really dropped now that it has turned so cold. I just want to sleep all the time.

7 I've always found that using ____________________ is a great way to encourage language learners.

8 Welcome to our management ___________________. You're going to learn how to be great managers.

9 Staff at this __________________ look after animals when they have been abandoned or badly treated.

GRAMMAR CHECKPOINT

GRAMMAR

See Grammar Reference page 281.

PREPOSITIONS OF TIME

ACTIVITY 3

Read and complete the sentences using *on*, *at* or *in*.

EXAMPLE David will be here _on_ New Year's Day.

1 I bought my dog _________ 2012.

2 I like to take my dog for walks ___________ the weekend.

3 The park is busy ___________ Wednesdays.

4 After we go for a walk, we eat lunch ___________ the afternoon.

5 Most dogs stay awake in the day and sleep __________ night.

6 Mine is such an early riser. She always wakes up ____________ six!

7 On the other hand, she is usually tired __________ the evenings.

8 She is quite old – she was born _________ the early 2000s.

GRAMMAR CHECKPOINT

GRAMMAR

See Grammar Reference pages 281–282.

a

b

c

d

e

PREPOSITIONS OF PLACE AND MOVEMENT

ACTIVITY 4

1 Read the speech about the pet show and fill in the missing prepositions.

Welcome, everybody, [1]________ the City Park Pet Show. My name is Mrs Orion and I hope that everyone here enjoys themselves today [2]________ this lovely park. Our Pet Show is always wonderful. I'm going to explain how this year's show is being organised, so I need you all to listen carefully. I want you to know which area you need to go [3]________ when I've finished talking!

So, we have divided the showground [4]________ four different areas. Those of you entering dogs for the agility event will be in the far right-hand corner of the field. There are lots of obstacles there so that dogs can run [5]________ them or jump [6]________ them. There are also gates for them to run [7]________ .

Those of you who have brought your dogs along for the other parts of the show need to go [8]________ the area [9]________ the entrance – it is just [10]________ it. Those of you with cats need to move to the back area to the left of the park, and those of you entering rabbits, other small animals and birds, you have a special area [11]________ the marquee.

The marquee is also where refreshments will be available after the judging has taken place. There will be tea, coffee and soft drinks, as well as a selection of cakes and biscuits. All profits from the sale of refreshments, as well as from the competition itself, will go to a local animal charity.

2 Listen and check.

ACTIVITY 5

Look at the pictures (a–e) in the margin and make sentences about them using the prepositions in the word box.

EXAMPLE *The dog is jumping through a hoop.*

above	behind	beside	between	in	in front of	
into	near	on	out of	towards	under	through

ACTIVITY 6

Choose the correct preposition of place and movement.

EXAMPLE The dogs enter _through_ the gate.

a (through) b in c above d onto

1 Please stay ______ the coach until we reach the pet show.
a on b onto c in d into

2 Once we arrive, you can get ______ the coach.
a away from b through c off d out of

3 Please sit down ______ the allocated chair to view the performance.
a on b in c over d at

4 At the start of the show, the dogs run ______ the park.
a off b over c onto d around

5 Then they jump ______ the hurdle.
a over b into c on d around

6 Finally, they race ______ the finish line.
a into b towards c in d at

7 The trophy is kept ______ a wooden case.
a on b by c in d under

8 When the winner is ready, the trophy is taken _______ the case.
a away from b out of c out d out to

9 Refreshments are served ______ the table.
a under b on c over d in

10 The food is kept ______ the dogs.
a away from b out of c off from d away to

GRAMMAR GAME

▼ PLACE THE OBJECT

- Working in pairs, stand up and choose an object, e.g. a rubber or a pencil sharpener.
- Take it in turns to choose a location in the classroom using one of the following prepositions of place: *in*, *on*, *over*, *above*, *between*, *under*, *behind*, *in front of*. Your partner then has to place the object in the location that you have specified.
- If your partner makes a mistake while placing the object, you gain a point.
- Whoever has the most points when the teacher ends the game, wins!

SELF-EVALUATION

Tick the relevant boxes.

I now feel confident about ...	STRONGLY AGREE	AGREE	DISAGREE	STRONGLY DISAGREE
▶ TALKING ABOUT ANIMALS AND PETS				
▶ IDENTIFYING DETAILS IN SPOKEN TEXTS				
▶ UNDERSTANDING THE DIFFERENCE BETWEEN STATED AND IMPLIED MEANINGS				
▶ USING NEW VOCABULARY (COLLOCATIONS: HEALTH AND TRAINING)				
▶ USING PREPOSITIONS OF TIME, PLACE AND MOVEMENT				

If you ticked 'disagree' or 'strongly disagree', you need to revise these parts.

LISTENING PART 3

GAMES

Assessment Objective 3C

Understand a conversation where information is being negotiated and exchanged

Assessment Objective 3D

Identify a speaker's viewpoint and attitude, stated and implied

LEARNING OBJECTIVES

- Talk about games
- Prepare for Part 3 of the Listening exam
- Consider the difference between statements and implications
- Identify facts and opinions, including stated and implied opinions
- Build new vocabulary (adjectives and adverbs)
- Use adverbs of frequency
- Use intensifiers

PREPARING THE WAY

Discuss the questions.

- What is the difference between a game and a sport?
- Do you like gaming? Why / Why not?
- What are the most popular games in your country at the moment? What are they about?

ACTIVITY 1

SKILLS REASONING, ARGUMENTATION

1 Look at the pictures. Working in pairs, decide which years you think the games and sports were first played.

1700s 868 around AD 500 1950s 1400s 1990s

a

b

c
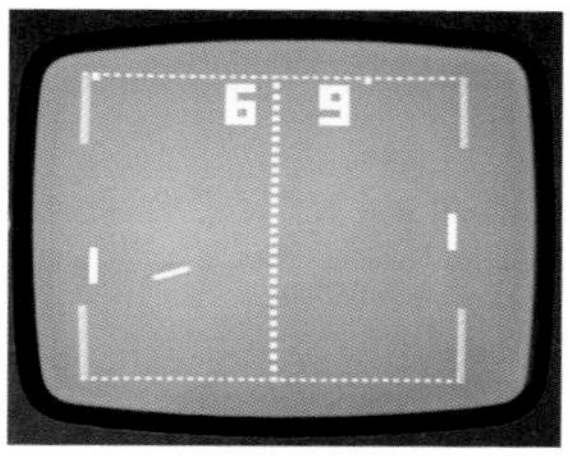

d

e

f

FOCUSING ON THE EXAM

- Part 3 (Listening) is worth 10 marks.
- It is based on a longer listening text, e.g. an interview.
- You need to complete the tasks given, e.g. multiple choice, note/sentence/chart/table/diagram completion, short-answer questions.
- You need to listen for and understand the viewpoint and attitude of the speaker(s), whether stated or implied.

EXAM SKILLS

STATEMENTS AND IMPLICATIONS

In the previous chapter, you looked at the difference between stated (**explicit**) information and implied (**implicit**) information. Sometimes people don't say things directly because they don't want to offend someone; at other times, it can be a way of making themselves sound better.

ACTIVITY 2

1 Listen to the recordings and complete the sentences.

1 There's _______________ with the antique vase I took to the auction house.

2 I managed to beat _______________ for push-ups at the gym today.

3 These cookies are really great. Your cooking _______________ improving.

4 You _______________ to reconsider that hairstyle.

5 I'm not sure an elephant _______________ best pet for you at the moment.

6 I've _______________ the whole house because you didn't get round to it.

SKILLS INTERPRETATION

2 Match the sentences (1–6) to their implied (hidden) meanings (a–f).

a You're really lazy!

b Oh dear! You look terrible!

c I dropped it on the way and it's now in 30 very small pieces.

d My physical fitness levels are fantastic.

e The ones you made before were awful!

f What on earth are you thinking?

ACTIVITY 3

Write five sentences with implied meanings. Ask your partner to work out what you meant to say.

EXAMPLE **Statement:** Your house is a little bit chilly with the windows open.

Implication: *Please close the windows, I'm cold!*

EXAM SKILLS

FACTS AND OPINIONS

Think about the difference between facts and opinions. Facts are often communicated by explicit statements and can be proved true or false. It is not so easy to prove whether or not an opinion is true. Opinions can be given through direct statements and they can also be implied by the choice of words.

SKILLS INTERPRETATION

ACTIVITY 4

Read a football fan's blog after a match. Underline the words which give you clues about the writer's opinion.

mistleyhome.com

THE MIGHTY MISTLEY HAVE BEEN ROBBED!

Weeley Wanderers 3 – Mistley United 0

Weeley Wanderers edge cup final in complete sham

The glorious Mistley United's series of victories came to an end today after a calamitous string of events led to an undeserved victory for Weeley Wanderers.

The heroic Mistley players battled fiercely for the whole 90 minutes, but ultimately were unable to take the win they so thoroughly deserved.

The first key moment of the game came in the tenth minute, when our boy Tom Mathews was unfairly sent off after the referee wrongly called for a handball when the ball clearly came into contact with his chest. What a joke!

And because of that, Weeley got a penalty and scored their first goal, putting our lads up against the wall.

Our luck didn't get any better when the next goal for Weeley came soon after: I blame the bad weather, several questionable decisions from the referee and an oddly-weighted ball. In the second half, things got worse. Manager James Humphries tried to save the day with some tactical and timely substitutions, but unfortunately luck, rather than skill, played a bigger part in the result.

The referee must have been blindfolded when he sent off Max Green, Mistley's inspirational captain. The filthy Weeley striker deliberately fell to the ground, he hadn't even been touched! In the final 15 minutes, we had our heads in our hands when Weeley scored again. I'd say the game was an utter sham!

A tragic day indeed, but heads up! Next year that cup will be ours!

1 Discuss in pairs.
- What do your underlined words have in common?
- Are there any words or phrases you don't know? Can you guess their meaning?
- Which team does the writer support?
- How do you know this? Does he ever directly state who he supports?
- What parts of speech are most of your underlined words (noun, verb etc.)?

2 Write a summary of the writer's opinion.

EXAM HINTS
- Make sure you don't miss out any questions.
- Remember that your answers need to come from the text. Other answers will not gain marks.

A03C A03D

SKILLS INTERPRETATION

LISTENING PART 3

▼ PRACTICE TIME

In this part, you will hear an interview with a writer.

For Questions 21–25, listen and answer the questions. You do not need to write in full sentences.

One mark will be awarded for each completed answer.

Interview with a writer

21 Why did Lance become interested in writing about the effect of video games on young people? (1)

....

22 What does Lance think of taking physical exercise too far? (1)

....

23 What leads to frustration for gamers, according to the interviewer? (1)

....

24 What is Lance's opinion about this frustration? (1)

....

25 What does Lance say can happen if games are played too much? (1)

....

EXAM HINT

Make sure that you identify only one answer for Questions 26–30.

Questions 26–30 must be answered with a cross in a box ☒. If you change your mind about an answer, put a line through the box ☒ and then mark your new answer with a cross ☒.

26 For Lance, learning is (1)

☐ **A** an adventure.

☐ **B** exam-focused.

☐ **C** about having a wide perspective on the world.

☐ **D** only useful because it improves your physical abilities.

27 According to Lance, what are the physical benefits of gaming? (1)

- [ ] **A** It makes you fitter.
- [ ] **B** It improves your eyesight.
- [ ] **C** It improves your listening skills.
- [ ] **D** It makes your reactions faster.

28 The interviewer feels that teenagers should be (1)

- [ ] **A** playing games indoors.
- [ ] **B** playing games outdoors.
- [ ] **C** studying for exams.
- [ ] **D** thinking of ideas for new games.

29 Lance says that certain games could improve people's health by (1)

- [ ] **A** quickly increasing fitness.
- [ ] **B** keeping young people's brains active.
- [ ] **C** measuring improvement in fitness.
- [ ] **D** encouraging ball games.

30 What does Lance think about the gaming industry? (1)

- [ ] **A** It benefits gamers only.
- [ ] **B** It would be exciting to work in the industry.
- [ ] **C** It is innovative.
- [ ] **D** It is losing influence in society.

(Total for Part 3 = 10 marks)

SKILLS SELF-MONITORING

HOW DID YOU DO?

- Check your score. What went well?
- Could you have done better? If so, how?

VOCABULARY AND GRAMMAR

VOCABULARY FOCUS

ADJECTIVES AND ADVERBS

SKILLS ANALYSIS

ACTIVITY 1

Write the adjective that relates to each adverb.

especially	*special*	firstly	________	probably	________
secondly	________	happily	________	quickly	________
certainly	________	definitely	________	greatly	________
well	________	simultaneously	________	normally	________
constantly	________	rarely	________	early	________

ACTIVITY 2

Listen to the extracts from the interview in Practice Time again and complete the sentences using the adverbs. You will not need to use all the adverbs.

firstly secondly normally necessarily probably certainly simultaneously especially definitely greatly

1 It can ________ offer all sorts of benefits.

2 It's __________the case that some people do get sucked into the gaming world and it has a negative impact on other areas of their life.

3 This is great, ________ for widening young people's knowledge of the world!

4 Learning for me means ________ gaining a wider knowledge of the world we're living in.

5 They show you different perspectives and even different landscapes you wouldn't ________ see.

6 The speed of your brain sending impulses to your body is ______ improved through gaming.

7 This is _____________ because video games operate on several levels ______________.

8 I don't think it _________ has a negative impact on learning.

ACTIVITY 3

Use the adverbs from Activity 2 to complete the definitions. You will not need to use all the adverbs.

1 When things happen at exactly the same time, they happen _____________.

2 Something that is likely to happen, will ______________ happen.

3 _____________ means that this comes before everything else.

4 If you ___________ eat something, you regularly eat it.

5 We use _______________ to emphasise that something is more important or happens more with one particular thing than others.

6 ______________ and ______________ mean that there is no doubt at all.

7 If something is not __________ true, it means it may not be true.

8 If you improve your skills _______, you improve them very much.

ACTIVITY 4

Circle the correct adverbs.

1 The traffic has **normally** / **greatly** improved since the new roundabout was built.

2 Fireworks went off **secondly** / **simultaneously** across the city to mark the new year.

3 It's **normally** / **probably** going to snow this weekend so I'd rather not go camping.

4 I'm **probably** / **normally** quite scared of flying, but I really enjoyed it this time.

5 He dislikes all his teachers, but **especially** / **certainly** his Physics teacher.

6 **Definitely** / **Firstly** I want to talk about the survey results.

7 The meal I had last night **simultaneously** / **certainly** made me ill.

8 I'm not **certainly** / **necessarily** hungry, but I could go and eat something.

ACTIVITY 5

Fill in the gaps with an adverb or adjective from Activity 1 on page 91.

1 Abed is ___________ that he saw a lion in his garden last night.

2 I suffer ____ from the cold so I'm not going to leave the house tonight!

3 I've never seen someone dancing and playing the guitar _____________ before.

4 I like playing lots of different sports, ________________ racket sports like tennis and badminton.

5 Jeff will _____________ be here soon. He promised he would come.

6 Today is very ___________ because it's my great-grandmother's hundredth birthday.

7 Alicia won _______ place in the race and her sister was only 20 seconds behind, in ______ place.

8 My parents ___________ have bread with their meals.

9 A _______ result of climate change will be more extreme weather, but we can't be certain.

10 It's totally __________ for young children to copy their friends so don't worry about it.

GRAMMAR CHECKPOINT

GRAMMAR

See Grammar Reference page 281.

ADVERBS OF FREQUENCY

ACTIVITY 6

Put these adverbs of frequency in the correct order, from the one that describes most frequent (1) to the one that describes least frequent (7).

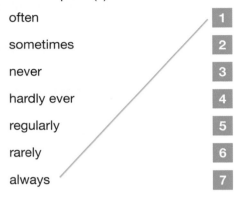

often	1
sometimes	2
never	3
hardly ever	4
regularly	5
rarely	6
always	7

SKILLS EXECUTIVE FUNCTION

ACTIVITY 7

▼ HOW OFTEN DO YOU …?

Ask your partner how often they do the following things. Answer your partner's questions, using adverbs of frequency.

- Play a sport
- Go to the shops
- Go for a walk
- Play a board game
- Go to school
- Play a computer game
- Visit another country
- Take a nap

GRAMMAR CHECKPOINT

GRAMMAR

See Grammar Reference page 280.

INTENSIFIERS

ACTIVITY 8

Fill in the gaps using the correct intensifiers.

EXAMPLE The board game party was not very good. _Hardly any_ people went.

a (hardly any) b some c a lot of d enough

1 The new Super Mario game has ______ of enemies, so it's very difficult.
a enough b some c very d a lot of

2 I will need ________ lives to complete this level.
a many b much c too many d too much

3 Can you help me find the hidden treasure? It's _______ hard to find.
a not very b really c too much d not enough

4 The final game is ________ fun _________. I didn't enjoy it.
a not … very b not … enough
c too … much d extremely … not

5 The game is _________ short. It only took two hours!
a quite b enough c too much d really

6 I like Mario, but Halo is _______ good too.
a quite b enough c too d not enough

7 There are ________ repetitive video games nowadays. Companies should be original!
a quite b too much c too many d not enough

8 Do you like board games? I find them ________ fun. We should play.
a enough b not enough c too much d so much

9 This game is _________ confusing.
a far too b enough c too much d too many

10 Let's play something else instead. I'm ________ bored.
a too much b so c not enough d too much

ACTIVITY 9

1 Ajit and Ben are playing an online game. Read their conversation and circle the correct intensifiers.

Ajit: Right, go through the door on the left very slowly. You need to look under the [1]**really / enough** big bag.

Ben: Okay. It's [2]**quite / a lot of** dark in this room. Do you mean this bag?

Ajit: Yes. Is there a torch under it?

Ben: Yes! Here it is.

Ajit: Great. Switch on the torch and keep looking out for snakes. They're [3]**much too / too many** dangerous for us to deal with.

Ben: I forgot about the snakes. If they arrive, I'll be in [4]**very / a lot of** trouble because I don't have [5]**too much / enough** anti-venom.

Ajit: Wait a second, what's in that bottle on the table?

Ben: I'm having a look. Oh, it's [6]**some / enough** more anti-venom. Well spotted, Ajit.

Ajit: That's [7]**very / far too** lucky – look behind you!

Ben: Oh no, there are snakes everywhere! There are [8]**so many / not enough** of them! This game is [9]**far too / a lot of** difficult for me.

Ajit: Come on, Ben! [10]**Hardly any / Too many** players get past this room, but you can do it. You're an [11]**extremely / enough** good player!

2 Listen and check.

SELF-EVALUATION

Tick the relevant boxes.

I now feel confident about ...	STRONGLY AGREE	AGREE	DISAGREE	STRONGLY DISAGREE
▶ TALKING ABOUT GAMES				
▶ RECOGNISING THE DIFFERENCE BETWEEN STATEMENTS AND IMPLICATIONS				
▶ IDENTIFYING A SPEAKER'S OPINION, WHETHER STATED OR IMPLIED				
▶ USING NEW VOCABULARY (ADJECTIVES AND ADVERBS)				
▶ USE SEPARABLE AND NON-SEPARABLE PHRASAL VERBS				
▶ USING ADVERBS OF FREQUENCY				
▶ USING INTENSIFIERS				

If you ticked 'disagree' or 'strongly disagree', you need to revise these parts.

LISTENING PART 4

SHOPPING

Assessment Objective 3B

Identify essential and finer points of detail in spoken material

Assessment Objective 3D

Identify a speaker's viewpoint and attitude, stated and implied

LEARNING OBJECTIVES

- Talk about shopping
- Prepare for Part 4 of the Listening exam
- Distinguish between essential and less important details
- Build new vocabulary (verbs and expressions: shopping)
- Use separable and non-separable phrasal verbs
- Use the passive

PREPARING THE WAY

Discuss the questions.

- Is shopping a chore or a hobby?
- Is shopping a skill? Can somebody be a 'good shopper' or a 'bad shopper'?
- Can people become addicted to shopping?
- What's your favourite place to shop?
- Do you enjoy buying gifts for people? Why / Why not?

ACTIVITY 1

SKILLS EXECUTIVE FUNCTION

Working in pairs, match the pictures (a–d) to the words in the word box.

CCTV	barcode	parking	sale

1 What do the signs in the pictures represent?

2 Where would you find them?

a

b

c

d

FOCUSING ON THE EXAM

- Part 4 (Listening) is worth 10 marks.
- It is based on a longer recording, e.g. a monologue or guided dialogue, usually covering a more academic topic.
- You need to complete the tasks given, e.g. multiple choice, note/sentence/chart/table/diagram completion, or short-answer questions.
- You need to be able to identify details (main points and more detailed points).
- You need to identify the viewpoint and attitude of the speaker(s), (expressed directly or indirectly).

EXAM SKILLS

IDENTIFYING IMPORTANT INFORMATION AND DETAILS

An important skill in Listening Part 4 is the ability to distinguish between the main message of a text and the details. When you have identified the details, you also need to be able to decide which details are more important. Some of the details will be essential to the main message or purpose and some will provide extra optional information.

Sometimes information is important because it is factual. Less important information may be linked to preferences or to areas of our lives that do not matter as much as others.

SKILLS DECISION MAKING

ACTIVITY 2

Look carefully at the online description of a jumper. Discuss in pairs.

- Which information is very important and which is less important?
- Is any information essential?

Women's jumper for sale

- Made in Wales
- Can be worn with skirts or trousers
- Size: 10
- Genuine wool
- Condition is nearly new
- Pale grey
- Dry clean only

I bought this for a party and only wore it once.

£10.00

SKILLS DECISION MAKING

ACTIVITY 3

1 You are flying to Spain to visit your aunt, who will collect you from the airport. Some information is missing from the transcript of the flight attendant's announcement. Copy the table below, then listen to the full announcement and make notes about the missing information in the first column.

Subject matter? Details?	Essential?	Less important?
1 destination – Madrid		

Flight attendant: Hello, everyone. My name is Mark and I'll be giving you some information about [1]_________. The first thing I need to tell you is that [2]_________ – and I should also mention that [3]_________, unfortunately, because we need to make a detour to avoid some storms, but that's not so bad as it will give you lots of extra time for in-flight shopping! [4]_________, but I'm sure you won't mind once you hear all about the fantastic bargains we've got in store for you today! For example, [5]_________ – isn't that great?

[6]_________, but before that, I want to let you know that [7]_________ – we want to make sure you enjoy these massive reductions.

[8]_________, as the plane is about to be cleared for take-off, but don't forget to get your credit cards out ready – it won't be long until you can start shopping. I bet you can't wait!

2 Working in pairs, discuss which information is essential and which details are less important.

A03B A03D

EXAM HINTS

- Use the sub-headings provided in the questions to help you search quickly for the relevant information.
- Use key vocabulary in the questions to help you listen for the relevant information.

AFTER EXAM CHECK

- Make sure you haven't written more than three words for any answer – if you do, your answer will automatically be discounted.
- Make sure that your writing is clear – your spelling is not tested in this section, but words need to be recognisable.

SKILLS SELF-MONITORING

LISTENING PART 4

▼ PRACTICE TIME

In this part, you will hear an extract from an interview on the topic of shopping.

For Questions 31–32 and 38–40, listen and complete the sentences below. Write no more than THREE words for each answer.

For Questions 33–37, complete the table. Write no more than THREE words for each answer.

One mark will be awarded for each answer.

Changes in shopping patterns

The shopper and the staff

31 The modern-day shopper often does research .... before buying products in the shops. (1)

32 Shop assistants are now trained more so they know .... the shopper. (1)

Advantages and disadvantages

Advantages of shopping online	Disadvantages of shopping online
33 Shoppers don't have to .... for hours at a time. (1)	**34** Impossible to .... before buying. (1)
35 Cheap unwanted purchases can be .... (1)	
36 Possible to see .... from other shoppers. (1)	**37** Less personal .... (1)

Changed relationships with shopping

38 Buying things in person might mean you spend less on .... (1)

39 Previously, people sometimes tried to .... for the best prices at markets. (1)

40 Looking at goods available online means customers won't .... unnecessarily. (1)

(Total for Part 4 = 10 marks)

HOW DID YOU DO?

- Check your score. What went well?
- Could you have done better? If so, how?

VOCABULARY AND GRAMMAR

VOCABULARY FOCUS

VERBS AND EXPRESSIONS: SHOPPING

ACTIVITY 1

1 Complete the extracts from the shopping interview with the verbs and expressions in the word box. Make sure you use the correct form.

bargain	find a good deal	make an investment	browse	order

1 Shoppers weren't very informed 50 years ago. They would just come into the shop and ________, not always knowing much about the product they were looking for.

2 They can find the product, ask any questions they might have and even ________ it online. The product will then be delivered a couple of days later.

3 Yes, that's true. But if the clothes are very cheap, some people are happy to try to ________ online, knowing that if they don't like what they buy, or it doesn't fit, it can be donated to charity and won't have cost them very much.

4 They haven't really ________ in these items, or not a big one, at least, so they're happy to give them away.

5 Yes. I remember I used to go to my local market to ________ over the prices of things I wanted to buy. That's something I miss with online shopping!

2 Listen and check.

ACTIVITY 2

Match each statement to the correct verb from Activity 1. Use a dictionary if you need to.

1 For me, shopping is about finding the best prices. I don't just buy the first thing I see.

2 Personally, I think markets are the most fun places to go shopping in! Sometimes there are no fixed prices, so you have to talk to the sellers to find a price. Sometimes they argue a bit, but I love the challenge!

3 My friend is starting a new business. I've given her some money to help get her started and I'll get a share of the profits later. She's told me that if the business is a huge success, I'll be a millionaire!

4 Often, I'll go to the shops just to look at what's around. I don't always buy things – I just like to look at what's for sale.

5 I never bother going to the shops. I always buy things online and have them delivered to my house. I love that feeling of having a package come to my door!

GRAMMAR CHECKPOINT

GRAMMAR

See Grammar Reference page 268.

PHRASAL VERBS (SEPARABLE AND NON-SEPARABLE)

ACTIVITY 3

Listen to more extracts from the shopping interview. Complete the text using the phrasal verbs, in the correct form.

shop around	queue up	sell off	sell out
splash out	try on		

1 Usually, they've already compared the price online from a dozen different stores and often they know the exact specifications of whatever they are buying. And they ______________ to get the best bargains.

2 Well, a lot of shops nowadays let their customers shop online. There's no need for the shopper to leave their house and to __________ for hours on end in a busy store.

3 I suppose that one thing that's not so good about internet shopping, especially with clothes or shoes, is that you can't ________ anything you might buy.

4 Not everyone enjoys online shopping. There's less human contact, and it's nice to be able to see what you're getting, for example if a supermarket decides to __________ food cheaply at the end of the day.

5 If you're handing over cash, that might be a reminder of what your purchases are really costing you. You might be less tempted to ____________ on luxuries and spend money you haven't really got!

6 True. Although at least you have fewer wasted journeys, as you can see immediately if an online shop has __________ of the item you want to buy from them.

ACTIVITY 4

Match the phrasal verbs to the correct definitions.

Phrasal verb	**Definition**
try on	try to find goods at a range of shops, perhaps to find the cheapest
sell off	wait in line
queue up	spend lots of money on something; to be extravagant
splash out (on)	no longer have goods for sale
sell out (of)	reduce stock by lowering prices
shop around	wear clothes or shoes briefly to see if they fit

ACTIVITY 5

Choose phrasal verbs from Activity 4 to fill in the gaps in the diary entry, using the correct form.

Date: 1 January

Today has been amazing. I wouldn't have believed it was possible – I've spent the whole day shopping! So rewarding!

I went online as soon as I woke up and managed to find those new boots I've wanted since last week. They were 10% off – I was really lucky they didn't [1] sell out. Maybe they were old stock that the shop wanted to [2] sell of? I don't mind – they're going to look great and that's what's important. I can't wait to [3] try on my new boots! And no [4] ________ and waiting either!

Of course, I needed a nap after all that excitement. Then I woke up at midday, had breakfast, and met up with some friends. We wanted to [5] shop around for some new clothes to wear to a party we're going to tonight. That's the great thing about being a celebrity, I can go shopping whenever I like and [6] ________ on anything I want to. I found a really nice dress. It cost a lot, but it will double in value as soon as I've worn it, now that I'm famous, so it was definitely worth it.

ACTIVITY 6

Discuss in pairs.

- Do you always try clothes on before you buy them?
- Do you prefer to shop around for a good deal or to splash out on something?
- Do people in your country queue up?

GRAMMAR CHECKPOINT

GRAMMAR

See Grammar Reference pages 271–272.

PASSIVE

ACTIVITY 7

Complete the table with the active forms of the verb *be*.

	Simple	Continuous	Perfect
Past			*had been*
Present	*am/are/is*		
Future		*will be being*	

ACTIVITY 8

Change these present simple sentences from the active to the passive. Remember to remove the sentence subject.

EXAMPLE In Japan, people buy more video games than in any other country.
In Japan, more video games are bought than in any other country.

1 In New Guinea, people speak more languages than in any other country.

2 In India, people read more books per year than in any other country.

3 In China, people drink more tea than in any other country.

4 In Switzerland, people eat more chocolate than in any other country.

5 In the USA, people watch more television than in any other country.

GRAMMAR CHECKPOINT

GRAMMAR

See Grammar Reference pages 271–272.

PASSIVE: ALL TENSES

ACTIVITY 9

Change these sentences from active to passive. Keep the sentence subject where a name is given.

EXAMPLE Caroline worked on the reports.

The reports were worked on by Caroline.

1 They are holding the meeting in Room C.

2 Paul has given the presentation already.

3 He knew nothing at that time.

4 She was mixing the chemicals.

5 Many people will hear the new album on the radio tomorrow.

6 They will have delivered the shipment by the end of the month.

7 Alia and Gill have already checked these reports.

8 They speak several languages in that country.

9 People will know the results of the election next week.

ACTIVITY 10

Read the diary entry in Activity 5 on page 103. Underline the sentences which are in the passive. How many are there?

SELF-EVALUATION

Tick the relevant boxes.

I now feel confident about ...	STRONGLY AGREE	AGREE	DISAGREE	STRONGLY DISAGREE
▶ TALKING ABOUT SHOPPING				
▶ RECOGNISING ESSENTIAL AND LESS IMPORTANT DETAILS				
▶ USING NEW VOCABULARY (VERBS AND EXPRESSIONS: SHOPPPING)				
▶ USING SEPARABLE AND NON-SEPARABLE PHRASAL VERBS				
▶ USING THE PASSIVE				

If you ticked 'disagree' or 'strongly disagree', you need to revise these parts.

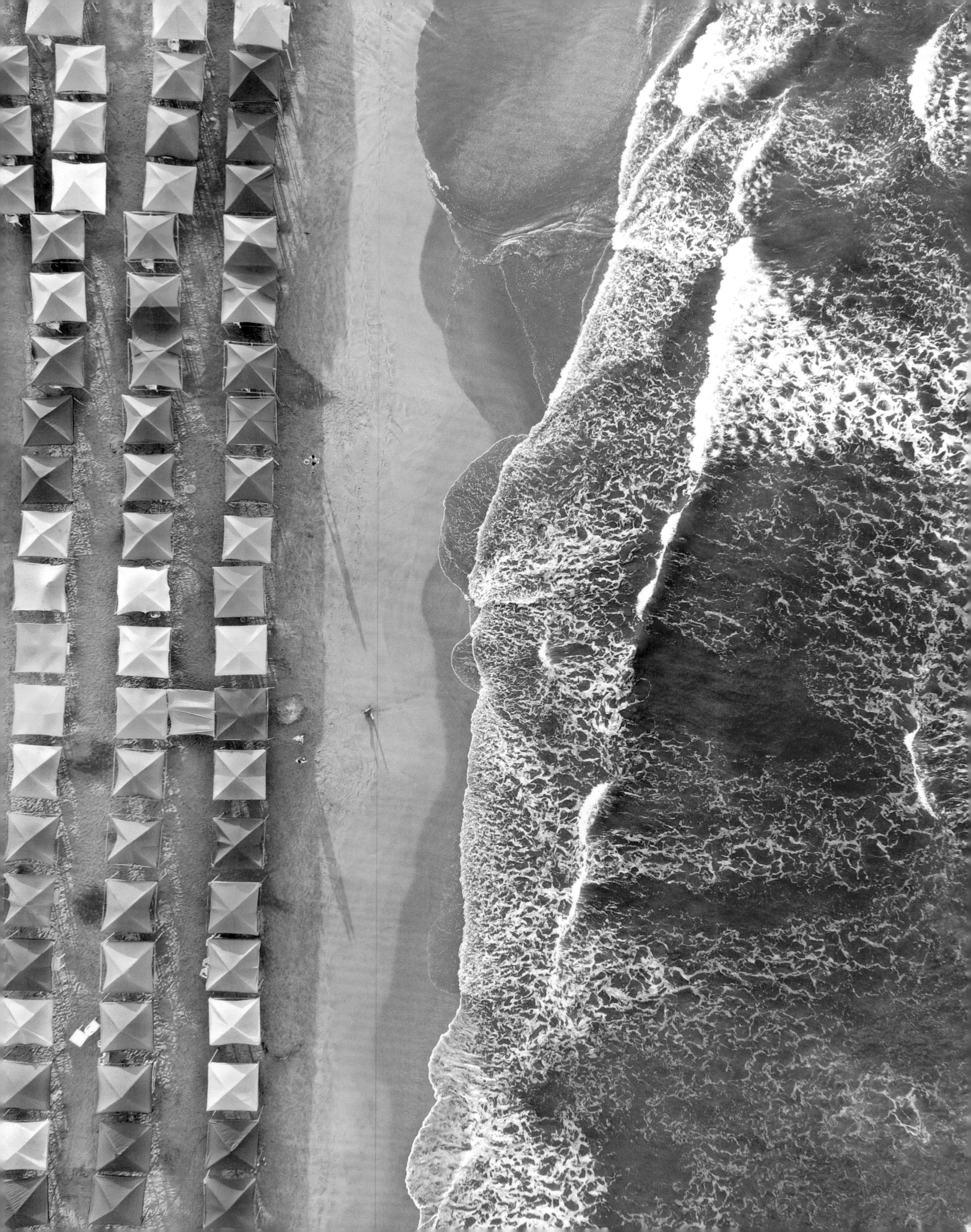

UNIT 4 SPEAKING PREPARATION

Assessment Objective 4A

Give information and express opinions on a range of topics at different levels of complexity

Assessment Objective 4B

Respond to a range of questions on a variety of topics

Assessment Objective 4C

Use a range of vocabulary, grammar and structures appropriately

This unit prepares you for the optional Paper 3 Speaking. In this exam, you will need to show that you can communicate comprehensibly and fluently.

There are three parts of the Speaking exam:

- Part 1: introductory interview
- Part 2: student talk
- Part 3: extended discussion.

In Parts 1–3 of the exam, you need to meet the Assessment Objectives AO4A, AO4B and AO4C. The AOs that will be tested in the exam are indicated at the beginning of the corresponding part of this unit.

The unit focuses on the core speaking skills that you need. Working through these activities will help you develop these skills.

SPEAKING

FASHION

Assessment Objective 4A

Give information and express opinions on a range of topics at different levels of complexity

Assessment Objective 4B

Respond to a range of questions on a variety of topics

Assessment Objective 4C

Use a range of vocabulary, grammar and structures appropriately

LEARNING OBJECTIVES

- Talk about fashion
- Prepare for Parts 1–3 of the Speaking exam
- Gain a better understanding of the skills required for the Speaking exam
- Identify intonation and stress
- Identify ways to improve English pronunciation
- Build new vocabulary (adjectives: fashion)
- Identify long and short vowels
- Use the past perfect
- Revise past tenses

PREPARING THE WAY

Discuss the questions.

- Is fashion important?
- Do you judge people by what they wear?
- Is it more important for clothes to be comfortable or to look good?
- Which celebrities do you consider the best-dressed?
- How has fashion changed in your country in the last 10 years?

ACTIVITY 1

1 Write a list of the key words you used in the discussion and categorise the words. You can use the suggestions in the word box.

types of clothing	descriptions of clothing	opinion words

2 Are your words mainly nouns, verbs, adjectives or other parts of speech?

3 Can you think of other categories under the topic of fashion?

4 Choose one of the categories listed in the word box above. Is it possible to use different parts of speech in this category? Use a dictionary to find three new words in that category.

ACTIVITY 2

1 Working in pairs, listen to the fashion show commentary and number the photos.

a 

b 

c 

d 

e 

f 

______ ______ ______ ______ ______ ______

2 Match the words to the correct image.

checks	handbag	denim	bling	chic	spotty

3 Listen again and check.

FOCUSING ON THE EXAM

- The Speaking exam is worth 40 marks.
- The Speaking exam is optional.
- There are three parts:
  - Part 1: an introductory interview (2–3 minutes)
  - Part 2: a talk (1 minute of preparation, plus a talk of 1–2 minutes)
  - Part 3: an extended discussion (5–6 minutes).
- During the brief preparation time for Part 2, you can take notes. The notes are collected in but they are not marked in any way.
- Your Speaking exam will be recorded and then marked externally.

EXAM SKILLS

SPEAKING SKILLS

You will need a range of skills for the Speaking exam. For example, you will need to:

- express your opinions and to do so in different ways
- show that you can develop your ideas; don't just give one-word answers
- listen carefully to the questions and answer them fully
- speak clearly and not too fast
- respond spontaneously to predictable and unpredictable questions. You can practise predictable questions with your classmates and your teacher. This will help to prepare you for the unpredictable questions as well.

Try not to be too nervous! The examiner is interested in you and wants you to succeed.

WATCH OUT!

Listen carefully and calmly to the examiner's questions. Try to pay attention to overall meaning of the question. Key words can be helpful, but don't panic if you can't identify all the key words.

ACTIVITY 3

1 Choose two of the topics listed in the word box and write three predictable questions for each topic.

food	pets	opinion words	sports	travel and holidays

2 Working in pairs, ask and answer each other's questions.

EXAM SKILLS

PRONUNCIATION SKILLS

Here are some tips to help you with English pronunciation.

- For every word that you write, you should also write down how to pronounce the word. You can use any system to do this as long as it works for you.
- Make lists of rhyming words (such as *head*, *bed*, *said*).
- Break words down into syllables and cross out any silent letters.
- Listen to recordings of native speakers talking and record yourself saying the same sentences. Compare the two and listen for the differences.
- Find out which English pronunciation problems are typical for students who speak your first language and practise correcting them.

ACTIVITY 4

For many students, reading and writing in English is a lot easier than speaking. Try saying the following sentence correctly.

English is tough – it can be understood through thorough thought, though.

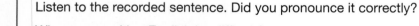

Listen to the recorded sentence. Did you pronounce it correctly?

Why can speaking English be difficult?

EXAM SKILLS

INTONATION AND STRESS

One aspect of speaking another language is **intonation**. This can be a very important aspect of the communication process.

In pairs, discuss how people use different intonation to show when they:

- ask a question
- read a list
- are really surprised
- are unsure if they have the right answer.

The meaning of a sentence can be changed by placing stress or emphasis on different words.

ACTIVITY 5

1 Listen to the sentences and tick the one you hear.

2 Match each of the differently stressed sentences in the tables to the correct meanings.

1	Meaning
a Excuse me, I paid for the green *shirt*.	i The salesperson has given the shirt to the wrong person.
b Excuse me, I paid for the *green* shirt.	ii The shopper's shirt is the wrong colour.
c Excuse me, *I* paid for the green shirt.	iii The salesperson has given the person the wrong piece of clothing.

2	Meaning
a Hello, can I have some of *those* bananas please?	i The customer wants bananas, not other fruit.
b Hello, can I have some of those *bananas* please?	ii Someone else has bananas and the customer wants some too.
c Hello, can *I* have some of those bananas please?	iii The customer knows exactly which bananas he or she wants.

3	Meaning
a *Huan* makes great tea.	i Huan makes better tea than some other people.
b Huan makes *great* tea.	ii Huan makes great tea but is not so good at making other drinks.
c Huan makes great *tea*.	iii Huan makes really very good tea.

4	Meaning
a *I* love the colour of the jacket.	i I love the colour of the jacket but I don't like the colour of the skirt.
b I love the colour of the *jacket*.	ii I love the colour of the jacket but don't like its style.
c I love the *colour* of the jacket.	iii I love the colour of the jacket even though other people don't.

SKILLS REASONING, ARGUMENTATION

EXAM HINTS

- Try to use a range of vocabulary, but make sure it is relevant to the topic. Remember, you can't bring a dictionary with you into the exam.
- Try to use a range of grammatical structures.
- Don't give one-word answers to the questions in Part 1. Try to make your answers interesting by adding information, e.g. personal opinion, experience and examples.

SPEAKING PART 1

▼ PRACTICE TIME

PART ONE

In this first part, I'd like to ask you some questions about yourself.

Let's talk about clothes.

- How often do you buy clothes?
- What sorts of things do you buy? (Tell me about that.)
- Do you prefer to buy your own clothes or for your family to buy them for you? (Why is that?)
- What is your idea of the perfect outfit?

Thank you. That is the end of Part One.

SKILLS REASONING, ARGUMENTATION

EXAM HINTS

- When you prepare your talk for Part 2, try to think of a small number of points you would like to express, with examples to support those points.
- Remember to include relevant detail.
- The ideas for the topic are there to help you, but you can use other ideas, as long as they are relevant to the main topic. Make it clear that your ideas are relevant.

SPEAKING PART 2

▼ PRACTICE TIME

PART TWO
STUDENT'S CARD

You are going to talk about **the role of fashion in your life**.

You can use some or all of the ideas listed below in your talk, but you must answer this question:

How important do you think fashion is to teenagers?

You must talk for 1 to 2 minutes. You have 1 minute to think and make notes before your talk begins.

Here are some ideas to help you:

- Appearance
- Links with identity
- Peer pressure
- Media pressure
- Other

SKILLS REASONING, ARGUMENTATION

EXAM HINT

Develop your answers in as much detail as you are able to, particularly in the extended discussion (Part 3).

SPEAKING PART 3

▼ PRACTICE TIME

PART THREE

We have been talking about **the role of fashion** and I would like to ask you some more questions on this topic.

- What sort of things do young people wear nowadays? (Tell me about that.)
- Which is your favourite fashion trend? (Tell me about that.)
- Which is your least favourite fashion trend? (Why is that?)

- Do you think teenagers worry too much about fashion? (Why is that?)
- What are some of the disadvantages of following fashion rules?
- Would it be better if everyone wore the same clothes?
- What is your opinion of fashion?
- Why do you think fashions change so much over time? (Tell me about that.)
- Do we judge others too much by what they wear?

SKILLS SELF-MONITORING

HOW DID YOU DO?

- Check with your teacher to see what you scored out of 40. What went well?
- Which part did you perform the best in? Why?
- Did you listen for the key words in the questions and focus on those?
- Did you listen carefully to the interviewer?
- Did you plan your talk using brief notes?
- Did you use a range of grammar and vocabulary when speaking?
- What do you need to improve for next time?

PRONUNCIATION

PRONUNCIATION CHECKPOINT

LONG AND SHORT VOWELS

HINT

Not all vowels in English are the same length – some are short (f**i**t) and some are long (f**ee**t).

ACTIVITY 1

Write each of the words from the word box in the correct column in the table.

hue	not	file	peach	cat	crime	bake	act	hide	map	cube	gene	toe	friend
pot	knight	huge	pain	ran	but	fit	know	shut	gas	said	tomb	slot	sweet
weight	nut	cute	ship	slow	kick	day	tread	bed	feel	rut	knot	no	

short *a* /æ/	long *a* /eɪ/	short *e* /e/	long *e* /iː/	short *i* /ɪ/	long *i* /aɪ/	short *o* /o/	long *o* /əʊ/	short *u* /ʌ/	long *oo* /juː/
had	*hate*	*head*	*heat*	*hit*	*height*	*hot*	*hope*	*hut*	*hue*

ACTIVITY 2

Cross out the silent letters.

EXAMPLE *bomb̸*

1 hour
2 doubt
3 receipt
4 night
5 calm
6 Wednesday
7 castle
8 psychology
9 science
10 knife

VOCABULARY AND GRAMMAR

VOCABULARY FOCUS

SKILLS INTERPRETATION

ADJECTIVES: FASHION

ACTIVITY 1

Read and listen to Samira's talk about fashion. Then answer the questions.

'The topic I've chosen to talk about is fashion, as I think it's a very important subject for teenagers like me. Looking stylish does matter to me – not because I'm very interested in clothes, but because it makes me feel like I fit in with my friends. It's funny how it always seems to be teenagers and young people who lead the way with fashion. Maybe that's because they are trying to find an identity, a sense of who they are.

I tend to dress differently around different people, because I try to adapt to the situation I'm in. If I'm going to a good restaurant with my parents, I try to look smart and wear nice shoes and a dress. My mum hates it if I wear old clothes. She says I look untidy and scruffy! But with my friends, I prefer to wear casual clothes like jeans, trainers and a T-shirt. Casual clothes are really comfortable but it's important to me and my friends that they're also stylish. I want to look like my friends but not too much like them, if you know what I mean. I want to be a little bit original in the things I wear. It would be really embarrassing if I showed up in exactly the same outfit as my friend! I think it's important to know what the latest trends are. No one wants to look old-fashioned. I also like wearing bright colours because I don't want to be drab and boring.

I end up spending about 4 hours shopping for clothes every month. That's probably less than some people my age, but I try not to let it take over my life. I think contemporary fashion is interesting, but a lot of it is overrated and not even that nice! Some people seem to buy it just because they feel they have to. There's huge pressure on people, especially people my age, to be stylish. Sometimes it feels as if there's a new trend every week and it's no accident. I think the fashion industry makes a lot of money out of the teen market. I guess that's the world we're living in, though.'

1 Why does Samira want to look stylish?
2 Why does Samira think young people lead fashion trends?
3 Why does Samira dress differently around different people?
4 How does Samira dress when she is with her friends?
5 How long does she spend clothes shopping per month?
6 What does she think of contemporary fashion?
7 What does she say about the fashion industry?

ACTIVITY 2

Write the words in the word box (from Activity 1) next to the correct definitions.

casual	comfortable	original	overrated	drab
embarrassing	stylish	old-fashioned	scruffy	smart

1 dull, boring and plain __________
2 easy to wear and designed for comfort __________
3 neat in appearance __________
4 not as good or important as some people think or say __________
5 shabby or looking uncared-for __________
6 out-of-date, belonging to the past __________
7 not formal __________
8 attracting attention in an unpleasant way __________
9 creative and different from others __________
10 looking cool by wearing the latest style __________

ACTIVITY 3

Circle the correct word from the pairs given in these sentences.

1 George's clothes are always so different and **original** / **comfortable**. He makes them out of unusual materials.
2 **Casual** / **Comfortable** clothes may not be appropriate for job interviews.
3 The fancy restaurant would not allow its customers to wear **scruffy** / **drab** clothes.
4 It was **embarrassing** / **smart** that they both arrived wearing the same trainers.
5 I really love wearing **comfortable** / **smart** clothes to relax in.
6 **Drab** / **Embarrassing** colours are really depressing.
7 Some people worry too much about buying **stylish** / **scruffy** clothes.
8 The trouble with spending a lot on the newest trends is that they become **old-fashioned** / **over-rated** within a few months.
9 I think that leather jackets are **embarrassing** / **overrated**. They're so expensive.
10 If you have an interview in an office environment, you should probably wear **casual** / **smart** clothes.

ACTIVITY 4

Fill in the texts using the adjectives from Activity 2 on page 115.

1 Look [1]________ enough for the office in a jacket you can wear for the after-work party. You won't feel [2]________ in front of your workmates if there's no time to change!

2 There's nothing worse than spending a lot on an [3]________ new trend, only for it to look [4]________ in a short space of time. Why not choose something completely [5]________ – a suit handmade just for you.

3 Love to be [6]________? Our range of relaxed and cool trousers will definitely fit the bill. There are lots of colours to choose from, so there's something for everyone!

4 Don't be caught out wearing [7]________ colours! Our range of hand-knitted jumpers will certainly brighten up your day – and not only are they colourful, they're also extremely warm and [8]________ to wear.

5 Worried about looking [9]________ when you're doing the gardening? Worry no more. Our stunning selection of [10]________ clothes is perfect for those times when you want to relax outside.

GRAMMAR CHECKPOINT

GRAMMAR

See Grammar Reference page 265.

PAST PERFECT

ACTIVITY 5

Which of these sentences is a correct past perfect sentence?

a I have gone out.
b I have went out.
c I had gone out.
d I had went out.
e I have been going out.

ACTIVITY 6

Which of these would you always find in a past perfect sentence?

a *to be* (in the present simple)

b *to do* (in the present simple)

c *to have* (in the present simple)

d *to be* (in the past simple)

e *to do* (in the past simple)

f *to have* (in the past simple)

g *will*

h the present form of the sentence verb

i the *-ing* form of the sentence verb

j the past participle form of the sentence verb

ACTIVITY 7

Complete the sentences using the past perfect.

EXAMPLE (+, the model, already appear)

The model had already appeared when Mark arrived at the show.

1 (–, he, meet)

____________ the designer before the party?

2 (+, she, wake up)

____________ just ____________ when I rang the doorbell.

3 (–, they, serve)

____________ already ____________ the refreshments by 12 o'clock.

4 (+, I, already leave)

________________________ home by the time the postman arrived.

5 (+, you, try)

____________________ contacting customer services before cancelling your order?

GRAMMAR CHECKPOINT

GRAMMAR

See Grammar Reference pages 263–265.

PAST TENSES

ACTIVITY 8

Read the text and choose the correct past tense from the options given.

Interviewer: Hey! We're here again with the glamorous Rachel Ritz, who [1] **has been / was** at the Gala Awards Night yesterday evening. Tell us about it, Rach.

Rachel Ritz: Oh, it was a fabulous evening; I [2] **have worn / was wearing** a pink dress that night, although it's interesting – pink is my favourite colour, but I had always worn silver dresses for previous awards ceremonies.

Interviewer: Why [3] **have you worn / did you wear** a silver dress for previous ceremonies, if your favourite colour is pink?

Rachel Ritz: Well, I was thinking that silver fits the occasion more, you know? But this time I [4] **wanted / was wanting** to go back to basics – back to pink!

Interviewer: So you enjoyed the evening?

Rachel Ritz: It was incredible. I think it [5] **had been / was** one of the best nights out I'd ever had.

Interviewer: It was that special?

Rachel Ritz: Oh, absolutely. It was one-of-a-kind.

Interviewer: What made it so good?

Rachel Ritz: I [6] **have been able to / could** meet so many celebrities – people I [7] **was watching / had watched** on television my whole life. We all had so much fun! The whole time I was there I was thinking: this can't be real, this is too special. But it was! I will never forget it.

ACTIVITY 9

Choose between the past continuous, past perfect and past simple to complete the following sentences. You may find two different tenses within the same sentence.

1 (+, she, sleep) (+, the alarm, go off)
____________ peacefully when ____________.

2 (+, he, go)
____________ to the party last night.

3 (+, they, do) (+, the show, take place)
What ____________ while ____________?

4 (+, the road, be) (+, it, rain)
____________ wet early this morning because __________ last night.

5 (+, she, travel) (+, she, get engaged)
____________ when __________ to her husband.

6 (–, Kate, win)
____________ never ____________ that award before today.

7 (+, you, do) (+, you, hear)
____________ when __________ the news?

8 (–, he, have) (+, he, be)
__________ dinner earlier so __________ happy when they gave him food.

9 (+, I, get) (–, I, remember)
When __________ to school, I realised that I __________ to do my homework.

10 (+, we, feel) (–, we, have)
__________ hungry by 12 because __________ breakfast.

GRAMMAR GAME

▼ TENSES DUELLING

- Line up in two queues, so that the students at the begining of each queue are facing each other.
- The teacher tells the first two students a person, tense and a verb, e.g. *he*, past simple, *sleep*.
- The first student who thinks of a full sentence using person, tense and verb raises their hand and says their sentence.
- If the sentence is correct and makes sense, the student opposite is eliminated from the game and must sit down. If it is incorrect, the student who spoke is eliminated.
- When all the students on one team are sitting down, the other team wins!

SELF-EVALUATION

Tick the relevant boxes.

I now feel confident about ...	STRONGLY AGREE	AGREE	DISAGREE	STRONGLY DISAGREE
▶ TALKING ABOUT FASHION				
▶ PREPARING FOR PARTS 1–3 OF THE SPEAKING EXAM				
▶ PRACTISING SPEAKING SKILLS				
▶ IDENTIFYING INTONATION AND SENTENCE STRESS				
▶ IDENTIFYING WAYS OF IMPROVING ENGLISH PRONUNCIATION				
▶ USING VOCABULARY (ADJECTIVES: FASHION)				
▶ IDENTIFYING LONG AND SHORT VOWELS				
▶ USING THE PAST PERFECT				
▶ USING PAST TENSES				

If you ticked 'disagree' or 'strongly disagree', you need to revise these parts.

UNIT 5 READING PRACTICE

Assessment Objective 1A

Understand the overall message of a text

Assessment Objective 1B

Understand in detail a range of texts, identifying finer points of detail

Assessment Objective 1C

Distinguish between facts, ideas and opinions

Assessment Objective 1D

Identify a writer's viewpoint and attitude, stated and implied

This unit provides further practice for Parts 1, 2 and 3 of the Reading section of Paper 1 Reading and Writing.

In the exam, you will need to show that you can:

- read in different ways for different purposes, for example scanning for synonyms, skimming for gist and analysing choice of vocabulary to identify implied meaning
- read and understand a range of materials used for informational or publicity purposes, for example timetables and brochures, identifying key information and making comparisons between short extracts
- read and understand a range of unseen texts, identifying overall themes
- read and understand a range of short opinion pieces, identifying the writer's viewpoints which may be stated explicitly or implied through the writer's choice of vocabulary
- read and understand a range of popular articles on a variety of factual, historical, geographical and technical themes.

The mark breakdown is:

- Part 1: 10 marks
- Part 2: 15 marks
- Part 3: 20 marks.

Note you can also gain marks for Reading in Part 6 of the Writing section of this exam.

READING PART 1

TRAVEL AND HOSPITALITY

Assessment Objective 1A

Understand the overall message of a text

LEARNING OBJECTIVES

- Talk about travel and holidays
- Revise the requirements for Part 1 of the Reading and Writing exam
- Practise two Part 1 sample questions
- Evaluate your exam practice
- Build new vocabulary (compound adjectives)
- Use modals of obligation, advice, permission

PREPARING THE WAY

Discuss the questions.

- Have you ever been abroad? Where to?
- Do you like the idea of living abroad?
- What is the most interesting city to visit in your country?
- Do you prefer quiet or active holidays?
- What is the best thing about travelling? What is the worst thing?

ACTIVITY 1

Listen to the radio interview with a tour guide and answer the questions.

1 What does Zelda say is the first advantage of her job as a tour guide?
2 Which countries has she visited?
3 What does Zelda see as the most impressive type of site to visit?
4 What kind of natural attraction does she mention?
5 Why would she like to visit the Oriental Pearl Tower?
6 Give an example from the interview of something that might go wrong with a holiday.
7 How might a hotel try to help customers who complain?
8 How can travellers avoid disappointing experiences on holiday?

EXAM REFRESHER

Part 1 (Reading and Writing) requires you to:

- understand the overall message
- read a short text made up of a number of paragraphs
- match pieces of information to paragraphs
- skim and scan for information
- sort information.

Reading Part 1 is worth 10 marks.

SKILLS CONTINUOUS LEARNING

ACTIVITY 2

Tick the statements that are correct for Reading Part 1.

- ☐ The first time you read the paragraphs, make sure you understand all the details.
- ☐ Use scanning skills: look for synonyms in the questions and text(s) to help you.
- ☐ If you can't decide between two answers, you should put crosses for both of them.
- ☐ Don't answer any questions you're not sure about.

EXAM HINTS

- Use skimming and scanning skills.
- Find lexical words in the text to help you.

READING PART 1

▼ PRACTICE TIME 1

Read the brochure below on the different visits offered by Lonsdale Tours, a tour company in London, and answer Questions 1–10.

London with Lonsdale Tours

A Portobello Road is the place to come if you love antiques. The world's largest market has more than 1000 antique dealers selling their goods here – no wonder it's a place where you can buy anything and everything!

B Shakespeare's Globe Theatre should be on every visitor's must-see list. It is a stunningly accurate reconstruction of the building where Shakespeare wrote and produced many of his plays. Don't let the fact that it is open-air put you off! The Shakespeare Globe Theatre Tour and Exhibition alone is worth a visit.

C The Shard – all 310 metres of it – offers what is simply the best view in the whole of London. Those with a head for heights can enjoy 360-degree views of the capital from its top floors, allowing them to see for up to 40 miles.

D Madam Tussauds is arguably one of London's most well known tourist attractions. The famous wax dummies are startlingly lifelike and you can impress your friends with a picture of your favourite film star – you can even stand right next to them if you want to! Although it's been open for over 200 years, its popularity shows no sign of fading.

E London's West End is famous the whole world over. Ever since the very first West End theatre, Drury Lane, opened in 1663, audiences have been flocking to see a range of plays, ballets, operas and musicals. It's a tradition that has only strengthened over time, attracting a whole host of talented directors, actors and producers.

F The Tower of London, on the north bank of the River Thames, has many fascinating things to see. It has a collection of over 23,500 royal jewels and there are always at least six ravens (a type of black bird) kept in the tower. People believe that if the ravens leave, the tower will fall! This must be on your list of places to visit!

G Visit the Natural History Museum if you would like to see dinosaur skeletons and a huge assortment of other exciting exhibits. Many of the displays are interactive and you will definitely be stunned by the range of different species on view here. This internationally-acclaimed museum is second to none.

H A cruise on the River Thames is an ideal way to experience London from a slightly different perspective. Climb aboard a riverboat and listen to your tour guide telling you the fascinating history of London's sights as you sail past them at a leisurely pace. What a wonderful way to see London's attractions – without having to walk a step!

I The London Eye, a giant wheel which gives its passengers a spectacular view as it rotates, is one of London's most striking features. Standing next to the River Thames, it is thought to be three times as tall as Tower Bridge. The London Eye took seven years to build.

J One really excellent way to see London is to take one of our special bus tours – you get all the views without tiring yourself out, which is great if you have children with you or find mobility a challenge. Another really good thing about our tours is that you can listen to our helpful commentaries in no fewer than 11 different languages as you are driven round the capital!

Questions 1–10

Identify which paragraphs (A–J) contain information listed in Questions 1–10 by marking a cross for the correct answer ☒. If you change your mind about an answer, put a line through the box ☒ and then mark your new answer with a cross ☒.

You must choose answers only from the information given in the leaflet.

Paragraphs may be used more than once or not at all.

1 Which paragraph refers to creatures from the past?

A ☐ B ☐ C ☐ D ☐ E ☐ F ☐ G ☐ H ☐ I ☐ J ☐ (1)

2 Which paragraph refers to an extraordinary view seen from different angles while moving?

A ☐ B ☐ C ☐ D ☐ E ☐ F ☐ G ☐ H ☐ I ☐ J ☐ (1)

3 Which paragraph refers to representations of famous people?

A ☐ B ☐ C ☐ D ☐ E ☐ F ☐ G ☐ H ☐ I ☐ J ☐ (1)

4 Which paragraph refers to a place to see a famous writer's stage?

A ☐ B ☐ C ☐ D ☐ E ☐ F ☐ G ☐ H ☐ I ☐ J ☐ (1)

5 Which paragraph refers to a place to find old objects for sale?

A ☐ B ☐ C ☐ D ☐ E ☐ F ☐ G ☐ H ☐ I ☐ J ☐ (1)

6 Which paragraph refers to exploring London's streets on wheels?

A ☐ B ☐ C ☐ D ☐ E ☐ F ☐ G ☐ H ☐ I ☐ J ☐ (1)

7 Which paragraph refers to precious objects?

A ☐ B ☐ C ☐ D ☐ E ☐ F ☐ G ☐ H ☐ I ☐ J ☐ (1)

8 Which paragraph refers to an area where you can watch different types of performance?

A	B	C	D	E	F	G	H	I	J	(1)
☐	☐	☐	☐	☐	☐	☐	☐	☐	☐	

9 Which paragraph refers to a skyscraper which offers visitors an extraordinary panorama?

A	B	C	D	E	F	G	H	I	J	(1)
☐	☐	☐	☐	☐	☐	☐	☐	☐	☐	

10 Which paragraph refers to specific arrangements for visitors from other countries?

A	B	C	D	E	F	G	H	I	J	(1)
☐	☐	☐	☐	☐	☐	☐	☐	☐	☐	

(Total for Questions 1–10 = 10 marks)
(Total for Part 1 = 10 marks)

REFLECT

- Check your work in pairs to see how many marks you scored out of 10. What went well? Could you have done better? If so, how?
- How well did you use your skimming and scanning skills?
- Which words did you look for? Were you looking for the right words?
- Did you find any of the vocabulary difficult to understand?
- Did you learn any helpful new words?

READING PART 1

▼ PRACTICE TIME 2

Read the leaflet below on the holidays offered by Halliday's Holidays and answer Questions 1–10.

Halliday's Holidays

A Check into our luxury hotel in the Swiss Alps, where you can enjoy a week-long skiing adventure! You can hit the slopes or unwind by a log fire with a cup of our famous hot chocolate. As well as your ski pass and your ski and snowboarding equipment, you receive personal tuition from our expert instructors, absolutely free of charge.

B Explore the pyramids! Our tour takes you through Egypt's most famous landmarks, including the tomb of Tutankhamun, the Valley of the Queens, the Great Sphinx of Giza and the Colossi of Memnon. When you're tired of seeing the sights, you can visit the colourful and busy markets in Cairo, or else enjoy the Egyptian heat with a spot of sunbathing by the pool.

C Enjoy a leisurely cruise around the Canary Islands! Embarking at Santa Cruz in Tenerife, you visit not only Gran Canaria but also La Gomera, La Palma and El Hierro. Luxuries like our 24-hour free on-board restaurant, your own private cabin, complimentary evening dance classes and our fully-equipped gym are all included in the price.

D Sign up now to enjoy the wonders of Tokyo! Stay in a five-star hotel right in the middle of this magnificent city, only 20 minutes from the Olympic Stadium. Enjoy our tours of Tokyo's cultural highlights or take advantage of your free passes to the nearby world-famous technology fair.

E If you're looking for a chance to get away from it all, why not fly with us to sunny Greece? With a range of friendly resorts to choose from, you will be able to relax to your heart's content, either by the pool or by the fabulous turquoise sea.

F If you're looking for spectacular views and incredible encounters with nature, you should visit Iceland. Our cruise ship will let you enjoy the beauty of this awe-inspiring terrain and marvel at the antics of dolphins, seals and a range of seabirds – all at a safe distance from the shore!

G France is a wonderful place to spend a vacation, with pretty countryside and amazing views. Visit the friendly villages or enjoy the fun and liveliness of a traditional beachside holiday. Or perhaps you could visit Paris, a city renowned for its culture the whole world over!

H For those who want a holiday that combines spectacular scenery with a rich variety of historical monuments, China is definitely a must-see destination. The remarkable thing about this country is that it's not just a feast for the eyes – Chinese cuisine is also legendary, which would be yet another reason to visit this extraordinary place.

I Come to Heidelberg! Germany's most beautiful city is a photographer's dream, with fairy-tale castles and picturesque houses on forest-covered mountains either side of a sparkling blue river. Take a ferry ride to enjoy the scenery and don't forget to sample some of the freshly-baked apple strudel on board.

J Have you ever wanted to explore the cobbled streets of Prague? Now you can make your dream a reality. Listen to the chime of the clock tower in the city centre and – if you enjoy local history – take the 'Moonlight Tour' through the dark and mysterious side streets and listen to stories of Prague's exciting past!

WATCH OUT!

Remember that you may not be asked about all of the paragraphs and some paragraphs might be used more than once.

Questions 1–10

Identify which paragraphs (A–J) contain information listed in Questions 1–10 by marking a cross for the correct answer ☒. If you change your mind about an answer, put a line through the box ⊠ and then mark your new answer with a cross ☒.

You must choose answers only from the information given in the leaflet.

Paragraphs may be used more than once or not at all.

1 Which paragraph refers to the wildlife of a coastline?

A	B	C	D	E	F	G	H	I	J	(1)
☐	☐	☐	☐	☐	☒	☐	☐	☐	☐	

2 Which paragraph refers to dining at no extra cost?

A	B	C	D	E	F	G	H	I	J	(1)
☐	☐	☐	☐	☐	☐	☐	☐	☐	☐	

3 Which paragraph refers to discovering a city at night?

A	B	C	D	E	F	G	H	I	J	(1)
☐	☐	☐	☐	☐	☐	☐	☐	☐	☒	

4 Which paragraph refers to a city with amazing photo opportunities?

A	B	C	D	E	F	G	H	I	J	(1)
☐	☐	☐	☐	☐	☐	☐	☐	☒	☐	

5 Which paragraph refers to a lively place to shop?

A	B	C	D	E	F	G	H	I	J	(1)
☐	☐	☐	☐	☐	☐	☐	☐	☐	☐	

6 Which paragraph refers to winter sports?

A	B	C	D	E	F	G	H	I	J	(1)
☐	☐	☐	☐	☐	☐	☐	☐	☐	☐	

7 Which paragraph refers to exceptional food?

A	B	C	D	E	F	G	H	I	J	(1)
☐	☐	☐	☐	☐	☐	☐	☒	☐	☐	

8 Which paragraph refers to the venue for an international sporting event?

A	B	C	D	E	F	G	H	I	J	(1)
☐	☐	☐	☐	☐	☐	☐	☐	☐	☐	

9 Which paragraph refers to the possibility of different types of swimming?

A	B	C	D	E	F	G	H	I	J	(1)
☐	☐	☐	☐	☒	☐	☐	☐	☐	☐	

10 Which paragraph refers to a bell that tells the time?

A	B	C	D	E	F	G	H	I	J	(1)
☐	☐	☐	☐	☐	☐	☐	☐	☐	☒	

(Total for Questions 1–10 = 10 marks)
(Total for Part 1 = 10 marks)

AFTER EXAM CHECK

- Make sure you have answered all the questions.
- Make sure you have marked a cross in the right box for each question.

EVALUATE YOUR EXAM PRACTICE

- How do your marks for the two Practice Time tests compare?
- Do you think your skimming and scanning skills have improved?
- What do you still need to work on?
- What could you do, inside or outside of lessons, that would help you?

VOCABULARY AND GRAMMAR

VOCABULARY FOCUS

COMPOUND ADJECTIVES

ACTIVITY 1

Read the Halliday's Holidays leaflet from Practice Time 2 again and find the compound adjectives, then match them to the correct definitions.

EXAMPLE Just out of the oven *freshly-baked*

1 full of trees forest-~~covered~~ covered

2 extremely impressive awe-inspiring

3 open all the time 24-hour

4 judged to be of the highest standard five-star

5 carried on a ship, plane, car, etc. on-loaded

6 known by people all over the world world famous

7 lasting seven days week long

ACTIVITY 2

Find the following compound adjectives in the Lonsdale Tours brochure in Practice Time 1 and the Halliday's Holidays leaflet in Practice Time 2. Write definitions for them, using a dictionary to help.

1 must-see

2 open-air

3 360-degree

4 well-known

ACTIVITY 3

1 Match the words to make a list of compound adjectives. Some words can be used more than once.

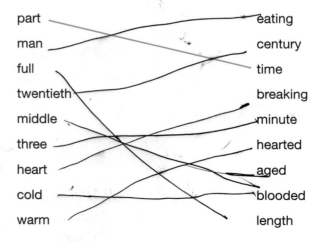

part	eating
man	century
full	time
twentieth	breaking
middle	minute
three	hearted
heart	aged
cold	blooded
warm	length

2 Draw a table like the one below. Use the compound adjectives from your list and sort them into the correct column in your table.

Compound adjectives – time	Compound adjectives – characteristics (physical or emotional)

ACTIVITY 4

Fill in the gaps with the compound adjectives.

non-stop 360-degree awe-inspiring
five-star freshly-baked mouth-watering
week-long well-known

1 I've been so busy with work this week – it's really been ____________. I'm looking forward to the weekend when I can have a break.

2 I know that this isn't a ___________ hotel, but the rooms should at least be clean and warm!

3 He was a ______________ businessman before he became president.

4 The mountains were really ______________. It was the most beautiful place I had ever seen.

5 Your dinner looks __________________. Is there any extra for me?

6 The bread was __________________ and it smelt delicious.

7 You must go to the top of the biggest skyscraper in Tokyo. There's a wonderful _____________ view.

8 I can't come to your wedding because I'm attending a ____________ training course in computer coding.

GRAMMAR CHECKPOINT

GRAMMAR

See Grammar Reference page 270.

MODAL VERBS (OBLIGATION, ADVICE AND PERMISSION)

ACTIVITY 5

1 Put these questions with modal verbs in order from least formal to most formal.

a **Could** you open the window?

b **May** I go to the toilet?

c **Can** we go outside?

2 Complete the sentences using the correct modal verb from the word box.

may	must	might

a We use may to show something is only possible.

b We use might to show politeness.

c We use must to show obligation.

ACTIVITY 6

Complete the polite sentences using the correct modal verb from the word box. Sometimes, it is possible to use more than one verb.

would	could	can	should	may	will

1 may I help you carry that?

2 I think we should have lunch sometime.

3 can you give me a lift?

4 Could I come in?

5 Would somebody lend me some money for the coffee machine?

ACTIVITY 7

Sort the modals of obligation and modals of permission from the word box into the correct columns.

could	can	ought	~~should~~	may	must	have to

Obligation	Permission
should	must
could	have to
can	ough
may	

ACTIVITY 8

Circle the correct modal verb for each sentence.

1 Dentists say you **should** / **must** floss twice a day.
2 **Would** / **Could I** give you a hand with that?
3 **Would** / **Must** you give me a hand with that?
4 You **mustn't** / **don't have to** use your mobile phones during lessons.
5 I **ought to** / **must** work tonight.
6 **Should I** / **Do I** book the restaurant for this evening?
7 We **have to** / **must** have coffee next week.
8 All right, I suppose you **can** / **might** go to the party.
9 The speed limit says you **must** / **should** drive at 75 kph or less.
10 **Can** / **Would** I offer you some advice?
11 **Might** / **Could** somebody let me know the time?
12 You **mustn't** / **don't have to** eat breakfast if you don't want to.
13 **Have I** / **Do I have to** finish today?
14 Excuse me, sir, **may** / **should** I help you?
15 **Could** / **May** you make dinner tonight?

GRAMMAR GAME

▼ LOCATION MODALS

With a partner, write five sentences describing a location using modal verbs:

- one sentence with *should*
- two sentences with *can*
- two sentences with *can't*.

EXAMPLE *Location: Paris*
You should see the large metal tower.
You can eat baguettes and cheese.
You can visit a famous art museum.
You can't go scuba diving.
You can't go snowboarding or skiing.

- Locations can be cities or countries.
- Don't make your clues too easy, e.g. don't use the name of famous monuments directly. Don't be too vague either – it must be possible to guess the answer! Check your sentences with your teacher when you have finished writing them.
- After your teacher has checked them, swap sentences with another pair and see if you can guess the city or country. You have two guesses. If your first guess is correct, you get two points; if your second guess is correct, you get one point.
- Swap sentences with all the other pairs in the class and give yourself points for correct guesses.
- Whoever has the most points at the end, wins!

SELF-EVALUATION

Tick the relevant boxes.

I now feel confident about ...	STRONGLY AGREE	AGREE	DISAGREE	STRONGLY DISAGREE
TALKING ABOUT TRAVEL AND HOLIDAYS				
TACKLING PART 1 OF THE READING AND WRITING EXAM				
UNDERSTANDING MY STRENGTHS AND WEAKNESSES FOR PART 1 OF THE READING AND WRITING EXAM				
USING NEW VOCABULARY (COMPOUND ADJECTIVES)				
USING MODAL VERBS OF OBLIGATION, ADVICE AND PERMISSION				

If you ticked 'disagree' or 'strongly disagree', you need to revise these parts.

READING PART 2

TECHNOLOGY AND THE FUTURE

Assessment Objective 1B

Understand in detail a range of texts, identifying finer points of detail

Assessment Objective 1C

Distinguish between facts, ideas and opinions

Assessment Objective 1D

Identify a writer's viewpoint and attitude, stated and implied

LEARNING OBJECTIVES

- Talk about gadgets and technology
- Revise the requirements for Part 2 of the Reading and Writing exam
- Practise two Part 2 sample questions
- Evaluate your exam practice
- Build new vocabulary (phrasal verbs)
- Use future simple, future continuous and future perfect tenses
- Use *going to*
- Use other ways of expressing the future

PREPARING THE WAY

Discuss the questions.

- Do you own any gadgets? Which is your favourite?
- What gadgets and technology would you like to be invented in the future?
- What technology and gadgets did you use when you were younger? Do they still exist?
- Do you think that some of the technology you currently use will disappear?

SKILLS CRITICAL THINKING

ACTIVITY 1

1 Listen to the author talking at a science-fiction interest group. Answer the questions.

1 Why was Abdu interested in science fiction as a child?

A It combines science and reading.

B He loved science.

C He loved reading.

D He liked thinking about other worlds.

2 Which area of science fascinates Abdu most?
A The theory of relativity
B Nuclear physics
C Time travel
D Splitting the atom

3 According to Abdu, how might time travel help us in the present?
A We could see that the past was better.
B We could take ideas from the past and maybe use them now.
C We could learn new ways of studying science.
D We could learn more about history.

4 What will Abdu upload to his website?
A The introduction to his new book
B His new book
C Some feedback on his new book
D The first chapter of his new book

5 How does Abdu see reading science fiction?
A As an indicator of future technologies
B As a way to relax
C As a source of inspiration
D As a source of excitement

2 Working in pairs, make a list of all the books, cartoons, films and television shows based on the future and/or technology that you are aware of. What do they have in common (e.g. maybe they all contain futuristic vehicles)?

EXAM REFRESHER

Part 2 (Reading and Writing) requires you to:

- read a longer text
- identify attitudes and opinions in the text
- identify different types of information
- complete gap-fill tasks such as completing sentences using information provided in the text as well as your comprehension and analytical skills
- complete other tasks, such as multiple-choice questions.

Reading Part 2 is worth 15 marks.

SKILLS CONTINUOUS LEARNING

EXAM HINTS

- Focus on the relevant parts of the text.
- Pay attention to the difference between facts and opinions.

ACTIVITY 2

Tick the statements that are correct for Reading Part 2.

- ☐ For short-answer questions, you can use your own words, but you must not write more than the specified number of words.
- ☐ Try to write a sentence for the three-word answers.
- ☐ If you aren't sure of the answers to multiple-choice questions, you should choose one anyway.

READING PART 2

SKILLS INTERPRETATION

▼ PRACTICE TIME 1

Read the article on driverless cars and answer Questions 11–25.

Driverless cars are going to save the world and I can't wait

By the end of this year, driverless cars will be cruising the streets of London. I'm quite excited about this. In fact, I'm really excited about this. This is a game changer.

For a long time, driverless cars have been a staple of sci-fi films. However, it now looks as if the future has arrived.

I don't think most people realise what an enormous change this is. The thing is, driverless cars are often presented simply as a technical development: first we got power steering, then we got airbags and now your car is about to be driven by a computer. But I think they're going to change the way we live and work – and almost entirely for the better.

For a start, the economic upsides are huge. Congestion is massively expensive, both in terms of direct costs (if you're sitting in traffic, you're wasting fuel and you're not working) and indirect costs (everything else).

How would driverless cars help reduce crowding, you ask. After all, if you need a car, you need a car whether you drive it or not. Well, the thing is driverless cars can drive much closer together. A University of Texas study suggests that if 90 per cent of cars on motorways were self-driving, road capacity would be doubled and delays would be more than halved. Basically, driverless cars could give us a free-flowing *M25. What's more, they'll free up so much extra capacity that we'll probably never need to build another road, depending on population levels.

That's only the beginning. They'll be driven much more fuel-efficiently too, which will mean less pollution. Free-flowing roads will result in much less stop-start driving and, on top of this, computers are better judges of how to drive efficiently than you or me. Of course, I do expect cars to be battery-powered fairly soon. But even so, the electricity to charge the batteries will have to come from somewhere and we're not likely to have a clean energy source for this for a while.

Still, can you imagine? All those roads in London which are currently snarled-up, diesel-choked hellholes will suddenly become much quieter – and much less polluted. This will also have the pleasant side effect of meaning that those of us who actually like walking or cycling will not have to do so in a soup of burnt hydrocarbons and road rage.

It'll also be much healthier for those in the cars. Driving many places in the UK is horribly stressful. Driverless cars will mean not only a smoother, faster journey, but more hours to use productively. Perhaps you'll do work. Perhaps you'll learn another language. Perhaps you'll read great novels. OK, so you probably wouldn't do any of these. You (and I) will spend the time glued to our phones dementedly using social media. But even so, arguing with strangers online over issues you half understand is better than getting into a real fight with the bloke who overtook you.

Even so, this still leaves the argument: 'What about my right to drive? I'm not letting a computer drive for me.' Well, leaving aside the fact that no-one actually has a human right to drive (that is why drivers are licensed), I doubt this is going to be much of an issue at all. People love convenience and ease more than they love abstract notions of rights (just look at how much people really care about online privacy).

EXAM HINT

Sometimes you will be given hints about places you do not know about or very difficult words.

As for the joys of driving down the open road? Please. Driving in most of the UK ceased to be a joy sometime in the 80s. It's a classic example of 'the tragedy of the commons' (as economists call it). Roads are too cheap (or poorly-priced) so they're overused and are now unpleasant for everyone.

Anyway, it's going to happen – and I think most of us will like it. I imagine that when my eldest son is my age, he'll be sitting in his driverless Audi with his friends, chatting away, nobody even looking at the road, and perhaps they'll starting reminiscing about their childhoods when people still drove themselves, and how absurd and dangerous and silly it all was.

Alex Proud,

The Telegraph

* M25 a motorway which circles London

EXAM HINT

Remember to only use a maximum of the specified number of words for short-answer questions.

Questions 11–20

Answer the following questions. For each question write no more than THREE words taken from one point in the text. DO NOT write full sentences.

11 How does the writer describe the change over to driverless cars? (1)

....

12 Where have driverless cars mainly appeared until now? (1)

....

13 What is the earliest change made to cars mentioned by the writer? (1)

....

14 What cost relating to energy is mentioned by the writer? (1)

....

15 What would increase if most cars on motorways were driverless? (1)

....

16 Which environmental improvement would driverless cars bring about? (1)

....

17 Which negative emotional state does the writer mention? (1)

....

18 How are people most likely to use the time gained by not having to drive? (1)

....

19 Which two advantages of not driving may appeal more than an idea? (1)

....

20 How does the writer describe driving before the 80s? (1)

....

(Total for Questions 11–20 = 10 marks)

SKILLS INTERPRETATION

Questions 21–25

Identify which of the options given for Questions 21–25 accurately completes the given statements by marking a cross for the correct answer ☒. If you change your mind about an answer, put a line through the box ☒ and then mark your new answer with a cross ☒.

21 According to the writer, the introduction of driverless cars is (1)

- ☐ **A** terrifying.
- ☐ **B** inevitable.
- ☐ **C** revolutionary.
- ☐ **D** fictional.

22 The first kind of benefit the writer mentions is (1)

- ☐ **A** a financial benefit.
- ☐ **B** an aesthetic benefit.
- ☐ **C** an environmental benefit.
- ☐ **D** a political benefit.

23 For the writer, a major advantage of using computers to drive will be (1)

- ☐ **A** cars using batteries.
- ☐ **B** fewer road accidents.
- ☐ **C** cars needing less maintenance.
- ☐ **D** more efficient driving.

24 The writer describes his current experiences of walking and cycling as (1)

- ☐ **A** healthy.
- ☐ **B** unpleasant.
- ☐ **C** relaxing.
- ☐ **D** noisy.

25 The writer imagines that, in the future, his son will think that people driving cars (1)

- ☐ **A** was a waste of time.
- ☐ **B** was a pleasant activity.
- ☐ **C** was ridiculous.
- ☐ **D** required skill.

(Total for Questions 21–25 = 5 marks)
(Total for Part 2 = 15 marks)

SKILLS SELF-EVALUATION

REFLECT

- What went well? Could you have done better? If so, how?
- Which aspects of the Practice Time test went better than last time?
- Did you find it easy to distinguish between fact and opinion?
- How many marks did you score out of 15?
- Identify one important target to aim for in your next Practice Time test.

EXAM HINT

Using highlighter pens may help you to identify the relevant sections of the text.

READING PART 2

▼ PRACTICE TIME 2

Read the article about artificial intelligence and answer Questions 11–25.

The Teaching Assistants of the Future?

TA's surprise identity surprises students

The world of education is changing fast. Students do an ever-increasing proportion of their learning online, and digital technology has transformed the ways in which knowledge in a range of subjects is taught. One subject that has, perhaps, changed more than most is computer science.

At Georgia Tech's College of Computing, in the USA, the changes have been particularly interesting and far-reaching. Professor Ashok Goel teaches computer science courses at the college, and for his students, the Knowledge Based Artificial Intelligence (KBAI) class is a compulsory element of the computer science programme and is essential for a science master's qualification. The fact that the course is compulsory causes problems because it means the volume of students taking the course at any given time is significant – approximately 300. To get support with their studies, these students post messages when they have queries, using online forums provided by the college. There are about 10 000 messages for each cohort of students. Staff need to respond to the messages so that the students on the course can access the help they need.

When the course was launched, Professor Goel had eight Teaching Assistants (TA's). However, even if he and these eight TA's had devoted all their time to the task, they still couldn't have dealt with the number of messages in the forum. So the school added one more TA, Jill Watson. Unlike her colleagues, Jill is not a human being, although most students don't realise that. She is actually a computer.

It's well known in the world of education that online classes struggle to keep students. They have low retention rates compared to face-to-face classes. This is often because students don't feel sufficiently supported. This is why Jill is so vital. To create her, Goel, together with some of his graduate students, identified the most commonly occurring questions that had been posted on the online forums since the KBAI course launched in 2014. (It is interesting to note that when online courses attract more students, the volume of questions increases, but the range of questions doesn't.) Once they had tracked down these questions, they were given to Jill along with the answers. How? Through a computer code written specifically for Jill by Goel and his team of researchers.

One issue, for example, that came up frequently for KBAI students, was where to locate relevant reading material. Goel and his team were able to program Jill to answer this question effectively because they could anticipate the question. Other questions on popular topics also emerged, which made the researchers' task much easier. However, even though the questions were often easy to predict, Jill didn't always tackle them correctly and her answers didn't always come out in quite the right way. Sometimes she would get stuck on a query, for example, if the wording of the question confused her. So the team created a hidden forum where she could practise and could go over the relevant material again until her answers were accurate enough to upload and pass on to students. Of course, all of this took time, and Jill made plenty of mistakes along the way. But every mistake she made gave the researchers another opportunity to fine-tune her responses. Soon they calculated that her answers had an accuracy rate of 97 per cent. At that point, Jill was allowed to respond to a student's query on her own.

As a student, it would be interesting to discover that the TA you'd written to, and who had helped you with your studies, was secretly a robot. The students in this case were told that Jill was a computer on 26 April and they were excited to hear the news. Overall it came as a huge surprise although one student, Tyson Bailey, had wondered about Jill as early as February. He later said he was aware that a course about artificial intelligence might make use of artificial intelligence in unexpected ways. He was certainly right!

Jill has gone from strength to strength, and is now a vital part of the teaching team. She will be back next term, although by then she will have a different name, and maybe a different gender!

SKILLS CRITICAL THINKING

EXAM HINT

The specified word limit may vary. For example, it could be two, three or four words. Make sure you pay attention to the word limit and do not exceed it.

Questions 11–20

Answer the following questions. For each question write no more than THREE words taken from one point in the text. DO NOT write full sentences.

11 Which Masters of Science programme are KBAI students following? (1)

....

12 How many posts do Goel's forums receive for each group of students? (1)

....

13 What is a problem that affects online classes? (1)

....

14 When did the KBAI class begin? (1)

....

15 What was written to enable Jill to answer the students' questions? (1)

....

16 What do the KBAI students frequently need information about? (1)

....

17 Where were Jill's first answers posted? (1)

....

18 When did Goel reveal the truth about Jill? (1)

....

19 Which student queried Jill's identity? (1)

....

20 When will Jill begin work again? (1)

....

(Total for Questions 11–20 = 10 marks)

SKILLS CRITICAL THINKING

Questions 21–25

Identify which of the options given for Questions 21–25 accurately completes the given statements by marking a cross for the correct answer ☒. If you change your mind about an answer, put a line through the box ☒ and then mark your new answer with a cross ☒.

21 Why did Goel employ a virtual TA for his online Master's course? (1)

☐ **A** The students' questions were too technical.
☐ **B** Teaching staff were too busy to deal with questions.
☐ **C** The students' questions were too hard.
☐ **D** There were too many questions.

22 What is the main reason given for students failing to complete online courses? (1)

☐ **A** Insufficient help is provided.
☐ **B** The workload is too heavy.
☐ **C** The work is too difficult.
☐ **D** There are too many computer problems.

23 If the number of students in an online class increases, what happens to the questions asked? (1)

☐ **A** The number of questions decreases dramatically.
☐ **B** The number of questions remains exactly the same.
☐ **C** There are more questions but a lot of them are similar.
☐ **D** There is a much bigger variety of questions.

24 When did Jill communicate directly with students? (1)

☐ **A** When the students asked for help.
☐ **B** When she was completely sure she had the right answer.
☐ **C** When the teachers were stuck.
☐ **D** When the human TAs believed she was ready.

25 How did students react to finding out that one of their teachers was not a real person? (1)

☐ **A** They were confused.
☐ **B** They decided to leave the course.
☐ **C** They felt cheated.
☐ **D** They reacted positively.

(Total for Questions 21–25 = 5 marks)
(Total for Part 2 = 15 marks)

SKILLS SELF-EVALUATION

EVALUATE YOUR EXAM PRACTICE

- How do your marks for the two Practice Time tests compare?
- When you read the questions, were you able to guess what sort of key words you could look for in the text to help you?
- Did you have enough time to read the text carefully? How will you make sure you use the time given most efficiently?
- What can you do, inside or outside of lessons, that would improve your reading skills and your exam performance?
- Identify one important target to aim for in your next Practice Time test.

VOCABULARY AND GRAMMAR

VOCABULARY FOCUS

PHRASAL VERBS

ACTIVITY 1

1 Match the phrasal verbs from the articles 'Driverless cars …' (pages 135–136) and 'The Teaching Assistants …' (pages 138–139) to the correct definitions.

Phrasal verb	Definition
get stuck on	search for and find
come out	increase or improve
go over	find it impossible to progress beyond a particular point
go up	revise or revisit
track down	appear, emerge

2 Can you think of any other meanings for the phrasal verbs listed above? You can use the following sentences to help you.

- Oh no! This stain won't come out!
- This cable car goes all the way up the south face of the mountain.

3 How many phrasal verbs can you think of using the verb *come*? Write sentences for each one you can think of.

ACTIVITY 2

Circle the correct words.

1 We've **gone up** / **been over** this issue several times and you still don't know what I'm talking about!

2 You should **come out** / **go up** with us tomorrow night – it'll be fun!

3 I've managed to **get stuck on** / **track down** that jacket I've been looking for everywhere!

4 The popularity of our website **went over** / **went up** by 50 per cent last month!

5 I always **go over** / **get stuck on** the same words in English, no matter how much work I do.

ACTIVITY 3

Complete the sentences using a phrasal verb from Activity 1 on page 141 in the correct form.

1 If you ____________ your English homework, just ask for help.
2 The science teacher insisted on ________________ the safety rules repeatedly.
3 Alejandro ________________ yesterday instead of staying at home to study.
4 The visitors from outer space could not ________________ anyone who spoke their language.
5 We wouldn't want the cost of space travel to ____________________ any higher.

GRAMMAR CHECKPOINT

GRAMMAR

See Grammar Reference pages 265–267.

WILL OR *GOING TO*

ACTIVITY 4

Circle the more natural response.

1 **Marco:** I feel like pizza for dinner.
  a **Rosa:** OK. I'll order some.
  b **Rosa:** OK. I'm going to order some.
2 **Rosa:** Someone's at the door.
  a **Marco:** Oh? Must be the pizza. I'll get it.
  b **Marco:** Oh? Must be the pizza. I'm going to get it.
3 **Marco:** Hi, Paolo. I'm going to have a party on Saturday. Do you want to come?
  a **Paolo:** Really? Sure, I'm coming for a while!
  b **Paolo:** Really? Sure, I'll come for a while!
4 **Paolo:** So, are you going to Marco's party on Saturday?
  Julia: I already have plans.
  Paolo: Really? What?
  a **Julia:** I'm going to watch a film.
  b **Julia:** I'll watch a film.

GRAMMAR CHECKPOINT

GRAMMAR

See Grammar Reference pages 265–266.

FUTURE SIMPLE AND FUTURE CONTINUOUS

ACTIVITY 5

Complete the sentences using the future simple or future continuous.

EXAMPLE (?, the plane, arrive)
When *will the plane arrive* ?

1 (–, Raul, disappoint) ____________ you again, I promise.

2 (?, you, do) What ____________ at this time tomorrow?

3 (+, they, make) ____________ a cake for the party tomorrow.

4 (?, you, sleep) ____________ at ten tonight?

5 (?, you, wear) What ____________ during the interview?

6 (+, I, wait) When your plane lands, ____________ at the Arrivals gate.

SKILLS CREATIVITY

ACTIVITY 6

Imagine how your life will be in 50 years' time, with all the new technology. Write a paragraph describing a moment in your future life, using the future continuous. You should consider:

- what you will be doing
- where you will be doing it
- the objects you will be using
- what you will be wearing
- what the people around you will be doing.

EXAMPLE *In 50 years' time, I will be ...*

GRAMMAR CHECKPOINT

GRAMMAR

See Grammar Reference pages 266–267.

FUTURE PERFECT

ACTIVITY 7

Write eight predictions about how technology will have changed in 50 years from now.

EXAMPLE *I think that in 50 years' time, computers will have stopped using cables.*

Here are some ideas for things that might change:

- food and drink
- accommodation
- sports
- environment
- transportation.

You should write your predictions in the future perfect.

GRAMMAR CHECKPOINT

GRAMMAR

See Grammar Reference pages 267–268.

OTHER WAYS TO TALK ABOUT THE FUTURE

ACTIVITY 8

1 Match the highlighted future expressions in the sentences (a–d) to the definitions (i–iv).

a I **should** be arriving at the train station by 5 p.m. today.

b I am **due to** be at the airport in 2 hours.

c Chen is **likely to** pass her ESL exam.

d They are **about to** leave the house.

i will probably

ii will, if everything goes according to plan

iii going to happen soon

iv scheduled to be

2 Look at the sentences (a–d) again.

- What forms of the verb are used after *should be*, *due to*, *likely to* and *about to*?
- Write four sentences, each containing one of the four future expressions.

ACTIVITY 9

Circle the correct phrases.

1 Johann **should be arriving** / **is about to arrive** at around ten o'clock tonight, I think.

2 Haley **should be doing** / **is about to do** her homework.

3 The class is **due to hand in** / **about to hand in** the assignment on 7 July.

4 It is **about to** / **likely to** rain today, according to the forecast.

5 Unless there's a delay, the plane **is likely to landing** / **should be landing** around seven.

6 I am not **due to finishing** / **likely to finish** my essay any time soon.

ACTIVITY 10

Find and correct the six remaining future tense mistakes in Daphne's email to a technical support centre. There may be more than one possible answer.

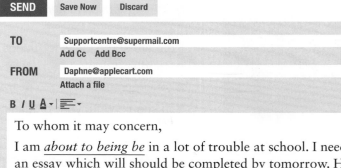

SEND | Save Now | Discard

TO Supportcentre@supermail.com
Add Cc Add Bcc

FROM Daphne@applecart.com
Attach a file

B I U A

To whom it may concern,

I am *about to being be* in a lot of trouble at school. I need to finish an essay which will should be completed by tomorrow. However, my computer isn't working, so tomorrow my teacher is due to be furious with me. Each time I press spellcheck, my essay turns into a series of random letters. I am about to crying. It will might be OK, if you could write me an email explaining that my computer is not working and so I won't be being able to complete my essay. I go to school at 7 o'clock, so please you will write the email before then.

Best wishes,

Daphne

GRAMMAR GAME

▼ FUTURE ACTION MIME

- Take three cards and write an action on each one (e.g. *sunbathing*), then lay them out on a table.
- Work in groups. One student takes a card and reads the action. They mime the preparation for the action (e.g. if the activity is sunbathing, you might mime laying a towel down on the floor and applying suncream). You cannot actually mime the action.
- The other students guess what you will be doing (e.g. 'he will be sunbathing').
- Whoever guesses correctly gains a point and takes the next card.
- Whoever has the most points at the end, wins!

SELF-EVALUATION

Tick the relevant boxes.

I now feel confident about ...	STRONGLY AGREE	AGREE	DISAGREE	STRONGLY DISAGREE
▶ TALKING ABOUT TECHNOLOGY AND GADGETS				
▶ TACKLING PART 2 OF THE READING AND WRITING EXAM				
▶ UNDERSTANDING MY STRENGTHS AND WEAKNESSES FOR PART 2 OF THE READING AND WRITING EXAM				
▶ USING NEW VOCABULARY (PHRASAL VERBS)				
▶ USING FUTURE SIMPLE, FUTURE CONTINUOUS AND FUTURE PERFECT TENSES				
▶ USING *GOING TO*				
▶ USING OTHER WAYS OF EXPRESSING THE FUTURE				

If you ticked 'disagree' or 'strongly disagree', you need to revise these parts.

READING PART 3

BUILDINGS

Assessment Objective 1B

Understand in detail a range of texts, identifying finer points of detail

Assessment Objective 1C

Distinguish between facts, ideas and opinions

Assessment Objective 1D

Identify a writer's viewpoint and attitude, stated and implied

LEARNING OBJECTIVES

- Talk about houses and other buildings
- Revise the requirements for Part 3 of the Reading and Writing exam
- Practise two Part 3 sample questions
- Evaluate your exam practice
- Build new vocabulary (nouns and verbs: buildings)
- Use conditionals

PREPARING THE WAY

Discuss the questions.

- What is the most famous building in your country?
- What is the most attractive building you've seen in real life?
- Do you prefer modern houses or old-fashioned houses?
- Do you prefer buildings in cities or buildings outside cities?

ACTIVITY 1

1 Match the pictures of the famous buildings (a–f) to:

- the correct names
- the correct countries.

a

b

c

d

e

f

Picture	Building	Country
a	Angkor Thom	Egypt
b	Himeji Castle	Italy
c	Burj Khalifa	Cambodia
d	Great Sphinx	India
e	Leaning Tower of Pisa	Japan
f	Taj Mahal	United Arab Emirates

2 Discuss in pairs.

- Which two of these buildings would you like to visit? Why?

SKILLS CRITICAL THINKING

ACTIVITY 2

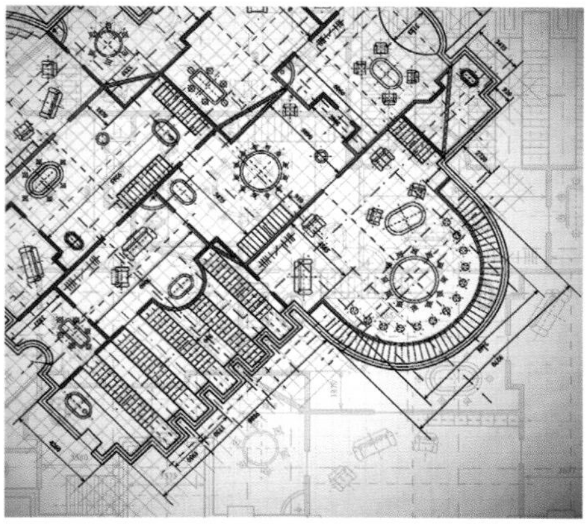

Listen to an interview with an architect. Answer the questions.

1 What should potential architects train themselves to notice?

2 What is people's usual response to buildings they see every day?

3 When are people more likely to notice the detail of buildings?

4 What two qualities should buildings have, as well as being original?

5 According to Gabriela, what item is essential for her as an architect?

EXAM REFRESHER

Part 3 (Reading and Writing) requires you to:

- read longer texts
- identify attitudes and opinions in the text
- identify different types of information
- judge whether some statements are true, false or have no evidence
- fill in missing words in a text
- choose the correct words from a list to complete a summary.

Reading Part 3 is worth 10 marks.

SKILLS CONTINUOUS LEARNING

ACTIVITY 3

Tick the statements that are correct for Reading Part 3.

☐ If some information suggested in the question is not given in the text, the information is probably false.

☐ Make sure you do not use more than the number of words specified in the question.

☐ In gap-fill activities, it is important to check that your answers fit grammatically.

☐ When you have to choose a word from a word box, there may be more than one possible answer.

EXAM HINT

Sometimes you can work out the meaning of words you don't know by reading the rest of the sentence or text.

READING PART 3

▼ PRACTICE TIME 1

Read about the Egyptian pyramids and answer Questions 26–45.

Pyramids

What does the word 'pyramid' mean?

The word 'pyramid' actually comes from the Greek word 'pyramis'. This means 'wheat cake'. The word 'pyramis' was used to describe the ancient Egyptian buildings because they reminded the Greeks of pointy-topped wheat cakes. The ancient Egyptian word for the pyramids was 'Mer'.

Why did the ancient Egyptians use the pyramid shape?

Egyptologists (people who study ancient Egypt) have developed many theories about why the tombs of their early leaders, the pharaohs, were built in the pyramid shape. Here are three different ideas:

- The pyramid represented the first land to appear at the beginning of time – a hill called 'Ben-Ben'.
- The pyramid had sloping sides so that the dead pharaoh could climb to the sky and live forever.
- The pyramid was designed to look like the rays of the Sun. The ancient Egyptians built pyramids as tombs for the pharaohs and their queens. The pharaohs were buried in pyramids of many different shapes and sizes from before the beginning of the Old Kingdom to the end of the Middle Kingdom.

There are about 80 pyramids known today from ancient Egypt. The three largest and best-kept of these were built at Giza at the beginning of the Old Kingdom. The most well-known of these pyramids was built for the pharaoh Khufu. It is known as the Great Pyramid.

The pharaoh Khufu, like the pharaohs before him, began planning his 'house of eternity' as soon as he took the throne. A spot was chosen for building on the west bank of the Nile. Cemeteries were usually built on the west bank because the Sun 'died' on the western horizon every night. Khufu's architects were wise and experienced. They knew the importance of building the pharaoh's final resting place so that its sides faced directly north, south, east and west. They planned a large pyramid – the largest one ever built in ancient Egypt. The outlines of the pyramid were measured and marked in the desert sand. Then building the foundations began. Large blocks of stone were cut from stone quarries nearby. They were dragged by groups of men across the desert to the site of the pyramid and set in place. Most of the workers were farmers who worked on building the pyramid during the flood season when their fields were under water.

After the first level of blocks was in place, the workers built ramps of mudbrick, limestone chips and clay. The workers dragged the large stones up the ramps to build the next level of the pyramid. For about 20 years, hundreds of men worked on building the pyramid. As they built each level, they also built up the ramps around the pyramid. When the pyramid was almost finished, a special block covered in shining metal (either gold or electrum) was placed on the top of the pyramid.

Then blocks of white limestone from quarries across the Nile were used to cover the pyramid. The blocks were trimmed to make the outside of the pyramid smooth.

Finally, the pyramid was finished. Khufu's pyramid was only part of the complex built for him at Giza.

This complex had many different parts:

- Three pyramids for Khufu's queens.
- Several deep pits containing boats that had been buried.
- A special temple where Khufu would be worshipped after he died.
- A path leading from the pyramid complex down to the valley temple.
- A valley temple where the pharaoh's funeral would begin.
- A small 'satellite' pyramid.

What is the Great Sphinx?

The Great Sphinx is a large human-headed lion that was carved from a mound of natural rock. It is located in Giza where it seems to guard the front of a large pyramid.

Legends have been told for many years about the Great Sphinx. These stories tell about the powers and mysteries of this sphinx. Some people even believe that there are hidden passageways or rooms underneath the Great Sphinx, but if this is true, no evidence of it has been found yet.

The beginning of one story about the Great Sphinx is written on a *stele between the sphinx's paws.

The story reads that one day, a young prince fell asleep next to the Great Sphinx. He had been hunting all day and was very tired. He dreamt that the Great Sphinx promised that he would become the ruler of Upper and Lower Egypt if he cleared away the sand covering its body (the Great Sphinx was covered up to its neck).

The rest of the story is gone, so if you want to work out the ending, you will have to use your imagination!
[from website 'Ancient Egypt']

* stele a stone slab that would stand upright in a temple or important place. The plural is 'stelai'. Important information was recorded on stelai.

SKILLS CRITICAL THINKING, INTERPRETATION

Questions 26–30

Read the statements below. Decide whether they are TRUE, FALSE or NOT GIVEN according to the text.

Mark a cross for the correct answer ☒. If you change your mind about an answer, put a line through the box ☒ and then mark your new answer with a cross ☒.

		True	False	Not Given	
26	The word 'pyramid' is Egyptian in origin.	☐	☒	☐	(1)
27	The shape of pyramids mimics the Sun's rays.	☐	☐	☐	(1)
28	About 80 pyramids have been discovered.	☐	☐	☐	(1)
29	Metal was used to make the tops of pyramids shine.	☐	☐	☐	(1)
30	A young prince cleared the Great Sphinx of sand.	☐	☐	☐	(1)

(Total for Questions 26–30 = 5 marks)

SKILLS CRITICAL THINKING, INTERPRETATION

A01B

EXAM HINT

The specified word limit may vary. For example, it could be two, three or four words. Make sure you pay attention to the word limit and do not exceed it.

Questions 31–40

Complete the following sentences using no more than THREE words taken from one point in the text.

31 Egyptologists specialise in learning about .... (1)

32 There are a number of different .... about the reason for the shape of Egypt's famous pyramids. (1)

33 As soon as Khufu became pharaoh, he started making arrangements for his '..'. (1)

34 Many of the builders of the Great Pyramid also worked as .... (1)

35 These men could not work during .... because their lands were flooded. (1)

36 Building the pyramids was a long and complicated process, which took about .... (1)

37 Khufu's construction was not only a pyramid, it also contained .... in which boats were found. (1)

38 After death, Khufu would be worshipped in a .... (1)

39 There are .... which tell mysterious stories about the Great Sphinx. (1)

40 One story was about a .... who went hunting. (1)

(Total for Questions 31–40 = 10 marks)

SKILLS CRITICAL THINKING, INTERPRETATION

A01B

Questions 41–45

Complete the summary of the text using words from the box below. Each word may be used once or not at all.

model	~~grave~~	levels	~~origin~~	elderly	beginning
~~ancient~~	statue	~~tombs~~	stages		

Pyramids are **(41)** ....ancient........ buildings and we are lucky that many have been preserved. Although pyramids are Egyptian, their name has a Greek **(42)** ....origin........ Pyramids are actually the **(43)** ....grave / ~~tombs~~........ of early pharaohs.

The best-preserved pyramid was built for the pharaoh Khufu and is situated at Giza. It took many years to build and contains many chambers. It is built on a number of different **(44)** ....stages........ and was finished off with white limestone. This had to be transported across the desert.

Another important legacy from early Egypt was the Great Sphinx. This is a huge **(45)** ....statue........ of a lion with a human head. It was carved from natural rock and is said to guard an important pyramid.

(Total for Questions 41–45 = 5 marks)
(Total for Part 3 = 20 marks)

EXAM HINT

Check that the words you choose from the word box fit grammatically into the summary text.

REFLECT

- Check your work in pairs to see how many marks you scored out of 20. What went well? Could you have done better? If so, how?
- How well did you identify attitudes and opinions in the text?
- How well did you identify different types of information?
- Were you able to distinguish between information which was true, false or not given?

READING PART 3

▼ PRACTICE TIME 2

Read the article about the Leaning Tower of Pisa and answer Questions 26–45.

Learning about the Leaning Tower!

Every country has its own popular tourist attractions, but not every tourist attraction is based on a mistake. And because of a mistake, thousands flock every year to the location of one of Italy's best-loved 'mistakes', the Leaning Tower of Pisa. Of course, the tower was not intended to lean – hence its original name was the *Torre di Pisa* or, in English, the Tower of Pisa.

Pisa is a province in the beautiful region of Tuscany, the origin of the Italian Renaissance, and a holiday destination that is popular with tourists, partly because of its sunny Mediterranean climate and partly because of its wealth of ancient monuments and museums. Of all of these, the tower stands out as the one that visitors most want to see. But what is the history of this extraordinary building? And how did its famous leaning habit come about?

First of all, the tower is not really a tower. Surprised? So are a lot of the tourists who flock there every year. It is actually a *campanile*, which is a bell tower. This is not the same as a regular tower (the clue is in its name!) and it's not, as many wrongly believe, the same as a belfry either. Belfries do have bells in the tower, but they are part of a bigger structure, whereas the Leaning Tower of Pisa stands alone. In fact, it's the way that the tower stands that has caused it to become so well known. We may not always be aware of it, but when we see a tower (or other tall building) we tend to assume that it will be straight and upright. This is what makes the leaning tower special. It goes against our expectations because – as its name suggests – it is leaning. The reason? Its foundation.

Construction of the tower was started as far back as 1173. All those centuries ago, the site and the foundations chosen for the tower had one fatal flaw: it was too soft to support the weight it had to hold. As time went on and further layers were added, the problem became even worse. It wasn't until quite recently, in the last century, that the tower finally became more stable, thanks to the efforts of hundreds of builders and engineers.

Of course, a lot of people are curious about the architect of this remarkable building. Many have speculated about the architect's identity and have looked for accurate records without much success. It seems that no one can say for sure who designed the building. An artist called Pisano, who specialised in bronze, was one candidate, especially when a cast bearing his name was discovered at the foot of the tower. However, it is believed that until 1595 there was a bronze door to the tower, which was destroyed, and it is possible that the cast was linked to that. Another possible candidate for the design the tower was Diotisalvi, who also lived and worked in the 12th century. The tower does not have a signature, though, and as Diotisalvi used to sign the buildings he designed it is probable that he was not the architect. Little is known about the builders either. Gerardo di Gerardo and Giovanni di Simone have both been named as possibilities, and either or both may have contributed to the building process; it is thought that di Simone, in particular, helped to complete it.

An interesting fact about the tower is that its famous tilt was not immediately visible, for the simple reason that it did not exist. The design of the tower was perfectly sound. It was five whole years after construction had begun, when the builders started to add the second floor, that the leaning quality was first noticed. The reason was simple: the land beneath it was not firm enough to support it. And this was where fortune was kind to the leaning tower. War broke out between Pisa and some neighbouring regions. It lasted for about 100 years, which meant the building of the tower was delayed. And while the people of Pisa were busy fighting, the foundation on which their tower had been built was settling. Without this pause in the building process, who knows what would have become of the famous tower?

Building resumed in 1272, with attempts made to counteract the leaning, which created the tower's notorious curve. Alterations have continued intermittently ever since, although the actual construction was finished after 199 years. A major restoration occurred in 1990, lasting for 11 years. Hopefully, generations to come will be able to enjoy the tower, just as we can today.

SKILLS CRITICAL THINKING, INTERPRETATION

A01C

Questions 26–30

Read the statements below. Decide whether they are TRUE, FALSE or NOT GIVEN according to the text.

Mark a cross for the correct answer ☒. If you change your mind about an answer, put a line through the box ☒ and then mark your new answer with a cross ☒.

		True	False	Not Given	
26	The Leaning Tower of Pisa is in Tuscany.	☒	☐	☐	(1)
27	The tower is actually a belfry.	☐	☒	☐	(1)
28	The ground where the tower was built caused problems.	☐	☐	☐	(1)
29	It is likely the tower's architect was Pisano.	☐	☐	☐	(1)
30	The tower took over two centuries to build.	☐	☐	☐	(1)

(Total for Questions 26–30 = 5 marks)

SKILLS CRITICAL THINKING, INTERPRETATION

A01B

EXAM HINT

The specified word limit may vary. For example, it could be two, three or four words. Make sure you pay attention to the word limit and do not exceed it.

Questions 31–40

Complete the following sentences using no more than THREE words taken from one point in the text.

31 The Tower of Pisa is now a .... in Italy. (1)

32 Tuscany is famous as the birthplace of the .... (1)

33 A 'campanile' is a type of ....bell tower.................................. (1)

34 The tower was not supported by a proper ....foundation.... because the ground under the construction was not hard enough. (1)

35 The tower eventually became .... in the 1900s. (1)

36 There has been a lot of speculation .... of the tower's architect. (1)

37 The fact that the tower has no .... means that Diotisalvi is probably not the architect. (1)

38 The war between Pisa and .... was indirectly responsible for the survival of the tower. (1)

39 The builders' efforts to straighten the tower resulted in its .... (1)

40 The tower underwent a .... between 1990 and 2001. (1)

(Total for Questions 31–40 = 10 marks)

SKILLS CRITICAL THINKING, INTERPRETATION

A01B

Questions 41–45

Complete the summary of the text using words from the box below. Each word may be used once or not at all.

appeal	shrouded	uncertainty	unevenness	attraction
delayed	unearthing	unevenly	prolonged	

The Leaning Tower of Pisa has a long and interesting history. It is lucky to have survived for so long and is only really here because a war **(41)** .... the building project. The tower leans because of the softness of the foundation it was built upon. This foundation settled **(42)** ....

There is some **(43)** .... about the identity of the architect. Several names have been put forward, but the truth is not really known; the identity of the builder too is **(44)** .... in mystery.

The tower was built in stages and has also been restored over a relatively long period of time; the major restoration period was 11 years long. Nowadays, the tower remains a popular **(45)** .... for visiting tourists.

(Total for Questions 41–45 = 5 marks)
(Total for Part 3 = 20 marks)

EVALUATE YOUR EXAM PRACTICE

- Which Practice Time test did you get a better mark for? Why?
- Do you think you were better at identifying attitudes and opinions and different types of information in the second text than in the first text?
- Did you find it easier to distinguish between information which was true, false or not given in the first or second text?
- What do you still need to work on?
- What could you do, inside or outside of lessons, that would help you?

VOCABULARY AND GRAMMAR

VOCABULARY FOCUS

NOUNS AND VERBS: BUILDINGS

SKILLS ANALYSIS

ACTIVITY 1

Read the 'Learning about the Leaning Tower' article again and underline the verbs and nouns that are linked with the ones in the table. Complete the table with the words you have found.

Verbs	Nouns
(to) found	*foundation*
(to) restore	~~storage~~ restortion.
(to) construct	construction
(to) locate	location.
(to) *speculate*	speculation
(to) complete	completion
destroy (to) ~~destruct~~	destruction
(to) constribute	contribution
(to) continue.	continuation

ACTIVITY 2

Match the words from Activity 1 to the correct definitions.

1 To damage something so badly that it no longer exists or cannot be used or repaired destruction.

2 The solid layer of cement, bricks or stones that is put under a building to support it foundation.

3 The state of being finished completion.

4 To find the exact position of something location.

5 To set up or establish contribution ~~construct~~

6 To build something such as a house, bridge or road construction

7 Something that you give or do in order to help something to be successful speculation.

8 The repairing of something such as an old building or a piece of furniture, so that it looks the same as when it was first built or made construction.

9 A particular place, especially in relation to other areas or buildings location.

10 A guess about the possible causes or effects of something without knowing all the facts ______

11 Something that continues or follows something, without stopping or changing continuation.

ACTIVITY 3

Circle the correct words in the news article.

SCHOOL DESIGNED BY STUDENTS!

When a local school had to be partially [1] **destroyed / completed** after major problems were found with its [2] **foundations / destruction**, the head teacher invited students to contribute to plans for its [3] **foundations / restoration**. 'We wanted our students to use their imagination and to come up with ideas that would really reflect their hopes and interests,' she said.

Students certainly seemed very excited about the idea and some say they can't wait for the final [4] **speculation / completion** of the project, scheduled for later this year.

Initially there was [5] **contribution / speculation** that the school would close and the remaining buildings would be sold off, as the school is in a prime location, but pupils, parents and teachers all campaigned against its closure and their efforts have now been rewarded.

'This school is an important part of the community and it's vital that it [6] **contributes / continues**,' said one parent, adding, 'I think the fact that the children have had a say in the new [7] **completion / construction** is brilliant. The school was always a good one and now the whole community feels even more committed to it. I really think it will go from strength to strength.'

ACTIVITY 4

Fill in the gaps using verbs or nouns from Activity 1 on page 155, using the correct form.

1 When buying a house, you need to think carefully about the ______. Is it convenient for your job and your children's school, for example?

2 The ______ of the Amazonian rainforest affects us all.

3 The United Nations was ______ in 1945.

4 The Eiffel Tower was ______ from wrought iron between 1887–1889 in Paris.

5 I don't like to ______, but I think she is going to lose the election.

6 Please could you ______ your forms and return them to me by 5 o'clock?

7 Greg is a great team player. He always has something to ______.

8 My job is to ______ old and damaged paintings. It's wonderful to see them come back to life!

9 The ______ of this construction project is essential for the future of this company. We cannot let it be stopped.

ACTIVITY 5

Can you think of any other nouns which end in *-tion*? Which verbs are they formed from? Working in pairs, make a list.

GRAMMAR CHECKPOINT

GRAMMAR

See Grammar Reference page 273.

ZERO CONDITIONAL

ACTIVITY 6

Make sentences in the zero conditional using elements from each column (several combinations are possible). Remember to use the correct form of the verbs.

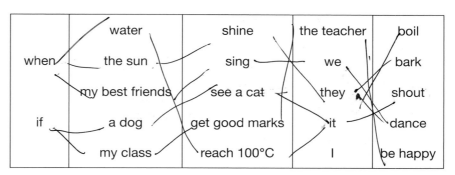

	water	shine	the teacher	boil
when	the sun	sing	we	bark
	my best friends	see a cat	they	shout
if	a dog	get good marks	it	dance
	my class	reach 100°C	I	be happy

EXAMPLE *When water reaches 100°C, it boils.*

GRAMMAR CHECKPOINT

GRAMMAR

See Grammar Reference page 273.

FIRST CONDITIONAL

ACTIVITY 7

Half of each of these first conditional sentences are missing. Try to complete the sentences with the other half.

EXAMPLE *If I have nothing else to do tonight*, I will watch a film.

what to do

1 If I don't know, I will ask the teacher.

2 If I argue with my friend, I will win.

3 If I break it, I will try to fix it.

4 If my school finishes early today, I will go home early.

5 If I feel bad., I get sick.

6 If it rains tomorrow, I won't go to school

GRAMMAR CHECKPOINT

SKILLS CREATIVITY

GRAMMAR

See Grammar Reference pages 273–274.

SECOND CONDITIONAL

ACTIVITY 8

Write five sentences describing your ideal home. Start the sentences using the second conditional.

EXAMPLE *If I lived in a different place, I would live in …*
If I could choose my ideal home, it would (+ verb) *…*

You should think about the following points.

- What type of building would it be (e.g. an apartment, a house, etc.)?
- Where would it be located?
- How many rooms would it have?
- Would it have any special rooms?
- Would there be any outdoor spaces?

ACTIVITY 9

1 Place the situations in the word box into the different columns, depending on how probable they are.

the weather is rainy this week	~~you win the lottery~~
you wake up early tomorrow	the dog eats your homework
you are able to turn invisible	you improve your English
aliens invade Earth	you make a mistake while speaking English
someone steals your pen today	nobody steals your pen today

Possible	Unlikely or impossible
	you win the lottery

2 Write nine second conditional sentences explaining what you would do in these hypothetical situations.

EXAMPLE *If I won the lottery, I would buy a house with a pool.*

GRAMMAR CHECKPOINT

GRAMMAR

See Grammar Reference page 274.

THIRD CONDITIONAL

ACTIVITY 10

Transform each past simple sentence into two possible third conditional sentences.

EXAMPLE I knew about the plumbing problems, so I didn't buy the house.
If I had known about the plumbing problems, I wouldn't have bought this house.
If I hadn't known about ...
I wouldn't have bought the house if ...

1 There was a traffic jam, so we took our usual route.
2 My friend missed his bus, so we missed the film.
3 Yoko ate two hamburgers for lunch, so she couldn't finish her dinner.
4 We didn't know it was your birthday, so we didn't buy a present.
5 It was very warm this morning, so I left my jacket at home.
6 The watch broke, so I had to send it back to the shop.

SELF-EVALUATION

Tick the relevant boxes.

I now feel confident about ...	STRONGLY AGREE	AGREE	DISAGREE	STRONGLY DISAGREE
▶ TALKING ABOUT HOUSES AND OTHER BUILDINGS				
▶ TACKLING PART 3 OF THE READING AND WRITING EXAM				
▶ UNDERSTANDING MY STRENGTHS AND WEAKNESSES FOR PART 3 OF THE READING AND WRITING EXAM				
▶ USING NEW VOCABULARY (NOUNS AND VERBS: BUILDINGS)				
▶ USING CONDITIONALS				

If you ticked 'disagree' or 'strongly disagree', you need to revise these parts.

UNIT 6 WRITING PRACTICE

Assessment Objective 2A

Demonstrate appropriate use of paragraphing, punctuation and spelling

Assessment Objective 2B

Write in a range of registers to fit the context and the audience

Assessment Objective 2C

Demonstrate a control of a range of vocabulary and a variety of grammatical structures

Assessment Objective 2D

Summarise information provided in text form for a given purpose and audience

This unit provides further practice for Parts 4, 5 and 6 of the Writing section of Paper 1 Reading and Writing.

In the exam, you will need to show that you can:

- write for a variety of audiences, such as friends and family, classmates or teachers
- write in a variety of styles ranging from informal to formal
- write for a range of purposes, for example to inform, persuade or entertain
- write on a range of topics
- write using a wide range of grammatical forms and structures
- write using a wide range of relevant and appropriate vocabulary
- summarise longer texts, selecting information that is relevant to the purpose of the summary and paraphrasing this information.

The mark breakdown is:

- Part 4: 10 marks
- Part 5: 20 marks
- Part 6: 25 marks.

WRITING PART 4

WORK AND JOBS

Assessment Objective 2A

Write using correct paragraphing, punctuation and spelling

Assessment Objective 2B

Write in a range of registers to fit the context

Assessment Objective 2C

Demonstrate control of a range of vocabulary and structures

LEARNING OBJECTIVES

- Talk about work and jobs
- Revise the requirements for Part 4 of the Reading and Writing exam
- Evaluate sample exam answers
- Practise two Part 4 sample questions
- Evaluate your exam practice
- Build new vocabulary (phrasal verbs: work)
- Use the perfect continuous

PREPARING THE WAY

Discuss the questions.

- Why do people work?
- In an ideal world, which jobs should people be paid the most for doing?
- What would be your ideal job?

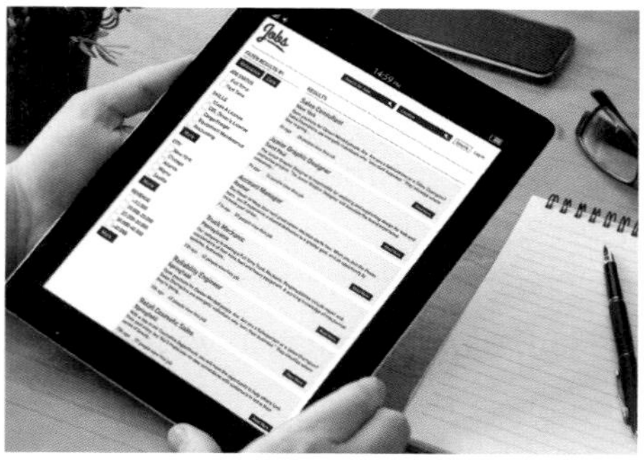

ACTIVITY 1

1 Read the questions and then listen to the podcast from a careers advisor.

a Why is getting a first job especially difficult?

b What are the advantages for employers of hiring younger workers?

c What steps can younger people take to help get their first job?

2 Discuss in pairs.

a What sort of work is available to young people in your country?

b Do young people make better employees than older ones? Why / Why not?

c What sort of work would you choose as your first job? Why?

EXAM REFRESHER

Part 4 (Reading and Writing) requires you to:

- write a short text, e.g. to a friend or family member
- consider the communicative qualities and organisation of your writing
- use an appropriate range of vocabulary and grammatical structures
- use a suitable format and style.

The assessment criteria for this part are:

- communication, content and organisation (5 marks)
- range and accuracy (5 marks).

SKILLS CONTINUOUS LEARNING

ACTIVITY 2

Tick the statements that are correct for Writing Part 4.

☐ Cover all three points fairly evenly.

☐ Use as many complex words as possible to show off your vocabulary.

☐ Make your writing very formal.

☐ Begin and end your writing in a way that is appropriate to the text type.

ACTIVITY 3

Read this Writing Part 4 task and the three openings from the three sample answers that follow.

> You have just started a new part-time job. Write an email to your friend, telling him/her about the work.
>
> In your email you **must** write:
>
> - when you started the job
> - what kind of work you have to do
> - what you like about it.
>
> You **must** write between **75 and 100 words only**. (10)

Discuss with your partner which one is best and why.

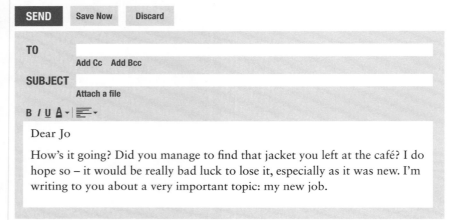

Student A

SEND Save Now Discard

TO
Add Cc Add Bcc
SUBJECT
Attach a file
B I U A

Dear Jo

How's it going? Did you manage to find that jacket you left at the café? I do hope so – it would be really bad luck to lose it, especially as it was new. I'm writing to you about a very important topic: my new job.

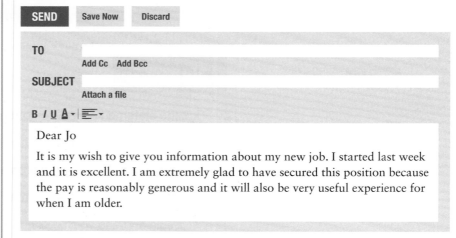

Student B

SEND Save Now Discard

TO
Add Cc Add Bcc
SUBJECT
Attach a file
B I U A

Dear Jo

It is my wish to give you information about my new job. I started last week and it is excellent. I am extremely glad to have secured this position because the pay is reasonably generous and it will also be very useful experience for when I am older.

EXAM HINTS

- Keep your writing relevant.
- Use the right register.

WATCH OUT!

Avoid exaggeration in your answers. Expressions like 'back-breaking work' or 'endless torment' would sound unnatural in this context. However, at the same time, you should avoid very simple expressions such as 'he tried hard' or 'she worked a lot'.

Student C

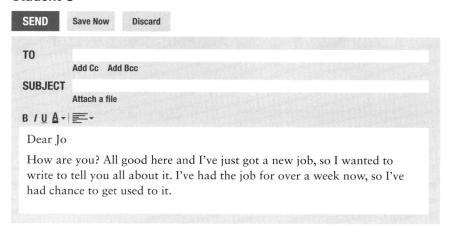

SEND Save Now Discard

TO

Add Cc Add Bcc

SUBJECT

Attach a file

B I U A

Dear Jo

How are you? All good here and I've just got a new job, so I wanted to write to tell you all about it. I've had the job for over a week now, so I've had chance to get used to it.

SKILLS CREATIVITY

WRITING PART 4

▼ PRACTICE TIME 1

You want to apply for a part-time job and need your friend's advice. Write an email asking him/her about part-time work.

In your email you **must** write:

- why you want a part-time job
- which jobs might be available in your area
- questions to ask for advice.

You **must** write between **75 and 100 words only**.

(Total for Part 4 = 10 marks)

REFLECT

- The task is divided into three bullet points. Did you cover each one?
- Did you give your email an appropriate opening and closing?
- Did you keep the language informal throughout?
- What went well? Could you have done better? If so, how?
- How many marks did you score out of 5 for:
  - communication, content and organisation
  - range and accuracy?
- Identify one important target to aim for in your next Practice Time test.

SKILLS CREATIVITY

A02A A02B A02C

WRITING PART 4

▼ PRACTICE TIME 2

You started a part-time job one month ago, but you do not like it and you want to leave. Write an email to your friend asking for his/her advice.

In your email you **must** write:

- what your new job is
- why you do not like it
- questions to ask for advice.

You **must** write between **75 and 100 words only**.

(Total for Part 4 = 10 marks)

EXAM HINTS

- Avoid using too many **metaphors** or **similes**.
- Avoid unnatural phrasing like:
  - *I miss you beyond imagining*
  - *my heart is breaking into pieces*
  - *unfaithfully yours.*

EVALUATE YOUR EXAM PRACTICE

- How do your marks for the two Practice Time tests compare?
- Did you improve? How and why?
- Which of the two assessment criteria did you find more challenging – communication, context and organisation or range and accuracy?
- What could you do, inside or outside of lessons, that would help you?

VOCABULARY AND GRAMMAR

VOCABULARY FOCUS

PHRASAL VERBS: WORK

SKILLS INTERPRETATION

ACTIVITY 1

Listen to the office discussion about workload and answer the questions.

1 What is the purpose of the meeting?

2 Why is Ralph reluctant to write a summary?

3 Which task is the person running the meeting particularly concerned about?

4 How has Ralph made the form-filling process faster?

5 When did Ralph tell David about his idea for reorganising the filing system?

6 Which idea didn't Ralph tell David about?

ACTIVITY 2

1 Read the transcript of the discussion in Activity 1 and underline the verbs from the table below.

2 Find and complete the phrasal verbs or expressions in the transcript and match them to the correct definitions.

Verb	Expression in text / phrasal verb	Definition
run	*run it by everyone* *run (something) by*	progress to a higher/better position
meet		resolve, discover
figure		be exhausted by work, usually over a longer period of time
get ahead		plan and produce
burn		explain or suggest an idea or proposal to someone
draw		give new information in a slightly formal way, in speech or in writing
fill		complete a form with missing information
fill		act as a substitute for someone
report		get together

Baljit: Right, well, thank you for coming, everyone. I didn't have time to draw up a proper agenda, but I think most of you are aware that I called this meeting to discuss how heavy our workload is at the moment and to try to decide what we can do about it. I thought it might be really useful if we could all meet up. Ralph, can you take notes? I've told David that we'll report back to him after our discussion, so it would be good to have something in writing.

Ralph: Sure. No problem. Do you want me to make a summary of the notes as well, though? I'm a bit snowed under at the moment.

Baljit: Yes please, Ralph. A summary would be great. We'll all appreciate that. Now the first thing I wanted to touch base about was these extra evaluations we've been asked to complete. You know, the ones on yellow paper where we have to record how we think the phone calls with our clients have gone.

Ralph: Um.

Baljit: Yes, Ralph?

Ralph: I was just going to say, I've come up with a system that lets me get ahead with filling in those evaluations. Perhaps I could run it by everyone?

Baljit: I see. And what system is that, then?

Ralph: Well, I normally write the same thing on every report. Spoke to client, it went well, client happy, the usual stuff.

Baljit: Yes. And?

Ralph: Well, so what I do now is, I fill one in and then photocopy it. That way I just have to put in the date and the client's name, rather than writing it all out in full every time. It's much faster.

Baljit: Hmm ... Yes, I can see that would be faster. I'm not sure how David would feel about it, though.

Ralph: Oh, he likes the idea. I told him all about it when the lift broke last week and we got stuck in between floors. I talked to him about that and about my idea for reorganising the filing system and about the scheme that I figured out to let us use the car park spaces more effectively. I could tell he was impressed with my ideas. He'll probably ask me to fill in for one of the managers next time they go on holiday. I made lots of suggestions to David. After 20 minutes, he just said, "Do whatever you like." It was a bit annoying, though, because the lift was mended before I could tell him about my idea for redesigning the staff canteen.

Baljit: Right.

Ralph: Yes. I talked to you about my idea for the canteen on Friday, if you remember?

Baljit: Friday. Oh. Yes. It was at going-home time, if I recall correctly.

Ralph: Five o'clock, yes.

Baljit: Well, it was five o'clock when you started. I seem to remember it was after six by the time you'd finished.

Ralph: Yes, well, that's me! I'm not afraid of hard work. I'll probably burn out by the time I'm thirty!

Baljit: Yes, Ralph. That would be a shame, wouldn't it?

ACTIVITY 3

Circle the correct phrases.

1 I need to **get ahead** / **report back** to Mike tomorrow as the project is in danger of going over budget.
2 If we don't **figure out** / **fill in** the forms, the whole system will break down.
3 With all of this extra work coming in this week, we're going to be **burned out** / **drawn up**.
4 Let's **draw up** / **meet up** as soon as possible before the 18th.
5 Can I **run something by you** / **get something ahead** that's been bothering me?

ACTIVITY 4

Read the telephone conversation. Fill in the gaps using the phrasal verbs from Activity 2 on page 167 in their correct form.

Roberto: Hello, Seb, how's it going? Still snowed under with paperwork?

Seb: Hello, Roberto. It's not too bad, thank you. I managed to [1]__________________ with the new project, so that helped.

Roberto: Great news. You said in your email that you wanted me to ring you. Is now a good time to talk?

Seb: Yes. I want to touch base with you about the new trainee, the one who's here on work experience.

Roberto: Oh, you mean Luis?

Seb: That's the one, yes. As his manager, how do you feel he's getting on?

Roberto: I think he's doing very well. He's very keen, he's gained a lot of experience and he's not afraid of hard work. I even got him to [2]__________________ for Lance when he was on holiday.

Seb: Oh?

Roberto: Yes. He visited our London branch and was able to [3]__________________ to the team here very successfully. He soon [4]__________________ how it was done.

Seb: That's good news.

Roberto: Yes, Luis said how much he enjoyed it – he seemed to feel it was the ideal job for him. He said he's even thinking of working with us here at Randall's Radios as a long-term career, if he gets the qualifications. I wonder if we could offer him a part-time job? We know he's a good worker.

Seb: Perhaps we could [5]__________________ to discuss it sometime soon. From our point of view there would be lots of advantages.

Roberto: Yes, true. I think it would be very useful to talk about it.

Seb: I'll add it when I [6]__________________ the agenda for our next meeting. There was something else I wanted to [7]__________________ you too, but I'm not sure what it was! Hope I'm not starting to forget things. That was what happened to Victor, just before he [8]__________________! Oh well, I'll ring you back if I remember it. Bye then, Roberto.

Roberto: Bye.

GRAMMAR CHECKPOINT

GRAMMAR

See Grammar Reference pages 265 (Present perfect continuous), 266 (Past perfect continuous) and 267 (Future perfect continuous)

PERFECT CONTINUOUS TENSES

ACTIVITY 5

Circle the most well-phrased sentence in each pair of sentences.

1 a I've had a job for ten years.
  b I've been having a job for ten years.

2 a How long have you known him?
  b How long have you been knowing him?

3 a Tim's eaten three burgers today.
  b Tim's been eating three burgers today.

4 a We decorated, so the walls still have wet paint on them.
  b We've been decorating, so the walls still have wet paint on them.

5 a What have you done all day?
  b What have you been doing all day?

6 a Sorry I'm so late. Did you wait long?
  b Sorry I'm so late. Have you been waiting long?

7 a I was working all of yesterday; I'm very tired.
  b I've been working all of yesterday; I'm very tired.

8 a Has Anusha arrived yet?
  b Has Anusha been arriving yet?

9 a Abasi has cooked for five hours and he's still not finished.
  b Abasi has been cooking for five hours and he's still not finished.

10 a I've been in Georgia for five years now.
  b I've been being in Georgia for five years now.

11 a I've written four pages already and I'm still writing.
  b I've been writing four pages already and I'm still writing.

12 a What did you do last summer?
  b What have you been doing last summer?

GRAMMAR GAME

▼ SENTENCE RACE

- Form two queues at the front of the class.
- The student at the front of each queue must answer your teacher's question, using the present perfect continuous.
- If you use the tense correctly, return to your seat. If you get it wrong, go to the back of the queue.
- When all of the students on one team have returned to their seats, they win!

ACTIVITY 6

Write:

- three true sentences about yourself in the present perfect continuous
- three true sentences in the past perfect continuous
- three true sentences in the future perfect continuous.

EXAMPLE *I have been living in Cairo for 6 months.*
By 2015, I had been studying English for 3 years.
Next Monday, I will have been working in this cinema for 7 weeks.

ACTIVITY 7

Conjugate the verbs in the past perfect continuous, present perfect continuous or future perfect continuous.

1 (+, I, live)
____________ in Hong Kong for seven months now.

2 (you, work)
How long ____________ here?

3 (+, they, building)
Next month, ____________ the property for a whole year.

4 (–, I, plan)
____________ on coming to the party, but then I found out there would be a band.

5 (+, he, act)
____________ in a very annoying way lately.

GRAMMAR GAME

▼ WHAT HAVE YOU BEEN DOING TODAY?

- Write five cards with different jobs on them (three common jobs and two unusual jobs) and give them to your teacher.
- One student goes to the front to take a card and describes what they have done that day. For example, *I have been helping sick people take medicine.*
- Other students guess what that person's job is.
- Whoever guesses successfully takes the next card.
- Whichever student has made the most successful guesses at the end, wins!

SELF-EVALUATION

Tick the relevant boxes.

I now feel confident about ...	STRONGLY AGREE	AGREE	DISAGREE	STRONGLY DISAGREE
▶ TALKING ABOUT WORK AND JOBS				
▶ TACKLING PART 4 OF THE READING AND WRITING EXAM				
▶ UNDERSTANDING MY STRENGTHS AND WEAKNESSES FOR PART 4 OF THE READING AND WRITING EXAM				
▶ USING NEW VOCABULARY (PHRASAL VERBS: WORK)				
▶ USING THE PERFECT CONTINUOUS				

If you ticked 'disagree' or 'strongly disagree', you need to revise these parts.

WRITING PART 5

TRANSPORT

Assessment Objective 2A

Write using correct paragraphing, punctuation and spelling

Assessment Objective 2B

Write in a range of registers to fit the context

Assessment Objective 2C

Demonstrate a control of a range of vocabulary and structure

LEARNING OBJECTIVES

- Talk about transport and travel
- Revise the requirements for Part 5 of the Reading and Writing exam
- Evaluate sample exam answers
- Practise two Part 5 sample questions
- Evaluate your exam practice
- Build new vocabulary (idioms and expressions: travel)
- Use possessives

PREPARING THE WAY

Discuss the questions.

- How many different forms of transport can you think of for land, air and sea?
- What is your favourite form of transport? Why?
- What is your least favourite form of transport? Why?
- If you could design a new form of transport, what would it be? Why?

ACTIVITY 1

1 Read the questions and listen to the discussion about Frank's new car.

2 Answer the questions.

a What two overall qualities of Frank's car is he proud of? Don't give specific details.

b Whose car has power steering?

c Why was Frank unhappy about the journey he took in Michael's car? Give three reasons.

d What is special about the windows in Frank's car?

e Why is this useful?

EXAM REFRESHER

Part 5 (Reading and Writing) requires you to:

- write a report, semi-formal letter or article
- use the suitable format and style.

The assessment criteria for writing are:

- content and communication (5 marks)
- lexical range and accuracy (5 marks)
- grammatical range and accuracy (5 marks)
- effective organisation (5 marks).

SKILLS CONTINUOUS LEARNING

ACTIVITY 2

Tick the statements that are correct for Writing Part 5.

- [ ] Cover all three points fairly evenly.
- [ ] Make your writing informal.
- [ ] Write a long introduction and conclusion.
- [ ] Begin and end your writing in a way that is appropriate.
- [ ] Make your writing semi-formal.

ACTIVITY 3

1 Read this Writing Part 5 task and the four opening extracts from four sample answers that follow.

You have been asked by your teacher to write a report on walking habits in your local area.

In your report you **must**:

- explain how popular walking is in your local area
- describe the best way to dress for walking safely
- give one health benefit of walking.

You **must** write between **100 and 150 words only**. (20)

Student A
Walking is really popular in my city. It's a really cool activity and load's of people enjoy it. It's the best way to get healthy and it really let's you chill. In my opinion, it's an awesome way to get around and more people should do it.

Student B
I am going to write my report on the topic of walking. First I am going to write about how popular walking is locally, then I am going to write about the best way to dress for walking safely, then I will describe one health benefit of walking.

Student C
Walking is quite a popular pastime locally. Large numbers of people walk to work in the city, especially when the weather is warm. This may be because they are keen to avoid traffic jams, so the city streets are full of people walking.

Student D
I walk to school every day and it's amazing – the views are really spectacular. Walking has lots of health benefits and keeps you fit. Come to my city and start walking! You definitely won't regret it, and it could be the start of a great new hobby. So, what's stopping you?

2 Discuss in pairs which opening is best and why.

- Are they suitable opening sections? Why/Why not?
- Are the register and tone appropriate?
- Would these answers score well against the four assessment criteria? (Content and communication; lexical range and accuracy; grammatical range and accuracy; effective organisation.)

SKILLS CREATIVITY

A02A A02B A02C

EXAM HINT

Organise your work so that the information is clearly visible to the reader.

WATCH OUT!

Remember to organise your work so that it is easy for the reader to see that you have addressed all points. Avoid copying wording from the question.

WRITING PART 5

▼ PRACTICE TIME 1

You have been asked by your teacher to write a report on the use of transport in your local area and to find out whether more people could walk or cycle.

In your report you **must**:

- explain what forms of transport local people currently use
- explain what stops people from walking or cycling
- give two advantages of changing to walking or cycling.

You **must** write between **100 and 150 words only**.

(Total for Part 5 = 20 marks)

REFLECT

- Did you cover each of the three points from the question?
- Did the organisation of your text help to show that you have covered the points?
- Did you use a range of vocabulary effectively?
- Did you use a semi-formal register consistently?
- Did you make any grammatical mistakes?
- How many marks did you score out of 5 for each of the four different assessment criteria?
- Identify one important target to aim for in your next Practice Time tests

SKILLS CREATIVITY

A02A A02B A02C

EXAM HINTS

- Remember to use the correct register consistently.
- Use the appropriate language for the task. For example, don't use wording suitable for a letter or speech if you are writing a report or article.

WRITING PART 5

▼ PRACTICE TIME 2

You have been asked to write an article for your school magazine with the title, 'My favourite journey'.

In your article you **must**:

- explain where you travelled from and to
- explain what form(s) of transport you used
- explain what you enjoyed about the journey.

You **must** write between **100 and 150 words only**.

(Total for Part 5 = 20 marks)

EVALUATE YOUR EXAM PRACTICE

- How do your marks for the two Practice Time tests compare?
- Did you improve? How and why?
- Which of the four assessment criteria did you find the most challenging?
- What could you do, inside or outside of lessons, that would help you?

VOCABULARY AND GRAMMAR

VOCABULARY FOCUS

SKILLS CRITICAL THINKING

IDIOMS AND EXPRESSIONS: TRAVEL

ACTIVITY 1

Listen to the discussion about a travel writer's experiences and answer the questions.

1 Why does Jack enjoy travel so much? Give four reasons.
2 How does he avoid jet lag?
3 What makes it easier for him to hitchhike?
4 Why did he begin his travels?
5 How did he overcome his culture shock?
6 How does he fund his trips?

ACTIVITY 2

Read the transcript of the interview on page 177 and match the expressions and idioms to the correct definitions.

Expression/idiom	Definition
get itchy feet	feel tired and confused after flying a very long distance because of the difference between time zones
be a culture vulture	be comfortable in a place
travel on a shoestring	become restless and want to visit lots of different places
have/get culture shock	relax by just looking at the people around you
feel at home	decide to do something because you suddenly feel like it
travel light	take very few possessions with you when you go abroad
have jet lag	spend very little money on a trip or holiday
see how the mood takes you	enjoy visiting attractions such as museums, galleries and theatres
watch the world go by	feel confused and challenged by being in a very different country or place

Sophia: So, with me here in the studio today is Jack Green, a well-known travel writer who is famous not just for travelling, but for travelling on a shoestring. Welcome to the studio, Jack.

Jack: Thank you very much, Sophia.

Sophia: I'd like to start by asking you why travel appeals to you so much.

Jack: I think it's the variety of countries I see and the range of people I meet. International food too! And also, I'm a culture vulture!

Sophia: You've travelled to a huge range of destinations, often in a short space of time. Aren't you constantly jet-lagged?

Jack: You might expect that, but no.

Sophia: How do you avoid it?

Jack: It's simple. I rarely fly.

Sophia: Ah, I see. And that must cut down costs.

Jack: Definitely. Also, I like to travel light. That means I can hitchhike. I couldn't really do that if I was carrying three huge suitcases!

Sophia: Good point. So, what motivated you to start travelling in the first place?

Jack: I guess I just got itchy feet. I was so sick of staying in one place.

Sophia: Mm, I know the feeling …

Jack: I wanted to visit other places, to experience the way that other people live at first hand. Of course, I got a real culture shock at first.

Sophia: I can imagine. How did you get past that?

Jack: One word: cafés! I just used to sit in the local café, wherever I was, and watch the world go by.

Sophia: Really? And how did that help you?

Jack: I'm not sure, to be honest. I think it just gave me a sense of being connected. It let me feel at home, somehow ... like less of a tourist. Often I'd get chatting to people at other tables, so it allowed me to spend time with local people.

Sophia: Sounds great!

Jack: Yes; it's a fantastic lifestyle. I just go where I like; see how the mood takes me and I get to write about it afterwards. That gives me the income that I need to pay for my next trip.

Sophia: What a brilliant way to make a living! Thanks for stopping by and telling us about it, Jack, and good luck with your next adventure!

Jack: Thank you, Sophia. It's been fun.

ACTIVITY 3

Complete the sentences using an expression or idiom from Activity 2 in the correct form.

1 Hassan can't come out tonight. He has just returned from China and he ____________________.

2 I love going to my local park and just sitting there and ____________________. People are so interesting to observe.

3 The worst ____________________ I ever had was when I spent a winter in Tajikistan. I struggled with the language and the weather.

4 My son will never settle down in one place. He always __________ and decides to move on.

5 Wow – only one tiny bag! You really know how to __________ .

6 I hate sitting on the beach and sunbathing all day – I prefer going to museums and galleries. I'm a real __________.

7 I lost my job this year so we'll have to __________ for our summer holiday.

8 I never know what I'm going to do from one day to the next when I'm on holiday. I prefer to just __________ me.

9 The best way to __________ when you're abroad is to take things that remind you of your friends and family. That way you'll never get homesick.

SKILLS REASONING, ARGUMENTATION

ACTIVITY 4

Discuss in pairs.

- Have you ever had culture shock? Where were you?
- Are you a culture vulture? What do you like doing on holiday?
- Have you ever had jet lag? What did you do to cope with it?
- Would you like to hitch-hike? Why/Why not?
- Do you prefer to plan your holidays or to see where the mood takes you?
- Do you travel light? What do you always take when you travel?

GRAMMAR CHECKPOINT

GRAMMAR

See Grammar Reference page 257.

POSSESSIVES

ACTIVITY 5

Complete the table using the correct possessive adjectives and pronouns.

Pronoun	Possessive adjective	Possessive pronoun
I	*my*	*mine*
you		
he		
she		
it		
we		
they		

ACTIVITY 6

Tick the correct sentences.

EXAMPLE a That's my bus. ✓
b That's mine bus.

1 a Is that pen yours? No, it's of her.
b Is that pen yours? No, it's hers.

2 a My sister's house is in Spain.
b The house of my sister is in Spain.

3 a He's a friend of us.
b He's a friend of ours.

4 a This is the boys' room. They're not home right now, though.
b This is the boy's room. They're not home right now, though.

5 a Is that his book or her book?
b Is that his book or hers book?

6 a That's the entrance of the hospital.
b That's the hospital's entrance.

7 a Have you seen the dog? I have its food.
b Have you seen the dog? I have it's food.

8 a Well, this is our house.
b Well, this is ours house.

9 a This part of the store is the man's section.
b This part of the store is the men's section.

10 a Can you see the leg of the table?
b Can you see the table's leg?

11 a This is a traditional Portugal's delicacy.
b This is a traditional delicacy of Portugal.

12 a That's Paul's mum's friend's car.
b That's the car of the friend of the mum of Paul.

ACTIVITY 7

The Lonsdale Tours leaflet contains eight mistakes relating to possession. Read it and correct the mistakes. The first has been underlined for you.

WELCOME TO LONSDALE TOURS

Hello, and congratulation<u>'s</u> on choosing Lonsdale buses! Our bus' company operates in the heart of the centre of London's. Enjoy you're tour through the capital cities beautiful streets and waterways in a traditional bright red London's bus, from which you'll be able to see world-renowned landmarks, famous peoples' houses and spectacular views of the River Thames. Our knowledgeable tour guides can point out tourist's attractions in 11 different languages.

Thanks for booking, and don't forget to bring your's ticket to the meeting point at 11 a.m. on the 17th.

SELF-EVALUATION

Tick the relevant boxes.

I now feel confident about ...	STRONGLY AGREE	AGREE	DISAGREE	STRONGLY DISAGREE
▶ TALKING ABOUT TRANSPORT AND TRAVEL				
▶ TACKLING PART 5 OF THE READING AND WRITING EXAM				
▶ UNDERSTANDING MY STRENGTHS AND WEAKNESSES FOR PART 5 OF THE READING AND WRITING EXAM				
▶ USING NEW VOCABULARY (IDIOMS AND EXPRESSIONS: TRAVEL)				
▶ USING POSSESSIVES				

If you ticked 'disagree' or 'strongly disagree', you need to revise these parts.

WRITING PART 6

MIND AND BODY

Assessment Objective 2A

Write using correct paragraphing, punctuation and spelling

Assessment Objective 2B

Write in a range of registers to fit the context

Assessment Objective 2C

Demonstrate a control of a range of vocabulary and structure

Assessment Objective 2D

Summarise information provided in text form for a given purpose and audience

LEARNING OBJECTIVES

- Talk about health
- Revise the requirements for Part 6 of the Reading and Writing exam
- Evaluate sample exam answers
- Practise two Part 6 sample questions
- Evaluate your exam practice
- Build new vocabulary (collocations: mind and body)
- Use linking words and phrases
- Use discourse markers

PREPARING THE WAY

Discuss the questions.

- Why is it important to stay healthy?
- What is the best way to stay physically healthy?
- What is the best way to stay mentally healthy?
- Do you think that your thoughts can affect your body? Why / Why not?

SKILLS INTERPRETATION

ACTIVITY 1

Listen to the TV interview and answer the questions.

1 Which two aspects of health has Dr Gupta been researching?
2 Whose emotional development does Dr Gupta's research focus on?
3 What happens to the immune system when people are stressed?
4 According to Dr Gupta, what is a main cause of problems related to identity?
5 According to the interviewer, what is responsible for many people's social problems?

EXAM REFRESHER

Part 6 (Reading and Writing) requires you to:

- write a summary of a text
- write in a formal or semi-formal register, usually for a teacher.

The assessment criteria for this part are:

- content and communication (5 marks)
- lexical range and accuracy (5 marks)
- grammatical range and accuracy (5 marks)
- effective organisation (5 marks).

Marks are also available for reading and extracting relevant material from the text as defined by the guidance given in the question (5 marks).

SKILLS CONTINUOUS LEARNING

ACTIVITY 2

Tick the statements that are correct for Writing Part 6.

- ☐ Cover all three points fairly evenly.
- ☐ Copy words and phrases from the text.
- ☐ Write a long introduction and conclusion.
- ☐ Include any extra information that you know about the topic.
- ☐ Organise your ideas effectively.

SKILLS CREATIVITY

A02A A02B

A02C A02D

EXAM HINTS

- Avoid copying wording from the text.
- Use your own sentence structures as well as your own wording.

EXAM HINT

Remember you may need to infer information from the text, i.e. understand meaning or implications that are not directly stated.

WRITING PART 6

▼ PRACTICE TIME 1

You are doing a project on teenage development. Read the text below and write a summary for your teacher.

Adolescence – a time of challenges

Adolescence can be one of the most challenging stages of life. Growing from a child into an adult and dealing with changes to emotions and attitudes isn't always easy. Relationships with friends, family and the world around you can also be difficult. To make things more confusing, these changes don't happen at once. From the age of about 11 to 21, a range of physical, emotional and social transformations will occur, leaving what may feel like a long-term state of confusion. So why is this?

Mood changes

Firstly, hormones, which are chemicals affecting growth and mood, increase and are constantly changing during teenage years. As long as the body is developing, hormone levels are likely to affect mood. This means that adolescents can suffer from dramatic alterations in mood without obvious reason. During this time of change, many teenagers also start experimenting with romantic relationships. This can add to the uncertainty and changes to emotions. Likewise, disagreements with friends and family and the pressures of school life may also cause uncertainty during this period. The teenager, therefore, may feel quite lonely and vulnerable at times.

A new identity

The teenage years span the gap between childhood and adulthood. Therefore, during this time, it's not surprising that identity can feel rather unstable. Teenagers are learning to understand different aspects of their personality and to figure out how they relate to family, friends and society. This period of learning and growth can also be a time of personal conflict. Often there is a split between the person the teenager is at home and the person he or she is at school or when they are when they are with friends. Still, teenagers must somehow learn to integrate these different identities – or, at least, to live with them. Whereas adults often manage this integration without thinking about it, the teenager may have difficulty dealing with the additional confusion.

Relating to others

Finally, when teenagers feel uncertain about their sense of personal identity, it becomes difficult for them to relate to others in a consistent way. On the other hand, adolescence can be a time of happiness, joy and freedom. Whereas adults have the responsibility of providing for their family and running a home, teenagers are often responsible only for themselves. Many adults look back on their teenage years with great affection, in spite of all the challenges and problems.

Becoming independent

At times, teenagers behave in ways that challenge the authority of their parents and teachers. The motivation behind this behaviour is usually the teenager's need to develop independence and try out new experiences. At this stage of development, parents and teachers must be able to accept that it's normal for teenagers to challenge boundaries. On the other hand, they must also provide guidance so that teenagers focus on positive goals and avoid developing poor habits.

In your summary you **must**:

- give **three** reasons why teenagers' moods may change dramatically
- give **two** ways in which identity and relationships can be difficult for teenagers
- explain why, according to the passage, teenagers may sometimes be difficult to live with.

You will be awarded up to **5 marks** for using relevant information from the text.

You **must** write between **100 and 150 words only**. You **must** use your own words where possible.

(Total for Part 6 = 25 marks)

REFLECT

- The task was divided into three bullet points. Did you cover all three?
- Did you use semi-formal language consistently?
- How many marks did you score out of 5 for the five different assessment criteria?
- Identify one important target to aim for in your next Practice Time test.

SKILLS DECISION MAKING

A02A A02B A02C A02D

ACTIVITY 3

Below are three possible responses to the first bullet point in this task. Discuss in pairs which response is best and why.

Student A
Hormones are chemicals affecting growth and mood. They increase and are changing during teenage years. While the body is developing, hormone levels affect mood. Adolescents can suffer from alterations in mood without reason and many start experimenting with romantic relationships. This adds to the uncertainty. Moreover, disagreements with friends and family and pressures of school cause problems. Teenagers may feel quite lonely.

Student B
There are several reasons for teenagers' mood swings. Firstly, their hormones are not stable. Hormones have an impact on mood, as well as growth. Romantic relationships can also be confusing and can affect moods. Thirdly, a teenager's friendships can change (perhaps significantly), so he or she may end up feeling isolated – not forgetting all of the pressure sometimes caused by school!

Student C

Teenagers change their moods very quickly a lot of the time; this is because they may have to deal with serious problems in their lives. For example, they may have a big argument with their friend or fail their exams at school. This could make them very worried. Also, their bodies are changing because of chemicals called hormones. Hormones are a kind of substance that travel round the body and they have an effect on cells and tissues. Although they are very necessary, changes in hormone levels can cause problems.

SKILLS CRITICAL THINKING

EXAM HINT

Identify the parts of the text which contain the relevant information.

WRITING PART 6

▼ PRACTICE TIME 2

You are doing a project on ways of improving physical and mental health. Read the text below and write a summary for your teacher.

Maintaining emotional health

We all know about the importance of maintaining our physical health, but studies suggest that emotional health is often neglected. How can we enjoy a better quality of life by improving this vital aspect of our well-being? The first step is to understand the ways in which the mind and body affect each other. Emotional health, as the term suggests, relates to the mind and the emotions.

Impact on physical health

You may not realise it, but many physical problems may be connected to your emotional health. Research suggests that the mind and body are linked. When you use your emotions to face challenges, you may find that your body also suffers. When you feel stressed, your immune system becomes weak, leaving you vulnerable to viruses such as colds and flu. You may also become careless when looking after yourself. For example, you might not be getting enough exercise not eating enough or getting enough nutritious food in your diet. If you have high levels of anxiety, you may develop physical illnesses or conditions, like ulcers.

Strategies for enjoying better emotional health

In spite of the above, there are steps you can take to improve your emotional health – and this is likely to mean that your physical health will improve as well.

Number 1: Don't * bottle up your feelings!

As long as your feelings are not identified or expressed, they'll have the power to make you feel anxious or unhappy. Whereas if you can understand why you are feeling troubled, that in itself is likely to reduce your stress levels.

Number 2: Talk things through

Talking to someone may also help, but it's important to talk to the right person. Although friends may provide a helpful social support system and may be great people to talk to in some situations, they may be out of their depth in others. Parents, too, can be a source of support, but you may not always feel comfortable telling them your innermost thoughts. This is where an external figure, like a therapist or doctor, may be of use, depending on what the problem is. Sometimes people who are outside of the situation can offer a fresh perspective that may be very helpful. Furthermore, expressing your feelings to somebody who won't judge you or react in a way that makes you feel worse can be useful. On the other hand, if you truly don't feel you can talk to anyone, sometimes writing your feelings down can also help.

Number 3: Build your resilience
Sometimes life may throw difficult things your way. This is an inevitable part of being human – no one's life is straightforward and easy all of the time. Consequently it isn't always possible to maintain a positive outlook or a regular routine. On the contrary, if something upsetting has happened, it is understandable that it will affect you and make you feel unhappy, and there is nothing wrong with that. Sometimes we need to give ourselves permission to feel sad, low or tired; these negative feelings are part of being human.

In conclusion, the important thing is to learn to recognise when we need help. For example, if our feelings of sadness are very severe, if they continue for longer than we would expect or if they prevent us from enjoying healthy relationships with others, then we can take that as a sign that it is time to seek help.

* bottle up to refuse to discuss things that make you angry or worried

WATCH OUT!

Copied phrasing (including from the bullet points in the question) will only count towards the reading mark out of 5. It will not gain you any writing marks (out of 20).

In your summary you **must**:

- state **three** ways in which negative emotions can affect physical health
- state **two** ways of dealing with negative feelings
- give **your predictions** about how young people will be taught about emotional health in the future.

You will be awarded up to **5 marks** for using relevant information from the text.

You **must** write between **100 and 150 words only**. You **must** use your own words where possible.

(Total for Part 6 = 25 marks)

EXAM HINTS

- Avoid copying too many words and phrases from the text and question.
- Do not introduce new information in your answer to the first two bullet points.
- Try changing sentence structures as well as wording.
- You will need to make inferences or predictions in your answer to the final bullet point.

EVALUATE YOUR EXAM PRACTICE

- Which Practice Time test did you get a better mark for? Why?
- Did you improve? How and why?
- Which of the five assessment criteria did you find the most challenging?
- What could you do, inside or outside of lessons, that would help you?

VOCABULARY AND GRAMMAR

VOCABULARY FOCUS

COLLOCATIONS: MIND AND BODY

ACTIVITY 1

1 Read the 'Maintaining emotional health' article on pages 185–186 again and match the words to form collocations found in the text.

emotional	problems
healthy	system
immune	routine
nutritious	outlook
physical	of life
negative	support
positive	health
quality	feelings
regular	relationship
social	food

2 Sort the collocations into the correct columns. Some collocations might fit in both columns. Use a dictionary to help you.

Mental health	Physical health
emotional health	

3 Discuss your answers in pairs. Are there any that you disagree on? Why?

ACTIVITY 2

Fill in the gaps with collocations from Activity 1 on page 187.

1 ______________ such as vegetables and wholegrains is a key weapon in the battle against ill-health.

2 I have a very ______________ with my hockey captain. We talk about our feelings and opinions instead of getting annoyed. My game is improving.

3 Without a healthy diet, plenty of exercise and supportive friendships, it can be hard to maintain a ______________ on life.

4 Because the mind and body are connected, emotional issues such as stress and anxiety can lead to ______________ as well.

5 Her ____________________ suffered a blow after the death of her husband. She's been depressed and anxious.

6 My ____________________ had really improved since I started working part-time. I eat better, I do more exercise and I see my friends and family more.

7 The __________________ can be weakened by emotional instability, which can lead to an increase in infections and diseases in the body.

8 Samuel seems very depressed. He's always talking about his ___________________ towards his life and I'm worried about him.

9 Emotional health can really improve if you manage to maintain a ___________________. Making sure you get up and go to bed at the same times every day can really help anxiety and insomnia.

10 People who move to a new town or country can become very isolated, which can lead to unhappiness. It's important to try to build up a _______________________ system as quickly as possible, even if it's only a small one.

SKILLS REASONING, ARGUMENTATION

ACTIVITY 3

Discuss in pairs.

- Which is more important: your physical health or your emotional health?
- How do you look after your physical and emotional health?
- How could you improve your physical and emotional health?

GRAMMAR CHECKPOINT

LINKING WORDS AND PHRASES

ACTIVITY 4

1 Sort the linking words and phrases in the word box into the categories in the table.

as long as although whereas in spite of
consequently furthermore in conclusion

Addition	Contrast
	although (+ VP)

2 Can you think of any other linking words or phrases that you can use for the four different purposes?

3 Which of the above phrases can be written before a verb phrase and which can be written before a noun phrase? Write *+ VP*, *+ NP* or *both*.

4 Look at the word(s) you have written in the Contrast column. Which word(s) could you use to complete the following sentences?

a _________ it's sunny outside, I'm going to bring my umbrella.

b My sister loves sport, __________ I hate it.

c Our dog is well-trained now, __________ his previous life on the street.

ACTIVITY 5

Fill in the gaps using the linking words and phrases in the word box. You will not need to use all the words and phrases in the word box.

~~so~~ as long as although for example whereas
in spite of because consequently on the other hand
furthermore on the contrary in conclusion

Ivan Pavlov was a Russian psychologist. Today he is mainly remembered for his experiments with animals. One of his most famous experiments was conducted in the 1890s and it involved dogs and a bell. He wanted to test a theory, ___*so*___ he did an experiment. Pavlov had noticed that every time he entered the room, his dogs began to *salivate, 1_______ they had not done this when he first began working with them. 2_______, he realised that, because he usually brought food into the room with him, his dogs had begun to associate him with food. For the experiment, every time he brought food for his dogs, he rang a bell.

Significantly, the dogs began to associate the sound of the bell with food. 3_______ they heard the bell, the dogs would salivate, 4_______ the fact that no food was present. 5_______, he found that this type of behaviour occurred in response to many types of activity – not just ringing a bell.

6_______, Pavlov's experiments were ground-breaking for what they taught us about animal (and human!) nature.

* salivate to produce saliva/moisture in the mouth

ACTIVITY 6

Correct the sentences, if necessary.

1 I'm tall, whereas both my parents are short.
2 Despite of the weather, we had a great time.
3 In conclusion, Pavlov was a great scientist.
4 I ate five sandwiches earlier, so I feel very full.
5 I will finish my English homework, as long as if nobody distracts me.

ACTIVITY 7

Complete the sentences with your own ideas.

EXAMPLE I'm hungry, so ...
I'm hungry, so you should make me dinner.

1 The experiment was a success, although ______________________.
2 __________________ so in conclusion, the party was a failure.
3 She discovered she could turn invisible, as long as ________________.
4 __________________ but in spite of this, we lost the match.
5 Many famous people are extremely intelligent. For example, ________.
6 __________________ even though I slept for 10 hours last night.
7 I don't dislike seafood; on the contrary ______________________.
8 Money doesn't buy happiness; on the other hand ________________.
9 We didn't finish in time because ______________________.
10 __________________ consequently we won't have school on the 14th.

GRAMMAR GAME

▼ LINKING WORDS

- Divide into two groups and give each student in each team a number starting from one.
- Take a card from the table in the middle. Each card has a linking word on it.
- Take it in turns to say the first half of a sentence and the linking word on the card you picked up.
- The student with the same number on the opposite team must finish the sentence for a point.
- Whichever team has the most points at the end, wins!

GRAMMAR CHECKPOINT

DISCOURSE MARKERS

ACTIVITY 8

1 Match the discourse markers to the correct uses. You can re-read the text in Activity 5 on page 189 to help you.

Discourse marker	Use
for instance	to introduce a similar point
so / therefore	to introduce a consequence
firstly, secondly, thirdly	to introduce an important point
because	to introduce a contrasting idea
likewise	to introduce an example
significantly	to introduce the last point
but / however	to introduce a reason
finally	to organise an argument into points

2 Scan the text in Activity 5. How many discourse markers can you find?

SELF-EVALUATION

Tick the relevant boxes.

I now feel confident about ...	STRONGLY AGREE	AGREE	DISAGREE	STRONGLY DISAGREE
▶ TALKING ABOUT HEALTH				
▶ TACKLING PART 6 OF THE READING AND WRITING EXAM				
▶ UNDERSTANDING MY STRENGTHS AND WEAKNESSES FOR PART 6 OF THE READING AND WRITING EXAM				
▶ USING NEW VOCABULARY (COLLOCATIONS: MIND AND BODY)				
▶ USING LINKING WORDS AND PHRASES				
▶ USING DISCOURSE MARKERS				

If you ticked 'disagree' or 'strongly disagree', you need to revise these parts.

UNIT 7 LISTENING PRACTICE

Assessment Objective 3A

Understand the overall message of a spoken passage

Assessment Objective 3B

Identify essential and finer points of detail in spoken material

Assessment Objective 3C

Understand a conversation where information is being negotiated and exchanged

Assessment Objective 3D

Identify a speaker's viewpoint and attitude, stated and implied

This unit provides further practice for Parts 1, 2, 3 and 4 of Paper 2 Listening.

In the exam, you will need to show that you can:

- listen to and understand short extracts and identify the item, place or event described
- listen to and understand informational broadcasts, such as extracts from radio programmes or podcasts, and identify key details and opinions in speech
- listen to and understand conversations or interviews and identify key information exchanged
- listen to and understand lectures on general interest topics, identifying facts and viewpoints.

The mark breakdown is:

- Part 1: 10 marks
- Part 2: 10 marks
- Part 3: 10 marks
- Part 4: 10 marks.

LISTENING PART 1

SPORT AND FITNESS

Assessment Objective 3A

Understand the overall message of a spoken passage

Assessment Objective 3B

Identify essential and finer points of detail in spoken material

LEARNING OBJECTIVES

- Talk about sport and fitness
- Revise the requirements for Part 1 of the Listening exam
- Practise two Part 1 sample questions
- Evaluate your exam practice
- Build new vocabulary (phrasal verbs: sport and fitness)
- Use modals in the past tense
- Use modals of deduction and speculation

PREPARING THE WAY

Discuss the questions.

- What is your favourite sport to play?
- What is your favourite sport to watch?
- What is the meaning of 'a sport'?
- Are the following activities sports: chess, jogging, flying a kite?
- Who is the most famous sportsperson in your country's history?

ACTIVITY 1

1 Match the pictures (a–f) to the words in the word box.

gymnastics cycling climbing skateboarding skiing windsurfing

a

______

b

______

c

______

d

______

e

______

f

______

2 Discuss in pairs.

- What equipment do you need for each of the sports in the pictures?
- Where can you do each sport?
- Have you ever done any of the sports?

3 Give each sport a rating from 1 to 6, where 1 = the sport you would most like to do and 6 = the sport you would least like to do. Then compare your list with a partner's and explain your ratings to each other.

EXAM REFRESHER

Part 1 (Listening) requires you to:

- match spoken information with written statements
- mark a cross to show the correct answer
- fill in a small number of words or write no more than three words.

Listening Part 1 is worth 10 marks.

SKILLS CONTINUOUS LEARNING

ACTIVITY 2

Tick the statements that are correct for Listening Part 1.

- ☐ If you can't decide between two answers, mark crosses for both of them.
- ☐ Miss out any questions you find difficult.
- ☐ Keep to the specified word limit.
- ☐ Don't worry about grammar. Concentrate only on vocabulary.

SKILLS PROBLEM SOLVING

A03A

EXAM HINT

Make sure you read the instructions carefully. Then you can look briefly at the list of places before listening.

LISTENING PART 1

▼ PRACTICE TIME 1

Section A

In this section, you will hear five short extracts in which people are talking about places to do sports and leisure activities.

Read the list of places below, then listen to the extracts.

For each question, 1–5, identify which place (A–H) is being described by each speaker by marking a cross for the correct answer ☒. If you change your mind about an answer, put a line through the box ☒ and then mark your new answer with a cross ☒.

Not all places are described and each place may be used more than once.

One mark will be awarded for each correct answer.

☐ **A** a sauna	☒ **B** a swimming pool
☐ **C** a tennis court	☐ **D** a skating rink
☐ **E** a football pitch	☒ **F** a bowling alley
☒ **G** a gym	☐ **H** a running track

1 Speaker 1 (1)

A	B	C	D	E	F	G	H
☐	☐	☐	☐	☒	☐	☐	☐

2 Speaker 2 (1)

A	B	C	D	E	F	G	H
☐	☐	☐	☐	☐	☐	☒	☐

3 Speaker 3 (1)

A	B	C	D	E	F	G	H
☐	☐	☐	☐	☐	☒	☐	☐

4 Speaker 4 (1)

A	B	C	D	E	F	G	H
☐	☒	☐	☐	☐	☐	☐	☐

5 Speaker 5 (1)

A	B	C	D	E	F	G	H
☐	☐	☐	☐	☐	☐	☐	☒

A03B

EXAM HINTS

- Listen to the text twice and read the questions before the recording begins.
- Respond to the questions as you listen.
- Pay attention to the specified word limit.

Section B

In this section, you will hear a ski instructor talking to some beginners before their first skiing lesson.

For Questions 6–10, listen and answer the questions below. Write no more than THREE words for each answer.

One mark will be awarded for each correct answer.

6 What will Kim not expect her students to manage yet? (1)

....

7 What is Kim's aim? (1)

....

8 What is the purpose of the first skill that students learn? (1)

....

9 What might expert skiers use instead of the snow plough? (1)

....

10 What happened to the beginners who didn't snow plough? (1)

....

(Total for Part 1 = 10 marks)

REFLECT

- Did you identify the main topic?
- Did you understand the main ideas?
- Did you listen for specific details?
- Did you get confused by any of the vocabulary?
- Did you use key words to help you match the information to the descriptions?
- What did you score out of 5 for:
  - listening for the overall message (Section A)
  - listening for detail (Section B)
- Identify one important target to aim for in your next Practice Time test.

SKILLS PROBLEM SOLVING

A03A

EXAM HINTS

- Listen for key vocabulary.
- Make use of the fact that you hear the text twice.

LISTENING PART 1

▼ PRACTICE TIME 2

Section A

In this section, you will hear five short extracts in which people are talking about extreme sports.

Read the list of sports below, then listen to the extracts.

For each question, 1–5, identify which sport (A–H) is being described by each speaker by marking a cross for the correct answer ☒. If you change your mind about an answer, put a line through the box ☒ and then mark your new answer with a cross ☒.

Not all sports are described and each sport may be used more than once.

One mark will be awarded for each correct answer.

A hang-gliding **B** water skiing

C rock climbing **D** scuba diving

E bungee jumping **F** white water rafting

G skateboarding **H** snowboarding

1 Speaker 1

A ☐ B ☐ C ☐ D ☐ E ☐ F ☐ G ☐ H ☐ (1)

2 Speaker 2

A ☐ B ☐ C ☐ D ☐ E ☐ F ☐ G ☐ H ☐ (1)

3 Speaker 3

A	B	C	D	E	F	G	H	(1)
☐	☐	☐	☐	☐	☐	☐	☐	

4 Speaker 4

A	B	C	D	E	F	G	H	(1)
☐	☐	☐	☐	☐	☐	☐	☐	

5 Speaker 5

A	B	C	D	E	F	G	H	(1)
☐	☐	☐	☐	☐	☐	☐	☐	

EXAM HINT

Use the speaker's intonation to help you make sense of the text and its details.

Section B

In this section, you will hear a professional trainer talking to gym users before a training session.

For Questions 6–10, listen and answer the questions below. Write no more than TWO words for each answer.

One mark will be awarded for each correct answer.

6 What can gym users access with the electronic card? (1)

....

7 What are gym users given in printed form each day? (1)

....

8 What is the first activity of the session? (1)

....

9 What physical reaction might this exercise cause? (1)

....

10 What can almost all the gym users lift after the first exercise? (1)

....

(Total for Part 1 = 10 marks)

EVALUATE YOUR EXAM PRACTICE

- How do your marks for the two Practice Time tests compare?
- Did you improve? How and why?
- Did you find one of the question types more difficult? Why?
- What could you do, inside or outside of lessons, that would help you?

VOCABULARY AND GRAMMAR

VOCABULARY FOCUS

PHRASAL VERBS: SPORT AND FITNESS

ACTIVITY 1

Match the phrasal verbs to the correct definitions.

Phrasal verb	Definition
catch up	participate
give up	do exercises to loosen the muscles
join in	do as well as expected
kick off	stop trying, accept defeat
knock out	eliminate from a contest
live up (to)	exercise
warm up	start a football match
work out	do enough or move fast enough to keep up with others

ACTIVITY 2

Circle the correct phrasal verbs.

1 It's really important to **work out** / **warm up** before playing basketball or you could strain a muscle.

2 The match hasn't **kicked off** / **caught up** yet due to ice on the pitch.

3 I'm not competitive, but I really hate it if my team is **worked out** / **knocked out** of a competition in the first round.

4 Please don't **give up** / **kick off** yet. You could still win the match.

5 I don't enjoy playing tennis in front of my coach. I'm always afraid I won't **join in** / **live up to** her expectations.

6 Samantha hates **working out** / **getting started**. She prefers watching TV and reading.

7 The French athlete **caught up** / **kicked off** at the last second and won the race.

8 Welcome to our dance class. I hope you'll all enjoy yourselves and **join in** / **catch up**.

ACTIVITY 3

1 Fill in the gaps in Akiko's email to her friend using the verbs in the word box in their correct form. You will not need to use all the verbs in the word box.

catch up	give up	join in	kick off	knock out
live up	warm up	work out		

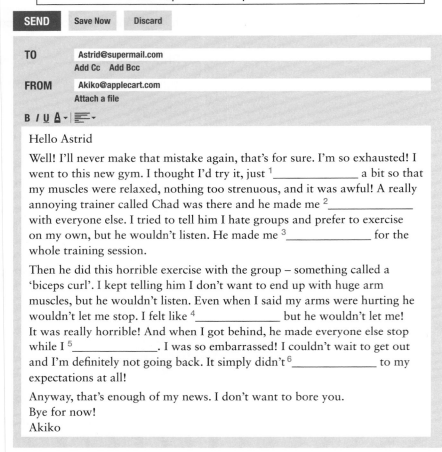

SEND Save Now Discard

TO Astrid@supermail.com
Add Cc Add Bcc
FROM Akiko@applecart.com
Attach a file

B I U A

Hello Astrid

Well! I'll never make that mistake again, that's for sure. I'm so exhausted! I went to this new gym. I thought I'd try it, just 1______________ a bit so that my muscles were relaxed, nothing too strenuous, and it was awful! A really annoying trainer called Chad was there and he made me 2______________ with everyone else. I tried to tell him I hate groups and prefer to exercise on my own, but he wouldn't listen. He made me 3______________ for the whole training session.

Then he did this horrible exercise with the group – something called a 'biceps curl'. I kept telling him I don't want to end up with huge arm muscles, but he wouldn't listen. Even when I said my arms were hurting he wouldn't let me stop. I felt like 4______________ but he wouldn't let me! It was really horrible! And when I got behind, he made everyone else stop while I 5______________. I was so embarrassed! I couldn't wait to get out and I'm definitely not going back. It simply didn't 6______________ to my expectations at all!

Anyway, that's enough of my news. I don't want to bore you.
Bye for now!
Akiko

2 Listen and check.

GRAMMAR CHECKPOINT

GRAMMAR

See Grammar Reference pages 269–271.

MODALS IN THE PAST

ACTIVITY 4

Change these sentences from the present into the past using the modals in the word box. Some options can be used more than once.

could(n't)	had to	didn't have to	should(n't) have
might have	must have		

EXAMPLE I can swim quite well.
I could swim quite well.

1 She should play football more.

2 Xavier must study for eight hours every day.

3 Juana can't swim very well.

4 Malek doesn't have to work very hard.

5 Pauline mustn't stay out after ten o'clock.

6 Hans might be sick.

7 Danielle can sing well.

8 Samira works until seven, so she must be at the office.

ACTIVITY 5

1 Put these phrases in order of how certain the speaker is. You should put them from least certain to most certain.

a He must have stayed here until seven.

b He stayed here until seven.

c He should have stayed here until seven.

d He might have stayed here until seven.

2 Are all of these sentences talking about the past?

ACTIVITY 6

Fill in the gaps in this gym user guide with the correct form of the modals in the word box. More than one answer may be possible.

can	can't	could	might	mightn't
mustn't	should	shouldn't		

Welcome to our gym! There are lots of things you [1]________ do here, but, equally, there are lots of things you definitely [2]________ do under any circumstances! Please check our dos and don'ts poster. We also suggest that you [3]________ really start exercising until you've been checked by your doctor, just to make sure that it's safe for you to do so. For example, you [4]________ have a health problem that you're not aware of and a doctor's check [5]________ show that up. It [6]________ feel necessary, but it's sensible to get yourself checked – otherwise you [7]________ have problems. You [8]________ just turn up and hope everything will be fine!

GRAMMAR GAME

▼ *SHOULD HAVE* AND *SHOULDN'T HAVE*

- Write five pieces of advice in the past tense on seperate cards, e.g. *You should have taken your sunscreen* or *You shouldn't have cloned the dinosaur.*
- Put your group's cards together on the table and mix them all together.
- One student takes a card at random and talks about when the advice would be useful, e.g. *I went to the beach last week and I spent three hours sunbathing. After I finished, my skin was completely red and I was burned all over. It was so painful.* You can't use any of the vocabulary already on the card!
- The other students try to guess the sentence that is written on the card, e.g. *You should have taken your sunscreen.*
- Whoever guesses the sentence correctly, takes the next card.

GRAMMAR CHECKPOINT

GRAMMAR

See Grammar Reference pages 270–271.

MODALS OF SPECULATION AND DEDUCTION

ACTIVITY 7

How certain is the speaker in each of the following sentences? Number the sentences from 1 (very certain) to 5 (not at all certain).

- Paul will be at home now. He finished school an hour ago.
- Kurt should have some gum. Ask him.
- Erica may know the answer. I'm not sure.
- Reyna must be on her way.
- Daniel might be at the gym. He's not answering his phone.

ACTIVITY 8

Choose the correct modal of speculation for the sentences below.

EXAMPLE Pauline has slept for two days straight. She **mustn't** / **can't** still be tired!

1 I think that I **will** / **must** arrive in about an hour.

2 Clive **must** / **can't** be happy right now. Somebody ate his lunch!

3 If I get a scholarship, I **may** / **can't** study abroad next semester.

4 I haven't seen him. He **might** / **mustn't** be at work or perhaps at the library.

5 Jacqueline hasn't left her room all day. She **may** / **must** be starving!

6 Randy **can't** / **mustn't** be home, he has work until two.

7 I **may** / **must** join you for dinner, if that's alright.

8 He **won't** / **mustn't** get sick. He is usually very healthy.

ACTIVITY 9

Fill in the gap in each sentence using an appropriate modal verb.

EXAMPLE He scored perfect marks on the exam. He *must* be a genius!

1 He hasn't done anything interesting all day. He ______ be bored.

2 Robert ________ be hungry. He hasn't eaten since yesterday.

3 That ________ be true! I don't believe it.

4 Look how nice that jacket is. It ________ be very expensive.

5 You ________ be that cold. The temperature is 30 degrees!

6 Clive is very hard-working. He ________ get good marks at school.

SELF-EVALUATION

Tick the relevant boxes.

I now feel confident about ...	STRONGLY AGREE	AGREE	DISAGREE	STRONGLY DISAGREE
▶ TALKING ABOUT SPORTS AND FITNESS				
▶ TACKLING PART 1 OF THE LISTENING EXAM				
▶ USING NEW VOCABULARY (PHRASAL VERBS: SPORT AND FITNESS)				
▶ USING MODALS IN THE PAST				
▶ USING MODALS OF DEDUCTION AND SPECULATION				

If you ticked 'disagree' or 'strongly disagree', you need to revise these parts.

LISTENING PART 2

SCIENCE

Assessment Objective 3B

Identify essential and finer points of detail in spoken material

Assessment Objective 3D

Identify a speaker's viewpoint and attitude, stated and implied

LEARNING OBJECTIVES

- Talk about science
- Revise the requirements for Part 2 of the Listening exam
- Practise two Part 2 sample questions
- Evaluate your exam practice
- Build new vocabulary (phrasal verbs: separable and non-separable)
- Use gerunds
- Use infinitives

PREPARING THE WAY

Discuss the questions.

- What is science?
- How has science helped people?
- How will science change the world in the next 50 years?
- Which is your favourite science subject, e.g. Physics, Chemistry or Biology? Why?

ACTIVITY 1

SKILLS REASONING, ARGUMENTATION

1 Look at the pictures. Working in pairs, discuss what the objects and places in the pictures have in common.

a

b

c

d
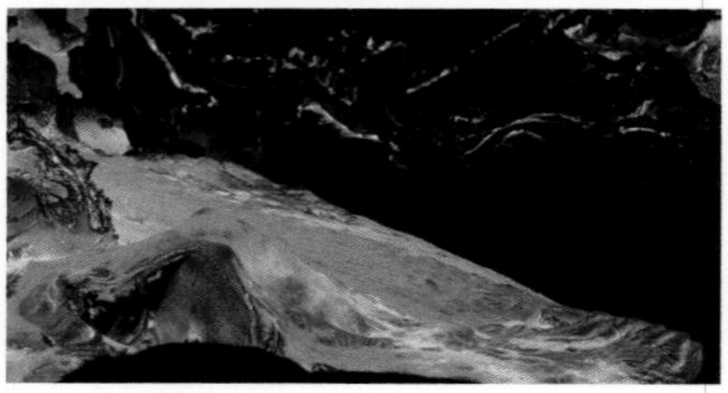

e

f

2 Tick the boxes that apply to each of the pictures (a–f).

	living	non-living	valuable	soft	dry to touch	hot to touch	cold to touch	dangerous	moves
a									
b									
c									
d									
e									
f									

3 Write one sentence describing each picture without mentioning the subject of the picture. Read the sentences to your partner without telling them what you are describing. Can your partner guess what you are describing?

ACTIVITY 2

Listen to the three speakers describing their own branch of science. Which pictures (on page 204) show what the scientists might study?

Speaker 1 __________ Speaker 2 __________ Speaker 3 __________

EXAM REFRESHER

Part 2 (Listening) requires you to:
- listen to a longer text
- complete a range of tasks
- identify information stated explicitly and implicitly.

Listening Part 2 is worth 10 marks.

SKILLS CONTINUOUS LEARNING

ACTIVITY 3

Tick the statements that are correct for Listening Part 2.

☐ Don't answer difficult questions.

☐ Don't worry about grammar. Concentrate only on vocabulary.

☐ You should listen for implicit information, such as the writer's opinion.

☐ If you can't decide between two answers in a multiple-choice question, you should mark crosses for both of them.

LISTENING PART 2

A03B

EXAM HINTS

- You will hear the text twice.
- Read the questions before the recording begins to play.
- Respond to the questions as you listen.

▼ PRACTICE TIME 1

In this part, you will hear a teacher giving a lesson about moles to a Biology class.

For Questions 11–18, listen and complete the student's notes. Write no more than THREE words for each answer.

One mark will be awarded for each correct answer.

Moles

Facts about moles

There are about **(11)** .... different types of mole. (1)

Moles can move a large amount of **(12)** .... quickly. (1)

Moles in captivity live for **(13)** .... than moles in the wild. (1)

Feeding habits

Apart from worms, moles also eat **(14)** .... (1)

They use a **(15)** .... chemical to help them store food. (1)

If they don't eat for 24 hours, moles can **(16)** .... (1)

Relationship with their environment

Moles survive underground because they can **(17)** .... there easily. (1)

They are not very popular with **(18)** .... (1)

SKILLS INTERPRETATION

A03B

Questions 19 and 20 must be answered with a cross in a box ☒. If you change your mind about an answer, put a line through the box ☒ and then mark your new answer with a cross ☒.

19 The teacher mentions a description of a fictional mole's home. What is her opinion of it? (1)

- ☐ **A** Children will enjoy it.
- ☐ **B** It isn't very pleasant.
- ☐ **C** It's lovely.
- ☐ **D** It's very detailed.

20 What is the speaker's opinion of moles? (1)

- ☐ **A** They're funny.
- ☐ **B** They're a nuisance.
- ☐ **C** They're sweet.
- ☐ **D** They're loving.

(Total for Part 2 = 10 marks)

REFLECT

- Did you understand the main ideas?
- Did you understand how different but related details were grouped together?
- Did you use key words to help you listen for information?
- Did you make notes while you were listening? Did these help you?
- Did you get confused by any of the vocabulary?
- How many marks did you score:
  - out of 8 for identifying the essential and finer points of detail (Questions 11–18)
  - out of 2 for recognising explicit or implicit viewpoints (Questions 19–20)?
- How could you do better next time?

SKILLS INTERPRETATION

A03B

EXAM HINTS

- Check that the words you use make sense within the sentence provided.
- Check that the newly completed sentence is grammatically correct.

LISTENING PART 2

▼ PRACTICE TIME 2

In this part, you will hear a man talking about gemstones.

For Questions 11–13 and 17–18, listen and complete the notes. Write no more than THREE words for each answer.

For Questions 14–16, complete the table. Write no more than THREE words for each answer.

One mark will be awarded for each correct answer.

Gemstones

Interesting facts

Created **(11)** .... underground. (1)

Precious stones are valuable because they are **(12)**
.... (1)

Often the biggest jewels are the most **(13)** .... (1)

Famous gems

Gem type	Place discovered	Year discovered	Weight	Measurements
Giant pearl	Mongolia		6 tonnes	**(14)** .... (1)
Largest gem ever found: Topaz	**(15)** .... (1)		Over 270 kg	
Largest high-quality gem: Aquamarine	Brazil	**(16)** .... (1)	103 kg	

Physical properties

(17) .... are needed for gem formation. (1)

Diamonds occur in rock near **(18)** .... (1)

A03D

Questions 19 and 20 must be answered with a cross in a box ☒. If you change your mind about an answer, put a line through the box ☒ and then mark your new answer with a cross ☒.

19 What does the speaker say about most gems? (1)

- ☐ **A** He'd like to own them.
- ☐ **B** They'll never be discovered.
- ☐ **C** They're worth a lot.
- ☐ **D** They're very beautiful.

20 What does the speaker think about the secrets of the Earth? (1)

- ☐ **A** They are problems which won't be solved.
- ☐ **B** They make Geology interesting.
- ☐ **C** They are impossible to understand.
- ☐ **D** They make Geology easier.

(Total for Part 2 = 10 marks)

EVALUATE YOUR EXAM PRACTICE

- How do your marks for the two Practice Time tests compare?
- Did you improve? How and why?
- Which did you find more challenging: listening for the overall message or listening for detail? Why?
- Which questions did you find the easiest and the most difficult? Why?
- Have you done anything, inside or outside of lessons, that has helped you in this Practice Time test?

VOCABULARY AND GRAMMAR

VOCABULARY FOCUS

PHRASAL VERBS: SEPARABLE AND NON-SEPARABLE

ACTIVITY 1

Listen to the extracts from the monologue about gemstones. Use the verbs and the prepositions from the word boxes to complete the extracts with phrasal verbs in the correct form. You can use the words as many times as you need.

Verbs

come	dig	find	run	carry	back	work	run

Prepositions

with	out	up	out	into

1 I loved the idea of ______ things ______ about the Earth's secrets.

2 I wanted to search for precious stones and ______ them ______.

3 I wanted to ______ experiments ______, to ______ how different substances interact and form new substances.

4 The Hope Diamond … is also known for the legend that says it is cursed and that anyone who owns it will ______ serious problems.

5 Scientists are unlikely to ______ any basis for that particular belief, though!

6 There really aren't any facts to ______ it ______.

7 Imagine being the person to ______ that!

8 We probably won't ever ______ of uses for them.

ACTIVITY 2

Match the phrasal verbs from Activity 1 (using the infinitive form) to the following definitions.

Definition	**Verb**
to discover facts or information	______________
to support something with evidence	______________
to make a hole in the ground	______________
to find the answer or solution	______________
to do something that you have planned to do	______________
to no longer have something	______________
to encounter, perhaps unexpectedly	______________
to think of (an idea or solution)	______________

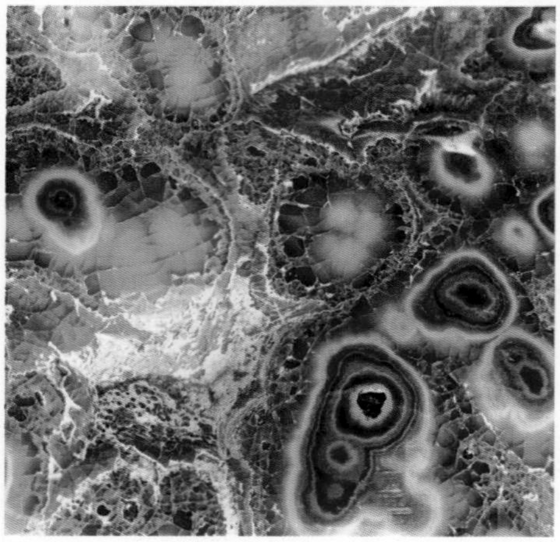

ACTIVITY 3

Circle the correct phrasal verb in each sentence.

1 There was a major problem with the experiment that the scientists were planning to **carry out** / **find out**.

2 They couldn't **run out** / **work out** a solution to the problem.

3 They tried to **dig up** / **run into** some new soil samples to help them.

4 There was one breakthrough, when they found they could **back up** / **dig up** their early findings with further evidence.

5 However, they were aware that time would soon **carry out** / **run out**.

6 In the end, they **backed up** / **came up with** the best solution possible, but it wasn't ideal and the quality of their research was affected.

7 Luckily, the youngest scientist on the team **found out** / **worked out** about a major problem with the samples that was affecting the experiment.

8 The researchers **came up with** / **ran into** some difficult obstacles when conducting their research.

ACTIVITY 4

Fill in the gap in each sentence using the correct form of a phrasal verb from the previous activities.

1 The doctor said that they've __________ a new type of treatment for my illness.

2 Could you get some more milk from the supermarket? We've __________.

3 Have you heard how many gold coins were __________ from the football pitch last week? Apparently, they date from Roman times.

4 We'll need to __________ some tests to find out if the building is safe to enter.

5 I __________ some real problems when I started building a metal detector.

6 Roberta thinks she's made a really interesting discovery about bees, but she doesn't yet have the data to __________ it __________.

7 I can't __________ if it's going rain or snow later. What do you think?

8 Can you __________ if James is free this weekend? I want to invite him to the cinema.

GRAMMAR CHECKPOINT

GRAMMAR

See Grammar Reference pages 259–260.

GERUNDS AND INFINITIVES

ACTIVITY 5

Sort the verbs into the correct columns. Some words will appear in both columns.

stop plan enjoy remember promise avoid
recommend suggest hope forget help

verb + infinitive (e.g. *to do*)	verb + gerund (e.g. *doing*)
plan	*enjoy*

ACTIVITY 6

Circle the correct words in each sentence.

1 Stefan promised **to break down** / **breaking down** the results of the experiment in the morning.

2 He denies **to find out** / **finding out** the secret information.

3 Let's not just wait **to run out** / **running out** of materials; let's order some more!

4 Chen chose **to conduct** / **conducting** the investigation a week later than we had planned.

5 I remember **to see** / **seeing** the report on my desk.

6 Maria didn't remember **to buy** / **buying** the chemical we needed. She should have made a shopping list.

7 Amani stopped **to rest** / **resting** because he was tired.

8 Zalfaa stopped **to rest** / **resting** when her break ended.

9 You suggested **to make** / **making** a change to our investigation procedure, didn't you?

10 Jiao and Liang hope **to publish** / **publishing** their results next month.

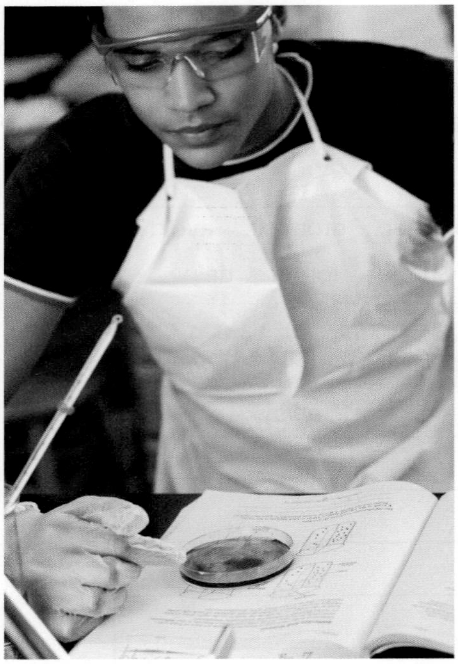

ACTIVITY 7

Fill in the gaps in each sentence using the verbs given in brackets. Write each verb in the correct form (gerund or infinitive).

Five tips to become a better scientist

1 Preparation. We suggest __________ (write) every detail of your planned experiment in advance, so that you remember __________ (complete) each part of the process and don't forget __________ (carry out) an important step.

2 Try out new things – you can't hope __________ (discover) something new if you don't experiment with new ideas.

3 Have an open mind. You can't anticipate __________ (get) all the results that you will need, so you should plan __________ (adapt) when it's necessary.

4 Be careful. We recommend __________ (take) regular breaks and checking all of your results carefully.

5 Love your work! If you don't genuinely enjoy __________ (perform) science experiments, you can't expect __________ (be) a very good scientist. It's important to appreciate your own work – and look forward to the results.

GRAMMAR GAME

▼ VERB RELAY

verb + ing	verb + ing
infinitive	infinitive

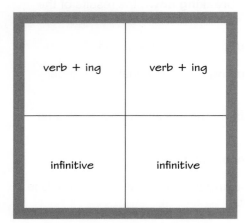

- Form two teams and give each a team name.
- Divide the whiteboard into four equally-sized squares like the example on the left.
- Write simple verbs like *hope* or *enjoy* on separate pieces of paper. You can use verbs from Activity 5 on page 211 if you like. Fold the pieces of paper and put them on a table at the front of the classroom.
- Each team should line up in front of their side of the board. The first student on each team should have a whiteboard marker.
- When the game begins, the first student on each team approaches the table, takes a piece of paper and, without consulting their team, writes the verb in the gerund or infinitive square on their side of the whiteboard, then gives the whiteboard marker to the next student on their team and goes to the back of the line.
- The game continues in this way until your teacher says that time is up.
- The team which has the most correctly written phrases on their side at the end, wins!

SELF-EVALUATION

Tick the relevant boxes.

I now feel confident about ...	STRONGLY AGREE	AGREE	DISAGREE	STRONGLY DISAGREE
▶ TALKING ABOUT SCIENCE				
▶ TACKLING PART 2 OF THE LISTENING EXAM				
▶ USING NEW VOCABULARY (PHRASAL VERBS: SEPARABLE AND NON-SEPARABLE)				
▶ USING GERUNDS				
▶ USING INFINITIVES				

If you ticked 'disagree' or 'strongly disagree', you need to revise these parts.

LISTENING PART 3

PEOPLE AND LANGUAGE

Assessment Objective 3C

Understand a conversation where information is being negotiated and exchanged

Assessment Objective 3D

Identify a speaker's viewpoint and attitude, stated and implied

LEARNING OBJECTIVES

- Talk about language
- Revise the requirements for Part 3 of the Listening exam
- Practise two Part 3 sample questions
- Evaluate your exam practice
- Build new vocabulary (suffixes)
- Use relative pronouns and relative clauses
- Use defining and non-defining relative clauses
- Use reported speech

PREPARING THE WAY

Discuss the questions.

- Is it important to be able to speak more than one language? Why / Why not?
- Is language unique to humans?
- Do you think communication between people from different cultures is easy?
- Can humans communicate with other species?

ACTIVITY 1

SKILLS PROBLEM SOLVING

1 Match the pictures (a–f) to the descriptions in the word box.

body language	Braille	computer code
semaphore	sign language	Chinese script

a 
____

b 
____

c 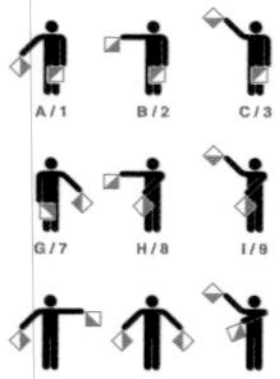

____

d 
____

e 
____

f 
____

2 Listen to the speakers and circle the correct option being described. If the description has no picture, circle 'Not given'.

1	Picture **c**	Picture **f**	Not given
2	Picture **a**	Picture **d**	Not given
3	Picture **a**	Picture **e**	Not given
4	Picture **b**	Picture **d**	Not given

SKILLS REASONING, ARGUMENTATION

3 Discuss in pairs.

- Who might use each of these languages?
- Are any of these languages specific to one country? Would you describe any of these languages as universal?
- Which of these languages can you use?
- Which of these languages would you like to learn? Why?

EXAM REFRESHER

Part 3 (Listening) requires you to:

- read the questions before the recording begins, listen to the text twice and respond to the questions as you listen
- identify information stated both explicitly and implicitly
- answer questions which have different formats, e.g. short-answer or multiple-choice questions. Other types of question could include table and diagram completion.

Listening Part 3 is worth 10 marks.

SKILLS CONTINUOUS LEARNING

ACTIVITY 2

Tick the statements that are correct for Listening Part 3.

- [ ] Try to scan the questions before the recording starts so you know what sort of information to listen for.
- [ ] You should always answer in full sentences.
- [ ] If your spelling is inaccurate, you may lose marks because the examiner may not understand your answer.
- [ ] Never give more than one answer for a multiple-choice question.

LISTENING PART 3

EXAM HINT

Note that you do not have to write full sentences.

▼ PRACTICE TIME 1

In this part, you will hear an interview from a podcast.

For Questions 21–25, listen and answer the questions. You do not need to write in full sentences.

One mark will be awarded for each correct answer.

Interview with a linguist

21 How does Jon define neologisms? (1)

....

22 How long has Jon been studying his subject? (1)

....

23 Where do the neologisms Wi-Fi and iPad come from? (1)

....

24 What does Jon think about 'blended' words? (1)

....

25 What has been a factor in change in language in modern times? (1)

....

A03C A03D

Questions 26–30 must be answered with a cross in a box ☒. If you change your mind about an answer, put a line through the box ☒ and then mark your new answer with a cross ☒.

26 Jon likes his job because he (1)

☐ **A** is always discovering new things.

☐ **B** can try out new ideas.

☐ **C** has a good salary.

☐ **D** lives close to work.

27 Jon says it's good to have neologisms because they (1)

☐ **A** describe new phenomena.

☐ **B** help with learning new languages.

☐ **C** give researchers more work.

☐ **D** make vocabulary more complex.

28 Words have transferred between different languages for (1)

☐ **A** the last few years. ☐ **C** centuries.

☐ **B** several decades. ☐ **D** 50 years.

29 Obsolete words are (1)

- [ ] **A** used occasionally.
- [ ] **B** used a lot.
- [ ] **C** part of everyday language.
- [ ] **D** almost never used.

30 The interviewer compares language change to (1)

- [ ] **A** types of plants.
- [ ] **B** natural species.
- [ ] **C** environmental change.
- [ ] **D** a zoo.

(Total for Part 3 = 10 marks)

AFTER EXAM CHECK

- Check that you answered all the questions.
- Read the instructions again and double-check that you followed them throughout the exam.

REFLECT

- Did you understand what sort of information was being exchanged in the conversation?
- Was there any negotiation in the conversation? Give reasons for your answer.
- Did you write full sentences or short answers for Questions 21–25? If you wrote short answers, did you include unnecessary words or leave out necessary words?
- What clues or key words did you listen for to help you answer the questions?
- Did you listen for different types of clues for the table and for the multiple-choice questions?
- How could you do better next time?

SKILLS INTERPRETATION

A03C

LISTENING PART 3

▼ PRACTICE TIME 2

In this part, you will hear a discussion between two English teachers.

For Questions 21–28, complete the notes in the table. You do not need to write in full sentences.

One mark will be awarded for each correct answer.

Discussion notes

	Female teacher	Male teacher
Country where they teach now	(21) .... (1)	(22) .... (1)
Typical student behaviour	(23) .... (1)	(24) .... (1)
Main reason for deciding to teach English	(25) .... (1)	(26) .... (1)
Main language problems their students have	(27) .... (1)	(28) .... (1)

SKILLS CRITICAL THINKING

A03C A03D

Questions 29–30 must be answered with a cross in a box ☒. If you change your mind about an answer, put a line through the box ☒ and then mark your new answer with a cross ☒.

29 Both teachers feel that language learning is (1)

☐ **A** stimulating.

☐ **B** boring.

☐ **C** a struggle.

☐ **D** fascinating and valuable.

30 Both teachers agree that the best way to learn a language is to (1)

☐ **A** meet lots of people abroad.

☐ **B** study the grammar in detail.

☐ **C** absorb yourself in the culture.

☐ **D** be confident when speaking.

(Total for Part 3 = 10 marks)

EVALUATE YOUR EXAM PRACTICE

- Which Practice Time did you get a better mark for? Why?
- What are the different challenges in listening to an interview and listening to a conversation between peers? Did you need to listen for different types of key words in the two recordings?
- When you read the questions, were you able to guess what sort of information to listen for or what type of key words might help you?
- What could you do, inside or outside of lessons, that would improve your listening skills and your exam performance?

VOCABULARY AND GRAMMAR

VOCABULARY FOCUS

SUFFIXES

ACTIVITY 1

Listen to the extracts from the interview with a linguist and write the words you hear with the following suffixes. They are in the order that you will hear them.

Extract 1: -ible __________ -ment __________ -ous __________

Extract 2: -ous __________ -tion __________ -ous __________

Extract 3: -ity __________ -tion __________ -able __________

ACTIVITY 2

Sort the words you identified in Activity 1 into the correct columns.

Nouns	Adjectives
	envious

ACTIVITY 3

Read the article and fill in the gaps with suitable nouns or adjectives, using the root words given in brackets.

THE GIRL WHO SPOKE TO DOGS

Oxana Malaya, who was born in the Ukraine in November 1983, was abandoned by her parents when she was very young. It was incredible that she survived at all, but what's even more [1]_________ (admire) is that this [2]_________ (courage) young girl had been raised almost exclusively by dogs.

Oxana was found by social workers at the age of eight, after neighbours became concerned. She was living alongside the family dogs in a kennel behind her house and did not have the [3]_________ (able) to use human language. Instead, she was capable only of growling and barking – her [4]_________ (communicate) was like that of a dog. She had picked up a number of dog-like habits and found it difficult to master language. Even after she was rescued it was obvious that her [5]_________ (develop) was still affected by her early experiences. She was understandably [6]_________ (nerve) of being around humans for a long time.

ACTIVITY 4

Re-write these sentences using nouns or adjectives with one of the suffixes given in brackets.

EXAMPLE The girl was generous. (-ity / -ment)
The girl showed generosity.

1 The fruit can be eaten. (*-ible* / *-able*)
The fruit is _______________.

2 She felt disappointed. (*-ion* / *-ment*)
She felt _______________.

3 He was full of suspicion. (*-eous* / *-ious*)
He was very _______________.

4 The kitten had a lot of curiosity. (*-ious* / *-ous*)
The kitten was very_______________.

5 The man showed courtesy. (*-eous* / *-ious*)
The man was _______________.

GRAMMAR CHECKPOINT

GRAMMAR

See Grammar Reference page 279.

RELATIVE PRONOUNS

ACTIVITY 5

Complete the table using the correct pronoun in the word box. You will need to use some of the pronouns more than once.

who where which when whose

That's the boy	*who*	helped me with my homework.
There's the beach		I lost my keys.
She's the doctor		wrote my prescription.
Those are the dogs		chased my cat.
That's the teacher		daughter goes to this school.
These are the chairs		I made by hand.
They're the customers		left without paying.
That's the day		I met your mother.
He's the teacher		marks my work.

GRAMMAR CHECKPOINT

GRAMMAR

See Grammar Reference page 279.

RELATIVE CLAUSES

ACTIVITY 6

Re-write each pair of sentences as one sentence, using a relative clause with a relative pronoun.

EXAMPLE That's the teacher. The teacher teaches French.
That's the teacher who teaches French.

1 English is a language. Many people learn English for work.

2 This is the café. We meet in the café once a month.

3 I need to find somebody with a car. Their car must be a red Porsche.

4 That's the computer. The computer is broken.

5 This is the book! I lost the book last week.

6 The expert on languages has arrived. He's giving a talk today.

7 I just got a new job. It's much closer to where I live.

8 Olaf is a Swedish man. I rent his flat.

GRAMMAR CHECKPOINT

GRAMMAR

See Grammar Reference page 279.

DEFINING AND NON-DEFINING RELATIVE CLAUSES

ACTIVITY 7

1 Some of the relative pronouns in the following sentences can be deleted and some can't. Delete any unnecessary pronouns from the sentences.

a This is the chocolate which I told you about.

b Saffron is the teacher who threw me out of her class.

c This is the school where I learn French.

d The book that they gave me was very helpful.

e Mateo is the boy who helped me with my schoolwork.

f Guillerme is the translator whom I met yesterday.

g Gabe lives in the same house that I live in.

h That's Stephanie, whose husband works with me.

2 Write four sentences: two with defining and two with non-defining clauses. You can use the Grammar Reference to help you.

GRAMMAR CHECKPOINT

GRAMMAR

See Grammar Reference pages 275–277.

REPORTED SPEECH

ACTIVITY 8

Change each statement into reported speech.

Original statement		**Reported speech**
'I like …'	→	I said *I like.*
'I have written …'	→	She said she ________.
'I am speaking …'	→	He said he ________.
'I thought …'	→	She said ________.
'I had listened …'	→	Leila said ________.
'He was reading …'	→	Helen said he ________.
'She will explain …'	→	Kenji ______________.
'You can translate …'	→	She ____ I ________.
'You must understand …'	→	He ____ we ________.

ACTIVITY 9

Change the statements into reported speech.

EXAMPLE **Marco:** I didn't understand anything people said to me.
Marco said he hadn't understood anything people had said to him.

1 **Julie:** I am learning to speak English.

2 **Gabi:** We live in Portugal.

3 **Sandra:** I'll see you later.
4 **Stefan:** Chen forgot her pen.
5 **Tanja:** I had eaten at the restaurant already.
6 **Mark:** I can fix the computer.
7 **Silke:** I must do my homework tomorrow or it'll be late.
8 **Yaz:** I was going to the beach.

SKILLS REASONING, ARGUMENTATION

GRAMMAR GAME

▼ AMONG THE STARS

- Divide into pairs. One person pretends to be a celebrity (choose a celebrity that you know a lot about), the other person pretends to be a reporter.
- The reporter asks the celebrity ten questions and tries to remember the answers without writing anything down. The celebrity has to answer the questions as if they were really the person they are pretending to be.
- Then each reporter talks to another reporter in the group. They tell them the questions and answers from their interview and the other reporter has to guess which celebrity they interviewed. If you guess correctly, you get a point. Try to use reported speech constructions in your statements, e.g. *she told me she was 48 years old …*
- After one round, celebrities and reporters should swap roles.

SELF-EVALUATION

Tick the relevant boxes.

I now feel confident about ...	STRONGLY AGREE	AGREE	DISAGREE	STRONGLY DISAGREE
▶ TALKING ABOUT LANGUAGE				
▶ TACKLING PART 3 OF THE LISTENING EXAM				
▶ USING NEW VOCABULARY (SUFFIXES)				
▶ USING RELATIVE PRONOUNS AND RELATIVE CLAUSES				
▶ USING DEFINING AND NON-DEFINING RELATIVE CLAUSES				
▶ USING REPORTED SPEECH				

If you ticked 'disagree' or 'strongly disagree', you need to revise these parts.

LISTENING PART 4

THE ENVIRONMENT

Assessment Objective 3B

Identify essential and finer points of detail in spoken material

Assessment Objective 3D

Identify a speaker's viewpoint and attitude, stated and implied

LEARNING OBJECTIVES

- Talk about the environment
- Revise the requirements of Part 4 of the Listening exam
- Practise two Part 4 sample questions
- Evaluate your exam practice
- Build new vocabulary (prefixes)
- Use *make* and *do*

PREPARING THE WAY

Discuss the questions.

- How would you define 'the environment'?
- What is a 'habitat'?
- What different types of habitat can you think of?
- What are the most serious environmental problems today?
- How can human beings take care of the environment?

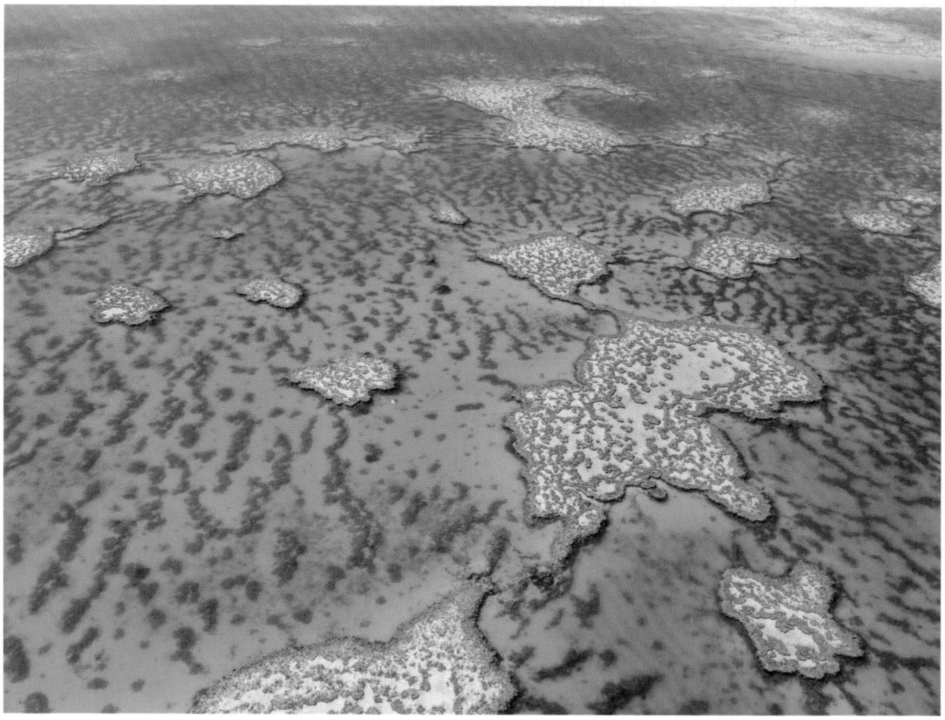

ACTIVITY 1

SKILLS REASONING, ARGUMENTATION

1 What sort of creature is this?

mammal	bird	reptile
fish	amphibian	

2 Working in pairs, complete the sentences with your ideas. You can use the words listed below to help you.

We think it:

- lives in (country and habitat) ______________
- eats ______________
- is **a predator / prey / a predator and prey**
- protects itself by ______________
- is a ______________.

Continents, countries and habitats
Greenland
South America
the jungle
Europe
ice and snow
dead trees
Cambodia

Creature
flamingo
capybara
toucan
potoo
garouper
salamander

Diet
fruit
insects
grass
fish

Ways of protection
being aggressive
being nocturnal
using camouflage
living underground

3 Do some research about a creature that is not very well known. Share your findings with your class.

EXAM REFRESHER

Part 4 (Listening) requires you to:

- listen to a longer recording, usually covering a more academic subject
- complete a range of tasks, e.g. multiple choice, note/sentence/chart/table/diagram completion, or short-answer questions
- recognise essential and finer points of detail
- recognise the viewpoints and attitude of speakers, which may be expressed directly or indirectly.

Listening Part 4 is worth 10 marks.

SKILLS CONTINUOUS LEARNING

ACTIVITY 2

Tick the statements that are correct for Listening Part 4.

- ☐ The headings of the table (if included) are important.
- ☐ Don't miss out any questions, even if they are difficult.
- ☐ You should not exceed the word limit if specified.
- ☐ Grammar is the most important part of your answer when completing a table.
- ☐ You should listen carefully to every word in the recording.

SKILLS INTERPRETATION

A03B A03D

EXAM HINT

Use synonyms to help you select the right information as you are listening.

LISTENING PART 4

▼ PRACTICE TIME 1

In this part, you will hear an extract from a podcast about a species of bird.

For Questions 31–32 and 38–40, listen and complete the sentences below. Write no more than THREE words for each answer.

For Questions 33–37, complete the table. Write no more than THREE words for each answer.

One mark will be awarded for each correct answer.

The wandering albatross

Facts and figures

31 The albatross has a .... of up to 3.5 m. (1)

32 The average lifespan is .... (1)

EXAM HINT

Pay attention to the instructions about how to complete the table. For example, do you need to complete sentences, or do you need to write notes? Is there a word limit for your answers?

Strengths and weaknesses

Strengths	Weaknesses
33 Ability to .... for a long time. (1) **35** Ability to drink .... (1) **37** Ability to .... food rapidly. (1)	**34** Difficulty flying after .... (1) **36** Likely to be caught in .... (1)

Breeding patterns and survival

38 .... is one factor in the birds' choice of habitat. (1)

39 They choose a partner for .... (1)

40 Many species are facing .... (1)

(Total for Part 4 = 10 marks)

REFLECT

- Did you listen for specific details?
- Did you get confused by any of the vocabulary?
- Did you use clues to help you match the information to the descriptions?
- Did you miss out any of the questions?
- Did you follow the instructions throughout?
- How could you do better next time?

SKILLS INTERPRETATION

A03B A03D

LISTENING PART 4

▼ PRACTICE TIME 2

In this part, you will hear an extract from a school talk by a marine biologist.

For Questions 31–32 and 38–40, listen and complete the sentences below. Write no more than THREE words for each answer.

Questions 33–37 must be answered with a cross in a box ☒. If you change your mind about an answer, put a line through the box ☒ and then mark your new answer with a cross ☒.

One mark will be awarded for each correct answer.

The deep sea

Environment

31 The 'deep sea' is far from the .... that is near the surface of the sea. (1)

32 Deep-sea creatures have .... to this environment. (1)

Deep-sea creatures

33 The hatchetfish is a successful hunter because it (1)

- ☐ **A** comes from the surface of the sea.
- ☐ **B** is shaped like a hatchet.
- ☐ **C** can look like light.
- ☐ **D** blocks out the light of the sun.

34 The colossal squid is different to squid on the surface because it (1)

- ☐ **A** is larger in size.
- ☐ **B** eats less.
- ☐ **C** is nocturnal.
- ☐ **D** has a smaller mouth.

35 Compared to their surface equivalent, amphipods in the deep sea can be (1)

- ☐ **A** 1 cm longer.
- ☐ **B** 10 ten times longer.
- ☐ **C** 3 times shorter.
- ☐ **D** 10 m longer.

36 The Mariana Trench (1)

- ☐ **A** has the deepest water on the planet.
- ☐ **B** is most western point in the Pacific.
- ☐ **C** has the largest surface area of all trenches.
- ☐ **D** has the toughest creatures in the world's oceans.

37 Forams are difficult to study because they (1)

- ☐ **A** do not have hard shells.
- ☐ **B** often bring disease to the sea surface.
- ☐ **C** do not usually survive on the sea surface.
- ☐ **D** cannot feed on the sea surface.

Studying the deep sea

38 It is impossible to .... the deep-sea environment to study its creatures. (1)

39 Most of the deep sea is still .... (1)

40 The deep sea is likely to contain new .... that haven't been discovered yet. (1)

(Total for Part 4 = 10 marks)

EVALUATE YOUR EXAM PRACTICE

- Which Practice Time test did you get a better mark for? Why?
- What did you find more challenging – hearing and understanding facts and details or deciding which facts and details were important? Did the questions help you to decide what was important?
- When you read the questions, were you able to guess what sort of information to listen for or what type of key words might help you?
- What can you do, inside or outside of lessons, that would improve your listening skills and your exam performance?

VOCABULARY AND GRAMMAR

VOCABULARY FOCUS

PREFIXES

ACTIVITY 1

Listen to the audio extracts from the marine biologist's talk and complete the sentences using the correct prefix from the box. You can use the prefixes in the box more than once.

anti-	dis-	im-	in-	under-	sub-	un-

1 … in case some of the students are __sure about what the job involves, could you start by explaining what a marine biologist does?

2 Well, marine biologists study the creatures and conditions under the sea, sometimes using specially-equipped __marines and cameras to explore.

3 This is the very __hospitable environment far beneath the surface.

4 ... it's easy to think that it would be __possible for anything to survive in such conditions, but this is far from the case.

5 But, of course, if you're expecting all deep-sea creatures to be enormous, then 30 cm might be a bit of an __-climax.

6 ... you've said that the inhabitants of this __water trench are quite different to those which are found on the ocean's surface.

7 ... they have a tendency to __integrate whenever brought to the surface.

8 The vast majority of the deep sea (and the Mariana Trench) remains __explored ...

ACTIVITY 2

Match the prefixes to the correct meanings.

Prefix	Meaning
anti-	under
dis-	not
im-	beneath
in-	opposite of
sub-	not
un-	against
under-	not

ACTIVITY 3

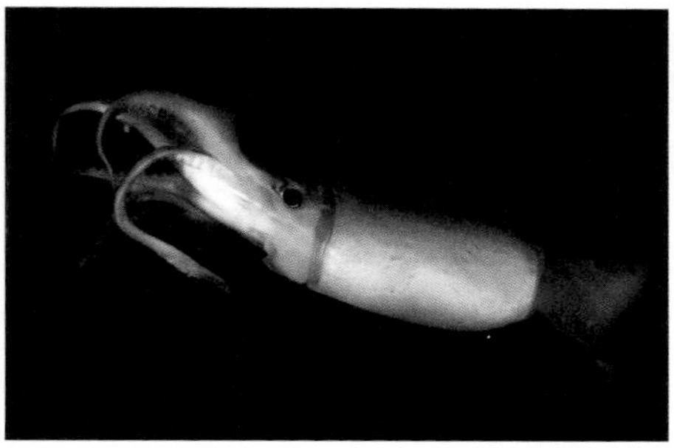

Circle the correct prefixes.

1 Because they live so far **sub-** / **under-** water, creatures such as the giant squid have evolved to be different to other sea creatures.

2 It was necessary to travel in a specially adapted **sub-** / **under-** marine in order to have any chance of seeing them.

3 Even this gave **de-** / **un-** expected results, though.

4 It was still very dark and it was a huge **anti-** / **dis-** climax.

5 The scientists were **dis-** / **un-** appointed not to see a giant squid during their deep-sea dive.

6 The squid seemed to have discovered a way to make itself **im-** / **in-** visible.

7 Unfortunately, the light source had accidentally been **anti-** / **de-** activated.

8 A follow-up dive has been planned and this time the light source's main lever has been adjusted so it will not remain **im-** / **in-** mobile at pressure.

HINT

Not all words that start with the same letters contain prefixes, e.g. *imagine* does not contain the prefix *-im*.

ACTIVITY 4

Can you think of any other words that use the prefixes from Activity 2 on page 229? Make a list with your partner.

GRAMMAR CHECKPOINT

MAKE AND *DO*

ACTIVITY 5

Sort the words in the word box into the correct columns, according to whether they come after *do* or *make*.

~~homework~~ a suggestion a crossword a choice a noise your hair lunch a favour a change an exam a cup of coffee a demand a course a job laundry a mistake an assignment a comment

do	make
homework	

ACTIVITY 6

Circle the correct verb in each instruction.

How to create your own aquarium

1 **Do** / **Make** plenty of research before you start.

2 Find a glass tank – it needs to be completely watertight, so you can't **do** / **make** it yourself!

3 Wash the gravel you will use in the tank carefully. You cannot **do** / **make** this enough times!

4 Put the layer of gravel on the bottom. **Do** / **Make** this carefully, watching out for any stones that might crack the glass.

5 Put the water in. You will need to **do** / **make** it safe for the fish.

6 Add water plants. It is important you **do** / **make** this a few weeks before adding any fish.

7 Leave the water to settle. You need to **do** / **make** this to make it healthier.

8 Add the fish. **Do** / **Make** sure you don't add too many – remember, they will grow.

9 Don't **do** / **make** the mistake of over-feeding or under-feeding your fish.

10 Remember to **do** / **make** the aquarium temperature constant and right for the species of fish.

11 There's a lot to **do** / **make** if you own an aquarium. Research is vital!

ACTIVITY 7

Fill in the gaps using *make* or *do* in the correct form.

SEND Save Now Discard

TO alishalisha@kooleroollie.com

Add Cc Add Bcc

SUBJECT Hiya!

Attach a file

B I U A

Dear Alisha,

I'm so excited. I've finally managed to set up my own aquarium! It was quite tricky to [1]___________ it properly, but I think it will be alright. To start with I [2]___________ a lot of research. I didn't want to at first, but my parents [3]___________ me. That was a good thing, it really [4]___________ help me to do some planning in advance. For instance, without the research I would have [5]___________ a huge mistake, right at the very start! Apparently, it's a mistake that a lot of people [6]___________ – I wanted to put the fish in as soon as the water was in the tank. That would have been a really bad thing to [7]___________, according to a lot of advice I've been given. I would have been [8]___________ life very difficult for the fish and giving them a very difficult start. The correct thing to [9]___________, in case you're wondering, is to [10]___________ the transition into the tank as easy as possible. You have to make sure they are not shocked when they enter the water, as it can take some time for them to adapt.

Why don't you come round to my place to see my aquarium? I'm sure you'd love it!

See you soon!

Maryam

SKILLS CREATIVITY, CO-OPERATION

ACTIVITY 8

1 Circle the correct verb in each sentence.

a Does it **do** / **make** a noise?

b What does it **do** / **make** if attacked?

c How does it **do** / **make** its home?

d Can it **do** / **make** any light? If so, how?

e What does it **do** / **make** to eat?

2 Design your own sea creature. Write a fact file about it for a nature magazine using the questions above.

3 Working in pairs, tell your partner about your sea creature.

GRAMMAR GAME

▼ *MAKE* OR *DO* RACE

Team A	Team B
make	make
do	do

- Get into two teams and give each team a name.
- Divide the whiteboard into four equally-sized squares like the example on the left.
- In the middle of the class should be a table with folded pieces of paper, on each of which is written a word which could come after *make* or *do*, such as *dinner* or *a speech*.
- Each team should line up in front of their own side of the board. The first student in each team should have a whiteboard marker.
- When the game begins, the first student on each team approaches the table, takes a piece of paper and (without consulting their team) writes the full *make* or *do* phrase with that word in the *make* or *do* square on their side of the whiteboard (e.g. *make dinner* in the *make* square). Then they hand the whiteboard marker to the next student and go to the back of the line.
- The game continues in this way until the referee says that time is up.
- The team with the most correctly written phrases on their side of the whiteboard at the end, wins!

SELF-EVALUATION

Tick the relevant boxes.

I now feel confident about ...	STRONGLY AGREE	AGREE	DISAGREE	STRONGLY DISAGREE
▶ TALKING ABOUT THE ENVIRONMENT				
▶ TACKLING PART 4 OF THE LISTENING EXAM				
▶ USING NEW VOCABULARY (PREFIXES)				
▶ USING *MAKE* AND *DO*				

If you ticked 'disagree' or 'strongly disagree', you need to revise these parts.

UNIT 8 SPEAKING PRACTICE

Assessment Objective 4A

Give information and express opinions on a range of topics at different levels of complexity

Assessment Objective 4B

Respond to a range of questions on a variety of topics

Assessment Objective 4C

Use a range of vocabulary, grammar and structures appropriately

This unit provides further practice for Parts 1, 2 and 3 of the optional Speaking Paper.

In the exam, you will need to show that you can:

- convey information in speech on a range of topics, using context-specific vocabulary
- express opinions about a topic, developing ideas through speech
- respond spontaneously to both predictable and unpredictable questions on a range of topics
- participate in extended discussions on a range of topics, from familiar to more abstract themes
- speak fluently and coherently, using a range of grammatical structures without undue hesitation or obvious searching for vocabulary.

SPEAKING

THE HOME

Assessment Objective 4A

Give information and express opinions on a range of topics at different levels of complexity

Assessment Objective 4B

Respond to a range of questions on a variety of topics

Assessment Objective 4C

Use a range of vocabulary, grammar and structures appropriately

LEARNING OBJECTIVES

- Talk about the home
- Revise the requirements for the Speaking exam
- Practise Speaking sample questions
- Evaluate your exam practice
- Build new vocabulary (adjectives: the home)
- Revise verb tenses

PREPARING THE WAY

Discuss the questions.

- What do you like a lot about your home?
- What do you like less about your home?
- Do you think home is always where you grew up?
- How long do you have to live somewhere before it feels like 'home'?
- Is it important to make your home reflect your personality?

ACTIVITY 1

1 Working in pairs, look at the pictures (a–f) and discuss:
- which house appeals to you most and why
- which appeals to you least and why.

a

____

b

____

c

____

d

____

e

____

f

____

2 Listen to the estate agent describing the houses. Write the words in the box below under the correct photo.

upside-down house	forest retreat	floral mansion
island home	remote cottage	house on stilts

SKILLS CREATIVITY

3 Imagine that you live in one of the houses in the pictures. Write:

- two reasons why you like living there
- two reasons why don't like living there.

Show your sentences to your partner. Can they guess which house it is?

EXAM REFRESHER

There are three parts to the Speaking exam:

- Part 1: an introductory interview
- Part 2: a talk
- Part 3: an extended discussion.

The Speaking exam requires you to:

- talk about a mixture of familiar and less-familiar topics
- answer a series of questions for Part 1 and Part 3
- prepare a brief talk for Part 2.

SKILLS CONTINUOUS LEARNING

ACTIVITY 2

Tick the statements that are correct for the Speaking exam.

- ☐ Listen for and pay attention to the key words.
- ☐ Listen to everything the interviewer says.
- ☐ You should try to speak for longer than the set times to get a higher mark.
- ☐ Prepare and take notes into the exam with you to remind you what to say.
- ☐ Take notes on the examiner's questions.
- ☐ You should plan your talk in Part 2 by using brief notes.

SKILLS CREATIVITY, COMMUNICATION, INTERPERSONAL SKILLS

SPEAKING PART 1

▼ PRACTICE TIME

PART ONE

In this first part, I'd like to ask you some questions about yourself.

Let's talk about homes.

- How much time do you spend at home?
- What sorts of things do you like doing there? (Tell me about that.)
- What do you like most about being at home? (Why is that?)
- What would be your idea of the perfect home?

Thank you. That is the end of Part One.

SKILLS CREATIVITY, COMMUNICATION, INTERPERSONAL SKILLS

SPEAKING PART 2

▼ PRACTICE TIME

PART TWO

STUDENT'S CARD

You are going to talk about the role of home in your life.

You can use some or all of the ideas listed below in your talk but <u>you must answer this question</u>:

How important do you think home is and why?

You must talk for 1 to 2 minutes. You have 1 minute to think and make notes before your talk begins.

Here are some ideas to help you:

- Family
- Relaxing
- Your own space
- Hospitality
- Other

SKILLS CREATIVITY, COMMUNICATION, INTERPERSONAL SKILLS

SPEAKING PART 3

▼ PRACTICE TIME

PART THREE

We have been talking about **the home** and I would like to ask you some more questions on this topic.

- Where do you live?
- Can you describe your neighbourhood to me?
- Are all the homes in your neighbourhood similar?

- Do you think that in general, young people spend enough time at home nowadays? (Why is that?)
- Do you think young people help out enough at home? (Why is that?)
- Do you think it is better to live within a family unit or to live alone? (Why is that?)
- What is the most important thing about a home – comfort, style or something else? (Why is that?)
- If you could live anywhere in the world, where would it be? (Tell me about that.)
- Why do you think so many songs and books are based on the idea of home?

EVALUATE YOUR EXAM PRACTICE

- Check with your teacher to see how many marks you scored out of 40. What went well?
- How good was your performance compared with the last time you practised?
- How many marks did you score for each of the three different parts?
- Did you listen for the key words in the questions and focus on those?
- Did you listen to everything the interviewer said?
- Did you plan your talk for Part 2 by using brief notes?
- Did you use a range of grammar and vocabulary?
- What do you need to improve next time?

VOCABULARY AND GRAMMAR

VOCABULARY FOCUS

ADJECTIVES: THE HOME

ACTIVITY 1

Listen to an interior designer talking about their design for the perfect kitchen and answer the questions.

1 What quality does the designer think is essential for the perfect kitchen?

2 What is the problem with kitchen appliances from the designer's point of view?

3 What does the designer think should be emphasised in a good kitchen design?

ACTIVITY 2

Listen to the designer again. Then write the correct words next to the definitions.

atmospheric	bold	characterless	cluttered	cramped
decorative	functional	minimalist	spacious	understated

1 Small, with little room to move ______________

2 Useful, serving a purpose ______________

3 Attractively large, with plenty of room to move ______________

4 Lacking in individualism or personality ______________

5 Full of objects that are unnecessary ______________

6 Pretty, ornate, attractive to look at ______________

7 Rather low-key and simple in style ______________

8 A style that is quite daring and makes a statement ______________

9 Having a distinctive feeling often created by the objects, colours and lighting ______________

10 A style of decorating that is very simple and uncluttered ______________

ACTIVITY 3

Circle the correct adjectives in Rachel's diary entry.

Dear Diary,

Today has been a disaster! I was meant to go to a fabulous lunch, but I couldn't get away in the end; my new interior designer turned up unexpectedly, which was wonderful, but he came up with the oddest ideas for my apartment!

I think of myself as being quite brave and [1]**bold / atmospheric** *when it comes to interior design, but I'm nowhere near as extreme as him. Apparently, he likes everything to be* [2]**cluttered / minimalist**, *with empty spaces everywhere – he seems to find every room in my apartment tiny and* [3]**cramped / spacious**. *He told me my front room was* [4]**cluttered / functional**, *just because I have lots of photos of myself on all the walls and have set out all the trophies that I won at school. He kept talking about clearing things out to make it look more* [5]**characterless / spacious**, *but I don't want to – I like having my belongings on display; they stop the rooms from looking* [6]**characterless / bold**. *And lots of the things he wanted to get rid of are really* [7]**decorative / minimalist** *too, like all of my mirrors – they're very pretty and some of them are quite valuable. He said I should stick to things that are* [8]**subdued / functional**, *but if I do that my apartment won't be at all* [9]**atmospheric / cluttered** *– it will just look boring and* [10]**decorative / subdued**.

I've decided to tell him to go and do his designing somewhere else!

ACTIVITY 4

Which adjectives best describe your bedroom? Underline the adjectives in the list below that apply and then write a sentence for each explaining why this is. Share your sentences with your partner.

My bedroom is:

- atmospheric / characterless
- bold / subdued
- cluttered / minimalist
- cramped / spacious
- decorative / functional.

GRAMMAR CHECKPOINT

GRAMMAR

See Grammar Reference pages 260–268.

TENSE REVIEW

ACTIVITY 5

Complete the tables using positive sentences, negative sentences and questions for each tense.

Positive sentences

walk

	Simple	Continuous	Perfect	Perfect continuous
Present	*I walk*	*I am walking*		*I was walking*
Past	*I walked*		*I had walked*	
Future				*I will have been walking*

Negative sentences

play

	Simple	Continuous	Perfect	Perfect continuous
Present				*I have not been playing*
Past	*I didn't play*			
Future				

Questions

listen

	Simple	Continuous	Perfect	Perfect continuous
Present				
Past				*Had you been listening?*
Future				

ACTIVITY 6

Answer the questions about the tenses.

1 Which tenses use the verb *to be* and the *-ing* form of the verb?
2 Which tenses use the verb *to have* and the participle form of the verb?
3 Which tenses use the verb *to do* in questions and negative forms?
4 Which parts of a sentence change when you change the tense?

ACTIVITY 7

1 Circle the correct tenses to complete this phone call between George and his mother.

Mum: Hey, where [1]**are you / are you being**? What [2]**do you do / are you doing**?

George: I'm out at the mall with my friends.

Mum: [3]**Will you be / Will you be being** home soon? I [4]**wanted / will want** to ask you about the housework. [5]**Will you be going / Weren't you going** to clean your room today? [6]**I've been waiting / I am waiting** to go in there with the vacuum cleaner for nearly a week.

George: Yes, I'll do it later.

Mum: What about the bathroom? I just went in there and I think you [7]**must have been showering / will have been showering** because the floor is covered with water … George?

George: Just a minute, please, Mum.

Mum: I don't understand where [8]**you are being / you've been** all day. It's Saturday, you don't have school. You know that [9]**we'll be eating / we had eaten** dinner in less than an hour, don't you? I [10]**will hope / had hoped** you would clean the oven before you left, but it seems the mall was more important. I [11]**am cleaning / will have cleaned** it all up by the time you get here! Can you at least unload the dishwasher? Oh, and it would be nice if you could get the clothes out of the washing machine as well. At this rate [12]**I'll have been eating / I will be eating** for half an hour by the time you get home. Hello, George, are you there? George!

2 Listen and check.

ACTIVITY 8

Complete the sentences using the correct tense.

1 (+, you, do)
What ____________ at the moment?

2 (–, I, go), (+, I, have)
In the end ____________ to the party last night. ____________ too much work.

3 (?, Fred, have)
How long ____________ his dog?

4 (+, we, eat)
At 7 o'clock tonight ____________. Dinner begins at 6.45.

5 (+, I, walk) (+, I, bump into)
_____________ along the street this morning when _____________ my friend Gabriel.

6 (–, Lucia, try)
_____________ Greek food before yesterday.

7 (+, Aisha, know)
_____________ Deema for three years.

8 (+, it, rain)
_____________ all morning! I hope it stops soon.

9 (–, Sam, read)
_____________ books normally. He prefers watching television.

10 (?, you, do)
What _____________? I'm a student.

GRAMMAR GAME

▼ VERB TENSE BASKETBALL

- Get into two teams and choose team names. Line up facing the whiteboard, a few metres away from the board.
- Divide the whiteboard into twelve squares, one for each of the tenses from Activity 5 on page 241.
- Your teacher will give you a piece of paper on which is written the function of a tense (e.g. *to describe a finished action in the past*). When it is your turn, say the function that you have and which tense it is.
- If you are correct, you can roll the piece of paper up into a ball and throw it at the board to try to hit the correct tense. If you hit the correct square, you gain a point.
- Whichever team has the most points at the end, wins!

SELF-EVALUATION

Tick the relevant boxes.

I now feel confident about ...	STRONGLY AGREE	AGREE	DISAGREE	STRONGLY DISAGREE
▶ TALKING ABOUT THE HOME				
▶ PREPARING FOR THE SPEAKING EXAM				
▶ USING NEW VOCABULARY (ADJECTIVES: THE HOME)				
▶ USING DIFFERENT VERB TENSES				

If you ticked 'disagree' or 'strongly disagree', you need to revise these parts.

GLOSSARY

antonym a word that means the opposite of another word

audience people who read someone's writing or listen to someone's speech

context the situation, events or information that are related to something and that help you to understand it; the words that come just before and after a word or sentence and that help you understand it

contractions shorter forms of a word or words

explicit expressed in a way that is very clear and direct

formal register formal language used in official or serious situations

genre a particular type of art, writing, music etc., which has certain features that all examples of this type share

implicit suggested or understood without being stated directly

implied not stated openly, but understood to exist or to be true

inference something that you think is true, based on information that you have

informal register an informal style of writing or speaking suitable for ordinary conversations or letters to friends

informal writing an informal style of writing suitable for letters to friends

intonation the way in which the level of your voice changes in order to add meaning to what you are saying, e.g. by going up at the end of a question

inversion the act of changing something so that it is the opposite of what it was before, or of turning something upside down

layout the way in which writing and pictures are arranged on a page

lexical words dealing with words, or related to words

metaphor a way of describing something by referring to it as something different and suggesting that it has similar qualities to that thing

paraphrase to express in a shorter, clearer or different way what someone has said or written

prediction a statement about what you think is going to happen, or the act of making this statement

purpose what something is intended to achieve

register the words, style and grammar used by speakers and writers in a particular situation or in a particular type of writing

scan to read something quickly

simile an expression that describes something by comparing it with something else, using the words 'as' or 'like', for example 'as white as snow'

skim to read something quickly to find the main facts or ideas in it

state to formally say or write a piece of information or your opinion

summarise to make a short statement giving only the main information and not the details of a plan, event or report

synonym a word with the same meaning as another word

viewpoint a particular way of thinking about a problem or subject

WRITING REFERENCE

INTRODUCTION

This Writing Reference section is a guide to the main features of:

- an informal email or letter
- a report
- an article.

You can also use this section to help you prepare for the exam. The criteria are broken down into the areas listed below. In Writing Part 4 the criteria are combined under two headings, whereas in Writing Parts 5 and 6 they are assessed separately.

These reference pages include key points for these four criteria, plus typical marked sample answers with a commentary.

There are also notes on the Summary which you are required to write in Writing Part 6. (Remember that Writing Part 6 carries 5 marks for reading as well.)

THE ASSESSMENT CRITERIA: AN OVERVIEW

Four main criteria are used to assess each of the three questions, but for Writing Part 4 they are combined into two assessment areas. For all questions, the criteria will always be interpreted according to the demands of the specific task.

COMMUNICATION AND CONTENT

Make sure you answer the question fully and respond to all three bullet points in the question. Your writing must communicate successfully, e.g. to give information, to explain something or to ask for something. Your writing must flow well. The tone and register need to be consistent and appropriate for the audience.

LEXICAL RANGE AND ACCURACY

This is about the words you choose and whether you spell and use them correctly.

You need to try to use a range of relevant vocabulary in your writing. Of course, more ambitious words can be more difficult to spell correctly. However, you should pay very careful attention to the spelling of simple, high-frequency words.

Avoid repetition. If you repeat the same words, you do not show a range of vocabulary. Also, the vocabulary you use must be relevant to the topic. Do not memorise an elaborate introduction, as it probably will not be related to the task. Topic-specific vocabulary is important but so too is the way it is used. The vocabulary throughout needs to match the purpose and nature of the task.

GRAMMATICAL RANGE AND ACCURACY

You need to use a range of structures and you also need to write accurately. The use of plurals, a variety of tenses and tense agreement are all assessed.

EFFECTIVE ORGANISATION

The writing needs to be well organised so that it can communicate clearly and successfully. You need to use tools like paragraphing and punctuation to make sure that the structure of your writing is suitable for its purpose.

You need to divide the content of your paragraphs in a logical way. You should use tools like linking words and summary words to help the reader follow your writing.

INFORMAL EMAIL OR LETTER

COMMUNICATION, CONTENT AND ORGANISATION

Note this is for an **informal** letter. In Writing Part 5, you may be required to write a **semi-formal** letter. That has different requirements – see Unit 2 Writing Preparation Part 5 (pages 48–57).

- Do not exceed the word limit or you will lose marks.
- Do not include a long or general introduction about your imagined reader's exams, recent holiday or family. That would not be relevant and would take up too much of your word count.
- You must cover all three bullet points.
- Your response must flow and it must communicate successfully.
- The email should be written in an informal register. Your audience is likely to be a friend or family member, so you need to sound friendly.
- Remember the piece will be short. You can only write 75–100 words in the exam so there is no time for a long introduction. You should move onto the set topic very quickly.
- You may decide to link your paragraphs to the bullet points. However, as the word limit is tight, you may prefer to write only one or two paragraphs rather than three.
- You do not need to create or write down an email address if you are asked to write an email.
- Try to use a range of punctuation. You may find that question marks and exclamation marks help to create a lively voice in your writing. Do not use them too much though, otherwise they lose their effectiveness. The key is variety.
- Remember to sign off at the end in an appropriate way. Do not leave the end blank or use a formal letter closure like *Yours sincerely*.

RANGE AND ACCURACY

- Use a range of vocabulary that is relevant to the task.
- Try to include a range of relevant words by avoiding repetition. Be especially careful not to repeat vocabulary that is used in the bullet points in the question.
- Avoid careless spelling errors, particularly on simple words.
- Although you probably won't use many complicated structures in an informal email or letter, it is still possible to use a range of different structures.
- Make sure your work is grammatically accurate and make sure that you use plurals and tenses correctly.

SAMPLE QUESTION

PART 4

Read this sample question for Writing Part 4.

You have decided to spend your pocket money on clothes. Write an email to your friend asking for his/her advice about the item of clothing you want to buy.

In your email you must write:

- why you want to buy clothes
- which items of clothes you want to buy and why
- questions to ask for advice.

You **must** write between **75 and 100 words only**.

Now read the two sample responses and the commentaries.

STRONGER ANSWER

SAMPLE ANSWER

Hello Akil,

Hope you are well.

I've decided to spend my pocket money on clothes, as I have grown taller, so some of my old ones don't fit well any more.

I looked through my wardrobe and realised that the best item to buy would be a jacket, as I would get more use out of that than anything else.

What do you think? I know you're very good at finding bargains, especially with clothes. Which shop should I try first? I hope you can advise me!

Talk soon,

Hanif

COMMENTARY

Communication, content and organisation

The student's answer is focused on the question and the non-specific contents (greeting and closure) are kept to a minimum. The register and tone are appropriate for an informal email and the bullet points are addressed one by one. There is a consistent sense of audience.

The structure is effective. A reasonable range of punctuation is used accurately.

Range and accuracy

Although the vocabulary is not wide-ranging, it is appropriate for the task requirements and avoids repetition. Spelling and usage are accurate.

A range of grammatical structures is used correctly.

WEAKER ANSWER

SAMPLE ANSWER

Hi Layla,

At last the indescribable tedium of exams is drawing to an end I can escape the back-breaking torture of endless revisions.

I want to buy some item of clothes with my money, The item of clothing I want to buy, and why, is I want to buy a jacket. I want to buy a jacket because I like to have a jacket always.

Do you think I should buy a jacket? Tell me why you think this.

Write me soon.

Habibah

COMMENTARY

Communication, content and organisation

The student's answer is generic and it is not focused specifically on the question. The register and tone are inconsistent (*indescribable tedium … I want to buy a jacket*). The opening section is not well-suited to an informal email and the ending is rather blunt (*Tell me why you think this*). The first bullet point is not addressed.

The organisation is adequate but punctuation is not always accurate (*money, The …*).

Range and accuracy

The vocabulary in the sections that are focused on the task is rather basic and limited (*I want to buy a jacket because I like to have a jacket always*).

The student's answer repeats the vocabulary provided in the wording of the bullet points. Usage is not always accurate (*I want to buy some item of clothes).*

There are grammatical errors (*revisions; Write me soon*) and a limited range of structures in the sections addressing the task.

REPORT

COMMUNICATION AND CONTENT

- You must provide content that addresses each of the three bullet points.
- Remember that sometimes bullet points (for any of the writing tasks) may cover two different points (e.g. what you want to do and why). Both points need to be answered to gain full marks.
- A good report is neutral and informative. Do not use emotional or strongly persuasive language. Your report should not sound like an advertisement.
- Successful communication in a report requires a consistent semi-formal register.
- Your writing should be impersonal. Avoid frequent references to personal experiences or preferences unless the question asks specifically for your own opinion.

GRAMMATICAL RANGE AND ACCURACY

- A report format gives you the opportunity to demonstrate a range of grammatical features. You could use the passive voice or more complex sentence structures than in the informal email or letter task.
- Semi-formal register often uses sentences with several clauses and a range of different sentence types. This makes grammatical accuracy more difficult, so be aware of your own limits.

LEXICAL RANGE AND ACCURACY

- The vocabulary should be relevant to the chosen topic. Spelling and usage must be correct.
- Do not overuse the vocabulary given in the bullet points.
- Words in a report are generally neutral. Avoid adjectives like *fantastic* and *wonderful*, which do not suit the tone of a report.
- Consider using words like *effective* or *satisfactory*. However, these are only examples and you must always make sure that your words fit the task and topic.

EFFECTIVE ORGANISATION

- You can use the organisational features of a report, such as sub-headings, bullet points and lists.
- Make sure that your use of organisational features does not limit your scope. You also need to include sentences that are long enough to show your command of the language.
- Remember to use paragraphs and punctuate your work clearly. Think about using discourse markers such as *however*, *alternatively* and *therefore*.

SAMPLE QUESTION

PART 5

Read this sample question for Writing Part 5.

You have been asked to write a report for the head teacher of your school about which charity the school should support in a fundraising event.

In your report you must:

- suggest one charity and give reasons for supporting them
- describe the work of the charity and why it is important
- explain what the charity will do with the money.

You **must** write between **100 and 150 words only**.

Now read the two sample responses and the commentaries.

STRONGER ANSWER

SAMPLE ANSWER

Report for Head Teacher

The charity I feel the school should support with the money from its next fundraiser is the Red Crescent. The reason I am suggesting this charity is because it doesn't just improve people's lives, it actually saves them.

The Red Crescent is responsible for looking after people who are sick or injured in many different countries across the globe. It is a vital organisation, because the work it does means that people are able to get help when they need it, particularly vulnerable people, like children, or those who are seriously ill.

With the money from the school's forthcoming fundraiser, the Red Crescent would be able to buy much-needed medicines and other supplies, it would also be able to deliver help to areas where people are suffering.

COMMENTARY

Communication and content

The response is focused on the question and all parts of all three bullet points are addressed. The register and tone are appropriate for a report. The sense of purpose and audience is clear and stays the same throughout.

Lexical range and accuracy

The vocabulary is reasonably varied and is appropriate for the task requirements. Spelling and usage of high- and low-frequency words (e.g. *vulnerable*) are accurate throughout.

Grammatical range and accuracy

A range of grammatical structures is used correctly (*The Red Crescent is responsible for looking after people who are sick or injured … ; It is a vital organisation, because … ; With the money from the school's forthcoming fundraiser, the Red Crescent would be able to buy …*).

Effective organisation

The student has divided their answer into paragraphs and the structure is effective. The paragraphs are helpfully organised in the same order as the bullet points. A range of punctuation is used accurately.

The content of each paragraph generally links together well (although links between paragraphs are not quite as effective as they could be).

WEAKER ANSWER

SAMPLE ANSWER

Report for Head Teacher

The charity the school should support is Red Crescent. The explaination which charity the school should support is because it is a good charity which does good work.

The Red Crescent is looking after sick people or injured people in many difference country. It works hard to make people better. It gives help to the people who have injurys.

The school's fundraiser is a cake stall. All the children will bake cakes and bring them to school to sell. The mony will help the Red Crescent do more, it will help them look after more people, it will also help them buy more medicines. This is why I think the school should give mony to the Red Crescent

COMMENTARY

Communication and content

The student's answer is partly focused on the question, but it also includes information (about the nature of the fundraiser) that was not asked for. The register and tone are appropriate for a report.

Lexical range and accuracy

The vocabulary is reasonably varied, but it is repetitive at times (*sick people or injured people*) and over-reliant on the wording of the bullet points. Spelling is not always accurate (*mony; explaination*).

Grammatical range and accuracy

A range of grammatical structures is used but there are some errors (*The explaination which charity the school should support*).

Effective organisation

The response is structured effectively and divided into paragraphs. These are helpfully organised in the same orer as the bullet points. Punctuation use is not always accurate (*… the Red Crescent do more, it will also help them …*).

The content of each paragraph generally links together well (although links between paragraphs are not quite as effective as they could be).

ARTICLE

COMMUNICATION AND CONTENT

- Make sure you cover the bullet points.
- Make your writing lively and engaging, so that it is suitable for an article and appeals to your audience. It should not sound like a report on the topic.
- Pay attention to the reader of your article, as you need to cover the bullet points in a way that is reader-friendly. Think about what the readers might understand and how they would respond.
- The task may require you to write in a way that is quite specific, e.g. informative and/or persuasive. Consider the target audience and their needs and experiences when you are writing.
- Rhetorical questions and exaggeration can make your writing livelier, but be careful not to overuse them.

GRAMMATICAL RANGE AND ACCURACY

- You need to use a range of structures and you also need to write accurately.
- You could use rhetorical questions to create a conversational tone or as a tool in an argument to persuade your reader.

LEXICAL RANGE AND ACCURACY

- Word choice needs to focus on the topic.
- Do not overuse the vocabulary given in the bullet points.
- Vocabulary choices in an article can be more opinion-based and descriptive than in the report task.
- Try to use more complex words than you would usually use in speech.
- Correct spelling and usage of simple, high-frequency words is very important.

EFFECTIVE ORGANISATION

- Try to think of a lively or interesting title or headline. Reading a range of articles in different publications will give you an idea about what to include in a headline.
- You could use a strapline, which is a line that goes below the title, to help make your article lifelike and engaging. This is optional.
- Do not use columns.
- Think about links between paragraphs as well as links within them.
- Try to use a lively range of punctuation.

SAMPLE QUESTION

PART 5

Read this sample question for Writing Part 5.

You have been asked to write an article for your school magazine to encourage your classmates to read more.

In your article you must:

- explain why reading is important
- explain what you enjoy about reading
- recommend two authors and explain why you like their work.

You **must** write between **100 and 150 words only**.

Now read the two sample responses and the commentaries.

STRONGER ANSWER

SAMPLE ANSWER

Reading matters ...

Not everyone enjoys reading, but maybe it's time to give it a second chance!

Reading is a vital skill in today's world. You need to be able to read, not just to enjoy literature, but also to understand written instructions, to follow directions – and even to read the messages on your mobile phone.

Personally, I love reading, as I find that it opens a series of doors into different places, real and imagined. It lets you visit so many countries and meet so many people. Some authors have a real gift for inviting you into their world.

Two I would really recommend, for different reasons, are Meera Syal and John Steinbeck. Meera Syal writes very vividly about the friendship between two young people from different backgrounds, whereas Steinbeck's books are set in America a long time ago, and I particularly like the way he describes the setting and countryside.

So what are you waiting for? Pick up a book right now!

COMMENTARY

Communication and content

The student's answer focuses on the question and covers all bullet points fully and evenly. The register and tone are appropriate for an article. The student adapts the wording to the form, e.g. in the inclusion of a strapline under the title of the article.

The audience is considered throughout.

Lexical range and accuracy

The vocabulary choices are confident and fairly wide-ranging (*imagined*; *inviting*; *vividly*) and are appropriate for the needs of the task. The candidate avoids repetition and spelling and word usage are accurate.

Grammatical range and accuracy

A range of grammatical structures is used correctly (*Two I would really recommend, for different reasons, are Meera Syal and John Steinbeck; Personally, I love reading, as I find that it ...*).

Effective organisation

The student's answer is structured effectively, matching the order of the bullet points, and a reasonable range of punctuation is used accurately (*So what are you waiting for? Pick up a book right now!*).

WEAKER ANSWER

SAMPLE ANSWER

Article on Reading

Reading is very good for you, It is a very good and it is very important You need reading in a lot of lessons which are taught at the school and you also must read in other times as well. I enjoy readings because it helps me and it is a good active to do with spare time. Many peoples do not read enoug. The two authors I reccomend are John Steinbeck and Meera Syal. I like John Steinbeck's books because they are exciteing and I like Meera Syal's books because they are very real to life and very exciteing also.

COMMENTARY

Communication and content

This answer is at the shorter end of the word range. It reads more like an essay than an article. The register and tone are reasonably consistent, but the first bullet point is not fully addressed.

Lexical range and accuracy

The vocabulary is sometimes repetitive and it is not particularly wide-ranging. Often the student repeats the vocabulary provided in the wording of the bullet points. Usage is not always accurate (*it is a good active to do with spare time*).

Grammatical range and accuracy

There are grammatical errors, such as misuse of the definite article (*taught at <u>the</u> school*), and a limited range of structures is used.

Effective organisation

The response is organised in a rather basic way and the two different paragraphs do not link very well together. Punctuation is not always accurate (*...you; It is*).

SUMMARY

GENERAL SKILLS

- Read the bullet points and summarise only the information asked about in the question.
- Put the information in the question into your own words.
- Organise it into paragraphs.
- Organise the paragraphing in the same order as the bullet points if possible.
- Write in a formal or semi-formal way, as required.

THINGS TO AVOID

- Copying from the text.
- Missing out bullet points or parts of bullet points.
- Introducing new material (except for the third bullet point, which may ask you to speculate or make a prediction).
- Adding a general introduction or conclusion.
- Using words or phrases that sound unnatural or too formal.

GRAMMAR REFERENCE: CONTENTS

ARTICLES

There are two types of article: the **indefinite article** (*a, an*) and the **definite article** (*the*). We usually use articles before nouns (or adjective + noun).

*I've got **a** cat.*
*She needs **a** new jacket.*

*He bought **an** apple.*
*That was **an** interesting film.*

*Put your homework on **the** desk.*
*Please pass me **the** blue pens.*

A AND *AN*

We use *a* before **singular nouns** that begin with **consonant sounds**, e.g.
***a b**ook*
***a d**esk*
***a h**ospital*
***a u**niform* (here, we pronounce the 'u' as a consonant)

We use *an* before **singular nouns** that begin with **vowel sounds**, e.g.
***an a**pple*
***an e**lephant*
***an h**our* (here, the 'h' is silent)
***an u**mbrella*

We usually use *a* and *an* when:

- it is not clear which person or thing we are talking about, e.g.
  *I want to buy **a** book.* (We do not know which book.)
  *It's raining. Have you got **an** umbrella?* (We do not know which umbrella.)
- we mention something for the first time, e.g.
  *I bought **a** book. The book is about animals.*
  *There's **a** pen under the desk. I think the pen belongs to Ali.*

THE

We usually use *the* when:

- it is clear which thing we are talking about, e.g.
  *Please hand me **the** book on the table.*
  *Is he **the** new Maths teacher?*
- we refer to things we have already mentioned, e.g.
  *I bought a book. **The** book is about animals.*
  *There's a pen under the desk. I think **the** pen belongs to Ali.*
- there is only one thing, e.g.
  *Did you see **the** Moon last night?*
  ***The** Sun is a star.*

We also use *the* with:

- time sequences, e.g. *in **the** beginning, at **the** end, in **the** past*
- dates, e.g. ***the** 1st of June, **the** 15th of March*
- parts of the day, e.g. *in **the** morning, in **the** evening, during **the** day*
- fixed time expressions, e.g. *at **the** moment, for **the** time being*
- seasons (optional), e.g. *in (the) spring, in (the) winter*
- musical instruments (after the verb *play*), e.g. *He plays **the** piano. She plays **the** violin.*
- historical events, e.g. ***the** Stone Age, **the** Industrial Revolution*
- ships, e.g. ***the** Titanic, **the** Bismark*
- public bodies, e.g. ***the** government, **the** police force*

ZERO ARTICLE

We do not usually use articles with:

- proper nouns, e.g.
  *I'm studying with **Sunil** tonight.*
  *My parents are from **Luxor**.*
  ***Mr Romero** is our English teacher.*
- plural countable nouns, e.g.
  *My aunt has five **cats**.*
  ***Computers** are getting faster and faster.*
  *Why do you have so many **watches**?*
- uncountable nouns, e.g.
  *I love playing **football**.*
  ***Water** covers 7 per cent of the globe.*
  *I eat **ginger** every day.*
- days, e.g.
  *I've got a cricket match on **Tuesday**.*
  *Let's meet on **Sunday** afternoon.*
- months, e.g.
  *We're going on holiday in **June**.*
  *My birthday is in **March**.*
- holidays, e.g.
  *I love **Chinese New Year**.*
  *My favourite holiday is **Diwali**.*
- school subjects, e.g.
  *The next lesson is **Science***
  *I think **History** is easy.*
- meals, e.g.
  *Let's have **breakfast**.*
  *What's for **dinner**?*
- abstract nouns, e.g.
  ***Happiness** is the key to life.*
  ***Curiosity** is more important than intelligence.*

- transport, e.g.
  *We travelled **by train**.*
  *I prefer going **on foot**.*

We do not use articles with some places (e.g. *bed*, *class*, *court*, *home*, *hospital*, *market*, *prison*, *school*, *town*, *university*) when we talk about their primary purpose, e.g.
*She's in **bed**.* (She is sleeping.)

*My grandma is in **hospital** for three weeks.* (She is sick.)

*He's already at **school**.* (He is studying.)

*My cousins are coming to **town**.* (They are visiting.)

WATCH OUT!

Note that we need to use *the* when we talk about the actual thing or place.
*Your shoes are under **the bed**.* (Where are the shoes?)
*I'm going to **the hospital** to see grandma.* (Where is he going?)
*There's a dinner at **the school*** on Saturday. (Where is the dinner?)
***The town** isn't very far from here.* (Where is the town?)

We do not usually use articles with most place names, but there are many exceptions. We use *the* when countable nouns like these appear in the place name, e.g. *bay*, *channel*, *gulf*, *kingdom*, *ocean*, *republic*, *river*, *sea*.

	Zero article	*the*
Continents	*Africa, Asia, Europe, South America*	
Countries	For most countries: *China, Egypt, Germany, Honduras, India, Kenya, Qatar, Spain*	For most plural country names: *the Bahamas, the Maldives, the Netherlands the Philippines*
		For islands, states, unions, kingdoms, republics: *the Czech Republic, the Democratic Republic of the Congo (The Congo* for short), *the Dominican Republic, the European Union, the Republic of the Sudan (Sudan* for short), *the Republic of Cyprus, the United Arab Emirates, the United Kingdom, the United States of America*
States/ counties/ districts/ municipalities/ provinces	Most states/ counties: *Bavaria, California, Cornwall, Famag, Umm Salal, Yunnan, Zamora*	*the Algarve, the (Scottish) borders*
Cities	Most cities: *Cairo, Beijing, Doha, Larnaca, London, Madrid*	*The Hague*
Universities	*Hong Kong University*	*the University of Hong Kong*
Geographical areas	*Central Asia, Northern Africa, Inner London*	*the Arctic, the Equator, the Middle East, the South Pole*
Lakes	*Lake Baikal, Lake Victoria, Lake Malawi*	
Oceans/seas/ rivers		*the Pacific Ocean, the Caspian Sea, the River Nile*
Mountains	*(Mount) Everest, Mount Fuji, Mount Kilimanjaro*	*the Jungfrau, the Matterhorn*
Mountain ranges		*the Alps, the Himalayas*
Islands	*Bali, Easter Islands, Hainan, Minorca*	*the Isle of Man*
Deserts		*the Gobi (Desert), the Sahara (Desert)*

NOUNS

Nouns are **people**, **places**, **animals** and **things**. There are four basic types of noun in English.

- **Proper nouns**: names of people and places that begin with a capital letter, e.g. *Anna*, *Aziz*, *Cairo*, *Egypt*, *Miss Smith*, *Lake Baikal*, *Mount Everest.*
- **Concrete nouns**: things that we experience through our senses (smell, sight, hearing, touch and taste), e.g. *cow*, *book*, *shoes*, *lamp*, *chocolate.*
- **Abstract nouns**: things that we do not experience through our senses (feelings, emotions, ideas, concepts, states etc.), e.g. *fear*, *happiness*, *friendship*, *charity*, *freedom.*
- **Collective nouns**: words for groups of people, animals or things, e.g. *family*, *band*, *company*, *team*, *herd*, *flock.*

COUNTABLE AND UNCOUNTABLE NOUNS

Countable nouns can be singular or plural, e.g.

*a **cup***	*two **cups***
*a **girl***	*four **girls***
*a **coin***	*eight **coins***

We form the plural of countable nouns in different ways.

Nouns	We should …	Examples
most nouns	+ *-s*	apple → *apples* bed → *beds* flag → *flags* book → *books* pen → *pens* lamp → *lamps* teacher → *teachers* key → *keys*
nouns ending in *o, s, x, z, ch* or *sh*	+ *-es*	potato → *potatoes* class → *classes* box → *boxes* buzz → *buzzes* beach → *beaches* dish → *dishes*
nouns ending in a consonant + *y*	- *y* + *-ies*	baby → *babies* city → *cities* family → *families* lady → *ladies* lorry → *lorries* pony → *ponies*

Some countable nouns have irregular plurals, e.g.

a leaf	*two leaves*	*person*	*four people*
a wolf	*four wolves*	*goose*	*six geese*
a knife	*six knives*	*a fish*	*two fish*
a man	*two men*	*a sheep*	*four sheep*

Uncountable nouns are nouns we cannot count. They do not have a plural form. They can be:

- materials, e.g. *cotton*, *metal*, *wood*
- liquids, e.g. *milk*, *soda*, *water*
- gases, e.g. *air*, *oxygen*
- grains and powders, e.g. *rice*, *wheat*, *sand*, *dust*, *flour*
- mass nouns, e.g. *fruit, furniture, transportation*
- natural phenomena, e.g. *rain*, *snow*, *sunshine*
- feelings, e.g. *anger, courage, happiness*

We can use *some* and *any* to refer to an indefinite amount, e.g.

- *Are there **any** oranges on the table?*
- *There are **some** oranges on the table.*
- *There aren't **any** oranges on the table.*
- *Is there **any** water in the fridge?*
- *There is **some** water in the fridge.*
- *There isn't **any** water in the fridge.*

Some nouns can be both countable and uncountable depending on the meaning.

Countable (single items)		Uncountable (substance or material)
*I found **two hairs** in my soup.*	hair	*He has black **hair**.*
*I'm writing **a paper**.*	paper	*I need some **paper**.*
*He ate half **a chicken**.*	chicken	*Do you want some **chicken**?*
*Can I have **two coffees**?*	coffee*	*Should I make some **coffee**?*
*This house has **nine rooms**.*	room	*There's not much **room** for a bed here.*
*I've been there **eight times**.*	time	*I don't have **time** to help you.*
*There are **five people** in the room.*	people	*The indigenous **people** of South America.*

*This applies to most drinks.

PARTITIVES

We can use **partitives** (e.g. *a cup of*, *a bag of*) with some uncountable nouns, e.g.

***a piece of** wood*	***a bag of** rice*
***a carton of** milk*	***a basket of** fruit*
***a bottle of** juice*	***a pile of** snow*

We can also use the adjectives in the table below to talk about the quantity of nouns.

Countable	a few	several	many / a lot of
Uncountable	little	much	a lot of

	Plural countable nouns	Uncountable nouns
Many	*many apples*	
Much		*much sugar*
A lot of	*a lot of apples*	*a lot of sugar*
Some	*some oranges*	
A few	*a few apples*	
A little		*a little sugar*

WATCH OUT!

Many people use *less* with countable nouns. This is a common mistake that we should avoid, e.g.

*There are **less** books here.* ✗

*There are **fewer** books here.* ✔

WATCH OUT!

These nouns are countable in many languages, but never in English: *information, advice, clothes, shopping, furniture, news, luggage.*

POSSESSIVES

We can talk about **possession** in different ways. When we talk about someone who owns something, we usually use *'s*, e.g.

*This is John**'s** pen.*

*Do you like Thomas**'s** dog?*

*I found Sara**'s** wallet.*

We can also use **possessive adjectives** and **possessive pronouns** to show possession.

Possessive adjective	Possessive pronoun
*This is **my** pen.*	*This pen is **mine**.*
*That is **your** dog.*	*It is **yours**.*
*It is **his** book.*	*That book is **his**.*
*This is **her** house.*	*The blue house is **hers**.*
*That's **our** new computer.*	*The computer is **ours**.*
*It is **their** problem now.*	*That problem is **theirs** now.*

OF

We can also use *of* to show possession. However, this is not common in English.

*He's a friend **of** John's.*

*This is a friend **of** hers.*

PRONOUNS

PERSONAL PRONOUNS

There are two types of **personal pronoun** in English: subject and object pronouns.

Subject pronoun	Object pronoun
I	me
you	you
he	him
she	her
it	it
we	us
they	them

We use **personal pronouns** to avoid repeating words. Compare the sentences.

Pedro made a cake for Maria, but Maria didn't like the cake, so Maria gave the cake back to Pedro and told Pedro that Maria didn't want to eat the cake.

*Pedro made a cake for Maria, but **she** didn't like **it** so **she** gave **it** back to **him** and told **him** that **she** didn't want to eat **it**.*

We can use **subject pronouns** to replace the subject of a sentence, e.g.

***Maria** enjoys tennis. **She** plays tennis three times a week.*

***Alex** is very tall. **He** plays on the basketball team.*

***That dog** is very cute. **It** will make a good pet.*

***Omar and I** like films. **We** go to see a film every weekend.*

***Lola and Joel** are learning to cook. **They** work at a seafood restaurant.*

We can use **object pronouns** to replace the object of a sentence, e.g.

*I gave **Pedro** a cap for his birthday. Elena gave **him** a T-shirt.*

*I took **my daughter** shopping. I bought **her** a book.*

*I bought **a ball** at the sports shop. I gave **it** to my brother.*

*My father will buy **my sister and me** a pet. He'll give it to **us** on Saturday.*

*She's teaching **Lola and Joel** to cook. She gives **them** lessons twice a week.*

We can use **personal pronouns** to replace people or objects. The word we use depends upon whether the **pronoun** is the **subject** or the **object** of the sentence.

DEMONSTRATIVE PRONOUNS

We use **demonstrative pronouns** to refer to people and things that are near or far away from us.

Near					
Singular	this	*girl*	*books*	*house*	*juice*
Plural	these	*girls*	*books*	*houses*	–

▶ Far away					
▶ Singular	that	girl	books	house	juice
▶ Plural	those	girls	books	houses	–

This *is a great book.*
This *is my juice.*
These *aren't my glasses.*
Are ***these*** *your shoes?*

That *is my uncle.*
That *is my house.*
Those *are my books.*
Are ***those*** *your pencils?*

REFLEXIVE PRONOUNS

These are the **reflexive pronouns**.

▶ Singular	myself	yourself	himself, herself, itself, oneself
▶ Plural	ourselves	yourselves	themselves

We use reflexive pronouns:

- when the subject and the object of the sentence are the same, e.g.
  I ***cut myself*** *while cooking dinner.*
  He ***helped himself*** *to some ice cream.*
  Please ***make yourself*** *something to eat.*
  We ***bought ourselves*** *something to eat.*
  Children, please ***behave yourselves****.*
- when the object of the preposition refers to the subject of the clause, e.g.
  Anna and Joel had to cook ***for themselves****.*
  Anil was feeling very sorry ***for himself****.*
  Deena is very pleased ***with herself****.*
- with *by* + reflexive pronoun to emphasise that an action was done alone and without help, e.g.
  I painted my room ***by myself****.*
  We fixed the car ***by ourselves****.*

We can use reflexive pronouns with most transitive verbs, but these are the most common: *amuse*, *behave*, *blame*, *cut*, *enjoy*, *express*, *help*, *hurt*, *introduce*, *kill*, *prepare*, *satisfy*, *teach*.

WATCH OUT!

A common mistake in English is to use an object pronoun instead of a reflexive pronoun, e.g.

You need to behave you. ✗
You need to behave yourself. ✔

VERBS

A verb is a word or phrase that we use to **express a state** or the **doing of an action,** e.g.

Mei-yin ***enjoys*** *painting.* (state)
I ***think*** *that's a good idea.* (state)
Sunil ***plays*** *football very well.* (action)
Sara ***wakes up*** *at 6.30 every morning.* (action)

We also use verbs to **express differences in time** (past, present, future), e.g.

I ***watched*** *a film last Saturday.* (past)
I'm watching *a film now.* (present)
I'm going to watch *a film tomorrow afternoon.* (future)

STATIVE VERBS

A verb that expresses a state is called a **stative verb**. Stative verbs usually occur in the simple form only and do not usually have an *-ing* form, e.g.

I ***like*** *jazz.*	✔	***I'm liking*** *jazz.*	✗
He ***owes*** *me money.*	✔	*He****'s owing*** *me money.*	✗
I ***don't mind*** *helping.*	✔	***I'm not minding*** *helping.*	✗

Some common stative verbs are:

- feelings, e.g. *admire*, *care about*, *dislike*, *hate*, *like*, *love*
- thinking or believing, e.g. *agree*, *appreciate*, *believe*, *consider*, *know*, *realise*, *understand*
- wants or preferences, e.g. *desire*, *need*, *prefer*, *require*, *want*, *wish*
- senses, e.g. *hear*, *notice*, *observe*, *see*, *smell*, *taste*
- being or seeming, e.g. *belong*, *come from*, *consist of*, *depend*, *happen to*, *own*

We can use some verbs to talk about both states and actions.

State	Action
*I **think** we should go to Thailand.*	*I'm **thinking** about our holiday.*
*Pedro **is** a silly boy.*	*You're **being** very silly!*
*The sauce **smells** nice.*	*Mum's **smelling** the sauce.*
*The dog **weighs** 15 kilos.*	*I'm **weighing** the dog.*
*Wow! You **look** great.*	*She's **looking** out of the window.*
*I **have** a cat.*	*I'm **having** a party.*
*Look! I **see** a butterfly.*	*I'm **seeing** the doctor after school.*

WATCH OUT!

Native English speakers use some **stative verbs** in the **continuous** form in informal speech, e.g.

*It's **looking** like rain today.*

This is very informal and should be avoided.

AUXILIARY VERBS

The main auxiliary verbs are *be*, *do* and *have*:

- ***be***: *am, is, are, was, were, being, been*
- ***do***: *does, did*
- ***have***: *has, had, having*

We use auxiliary verbs to give more information about actions and states. We use them in:

- tenses, e.g.

  *I'**m playing** football.* (present continuous)

  *My friends **didn't want** to play football.* (past simple)

  *Sunil **has played** football for 6 years.* (present perfect)
- questions, e.g.

  ***Are** you **going** to the party?*

  ***Do** you **like** pizza?*

  ***Have** you **eaten** lunch?*
- negative statements, e.g.

  *He **isn't coming** to the party?*

  *Sofia **doesn't like** parties.*

  *Marco **hasn't arrived** yet?*

WATCH OUT!

A sentence in English must contain at least one verb.

VERB FORMS

Every **verb** in English has five different forms.

Base	Infinitive	Past simple*	Past participle*	*-ing* form
ask	to ask	asked	asked	asking
begin	to begin	began	begun	beginning
clean	to clean	cleaned	cleaned	cleaning
drink	to drink	drank	drunk	drinking
eat	to eat	ate	eaten	eating
finish	to finish	finished	finished	finishing

Note the past simple and past participle have both regular (-ed*) forms and irregular forms (e.g. *began*, *begun*). A list of common irregular verbs and their forms is on pages 284–285.

GERUNDS AND INFINITIVES

The **gerund** is the *-ing* form of a verb (e.g. *drinking*, *playing*). The infinitive is the root form of the verb with *to* (e.g. *to drink*, *to play*).

GERUNDS

Some verbs are always followed by the gerund form of the verb.

admit	continue	finish	miss	put off
avoid	delay	hate	plan on	quit
begin	deny	imagine	postpone	recommend
complete	discuss	keep	practise	start
concentrate on	dislike	mention	prefer	suggest
consider	enjoy	mind	propose	think about

*Maria **enjoys hiking** very much.*

*I've just **finished eating** lunch.*

*Please **keep working**.*

*Would you **mind opening** the door for me?*

Note that verb-preposition combinations are also followed by a gerund, e.g.

*Please **concentrate on doing** your work.*

*I **plan on studying** after school.*

*She's **thinking about joining** a club.*

We use gerunds, not infinitives, after prepositions, e.g.

*I'll call you **after arriving** at the park.*

*I'll finish this **before going** to sleep.*

*You can't learn **without making** mistakes.*

We can also use gerunds as the subject of a sentence. e.g.

Exercising *is very good for you.*

Swimming *is my favourite activity.*

INFINITIVES

Some verbs are always followed by an infinitive.

agree	care	happen	offer
aim	choose	hesitate	plan
appear	continue	hope	prefer
arrange	decide	hurry	prepare
ask	deserve	intend	promise
attempt	expect	like	refuse
beg	fail	love	start
begin	forget	mean	wait
can't stand	get	need	want

Sara ***has agreed to help*** *me with my project.*

I ***hope to go*** *to Spain next year.*

Marco is ***planning to take*** *piano lessons.*

They ***wanted to go*** *to the football match.*

Some verbs can be followed by an object and then an infinitive.

allow	expect	love	require
ask	force	order	send
beg	hire	pay	teach
challenge	instruct	permit	tell
choose	invite	persuade	urge
command	lead	prepare	want
direct	let	promise	warn
encourage	like	remind	

Note that some of these verbs are included in the list above and may be used without an object.

He ***asked <u>me</u> to leave****.*

She ***begged <u>me</u> to come*** *to the party.*

They ***expected <u>their</u> team to win****.*

My father ***taught <u>me</u> to play*** *table tennis.*

Other verbs can be followed by either a gerund or an infinitive with no change in meaning.

begin   can't stand   continue   like   love   prefer   start

I ***like painting****.*

I ***like to paint****.*

I ***prefer cooking****.*

I ***prefer to cook****.*

It ***has started raining****.*

It ***has started to rain****.*

VERBS + GERUND, VERBS + *ING*

Some verbs change meaning when they are followed by a gerund or an infinitive, e.g.

- **forget**

I ***forgot meeting*** *her.* (I have no memory of meeting her before.)

I ***forgot to meet*** *her.* (I didn't meet her because I forgot.)

- **regret**

I ***regret not studying*** *harder.* (I'm sorry that I didn't study harder.)

I ***regret to tell*** *you that you have failed the exam.* (I'm telling you now and I'm sorry.)

- **remember**

She ***remembered walking*** *on the beach as a child.* (She has memories of the walks on the beach.)

I ***remembered to meet*** *my mum at the beach.* (She didn't forget to meet her mum.)

- **stop**

We ***stopped playing*** *football at 5 p.m.* (We finished the activity and went home.)

We ***stopped to play*** *football at 5 p.m.* (We interrupted an activity to play football.)

- **try**

He ***tried opening*** *the window.* (He opened the window because the room was hot.)

He ***tried to open*** *the window.* (He tried to open the window but couldn't.)

TENSES

Every complete sentence in English has at least one verb in it. Depending on the period of time we are talking about, we conjugate this verb in different ways. We call these **tenses**. There are twelve **tenses** relating to time in English: four **past tenses**, four **present tenses** and four **future tenses**.

	Simple	Continuous	Perfect	Perfect continuous
Past	*I ate.* *I did not eat.* *Did you eat?*	*I was eating.* *I was not eating.* *Were you eating?*	*I had eaten.* *I had not eaten.* *Had you eaten?*	*I had been eating.* *I had not been eating.* *Had you been eating?*
Present	*I eat.* *I do not eat.* *Do you eat?*	*I am eating.* *I am not eating.* *Are you eating?*	*I have eaten.* *I have not eaten.* *Have you eaten?*	*I have been eating.* *I have not been eating.* *Have you been eating?*
Future	*I will eat.* *I will not eat.* *Will you eat?*	*I will be eating.* *I will not be eating.* *Will you be eating?*	*I will have eaten.* *I will not have eaten.* *Will you have eaten?*	*I will have been eating.* *I will not have been eating.* *Will you have been eating?*

There are several key points to help remember the differences among tenses. We use a form of:

- *do* to form questions and negative statements in the present simple and past simple
- *be* and the *-ing* form of the verb to form continuous tenses
- *have* and the past participle form of the verb to form perfect tenses
- *will* and the simple form of the verb to form future tenses.

PRESENT SIMPLE

We use the **present simple** to talk about:

- facts which are always true, e.g.

  *Water **boils** at 100°C.*

  *The Earth **goes** around the Sun.*

  *There **are** seven continents.*
- situations that are true in the present period of time, e.g.

  *I **study** English and Maths.*

  *My mother **works** in a bank.*

  *She**'s** very tired.*
- habitual actions (often with adverbs of frequency and time), e.g.

  *Sara usually **plays** tennis three times a week.*

  *They often **go** hiking.*
- timetables and schedules, e.g.

  *The train **leaves** at 11 p.m. tonight.*

  *The concert **starts** at 7 o'clock.*

We form positive and negative statements in the present simple as shown in the table opposite (above).

Main verbs	I/You/We/They	**work** **do not / don't work**	at the hospital.
	He/She/It	**works** **does not / doesn't work**	
Verb *to be*	I	**am** **am not**	kind.
	You/We/They	**are / 're** **are not / aren't / 're not**	
	He/She/It	**is / 's** **is not / isn't / 's not**	

WATCH OUT!

Note that we often use contractions (e.g. *he's*, *aren't*) in spoken English and informal writing.

We form *yes/no* questions and answers in the present simple as shown in the table below.

Main verbs	**Do**	I/you/we/they	**work** at the hospital?	**Yes,**	I/you/we/they	**do.**
					he/she/it	**does.**
	Does	he/she/it		**No,**	I/you/we/they	**don't.**
					he/she/it	**doesn't.**
Verb *to be*	**Am**	I	kind?	**Yes,**	I	**am.**
					you/we/they	**are.**
	Are	you/we/they			he/she/it	**is.**
				No,	I	**am not.**
	Is	he/she/it			you/we/they	**are not / aren't / 're not.**
					he/she/it	**is not / isn't / 's not.**

In the present simple, we form regular verbs in the third person in different ways as shown in the table below.

Verbs	We ...	Examples
For verbs ending in ... *-ss* *-x* *-ch* *-sh* *-zz* *-o*	add *-es*	miss → *misses* relax → *relaxes* catch → *catches* wash → *washes* buzz → *buzzes* go → *goes*
For verbs ending in a consonant and *-y*	remove *-y* and replace with *-ies*	carry → *carries* cry → *cries* fly → *flies* hurry → *hurries* study → *studies*
For verbs ending in anything else	add *-s*	dance → *dances* enjoy → *enjoys* make → *makes* play → *plays* walk → *walks*

PRESENT CONTINUOUS

We use the **present continuous** to talk about:

- periods of activity which are ongoing, e.g.
  *I'**m studying** for exams this week.*
  *They'**re taking** an Art class.*
- actions in progress at the moment of speaking, e.g.
  *He'**s talking** on the phone.*
  *They'**re playing** at the park.*
- a current change, e.g.
  *Manchester **is playing** better recently.*
  *The weather **is getting** cooler.*
- repeated actions, e.g.
  *Sunil **is** always **complaining**.*
  *Anna and Marta **are** always helping people.*
- descriptions of pictures, e.g.
  *The man in the photo **is sitting** in a chair.*
  *That's me. I'**m holding** a big fish.*
- future plans, e.g.
  *My grandparents **are arriving** on Saturday.*
  *We'**re having** a party this weekend.*

We often use certain time expressions with the present continuous: *at the moment*, (*right*) *now*, *currently*.

We form positive and negative statements in the present continuous with:

- the present simple form of the verb *to be*.
- the *-ing* form of the main verb.

I	**am** **am not**	**reading** a book.
You/We/They	**are / 're** **are not / aren't / 're not**	
He/She/It	**is / 's** **is not / isn't / 's not**	

We form *yes/no* questions and answers in the present continuous as shown in the table below.

Am	I	**reading** a book?	**Yes,**	I	**am.**
Are	you/we/they			you/we/they	**are.**
Is	he/she/it			he/she/it	**is.**
			No,	I	**am not.**
				you/we/they	**are not / aren't / 're not.**
				he/she/it	**is not / isn't / 's not.**

Verbs	We ...	Examples
For most verbs	add *-ing*	cry → *crying* eat → *eating* go → *going* throw → *throwing*
For verbs ending in *-e*	remove *-e* and replace with *-ing*	hike → *hiking* give → *giving* make → *making*
For verbs ending in a vowel + a consonant (except *w*)	double the consonant and add *-ing*	drop → *dropping* run → *running* swim → *swimming*
For verbs ending in *-ie*	remove -*ie* and replace with -*ying*	die → *dying* lie → *lying*

PRESENT PERFECT

We use the **present perfect** to talk about:

- life experiences, e.g.
  *I'**ve been** to France three times.*
  *Deena **hasn't taken** her driving test.*
- periods of time that have not finished, e.g.
  *I'**ve** already **eaten** today.*
  *It **has rained** a lot this week.*
- recently completed actions that are still important, e.g.
  *I'**ve broken** my computer so I can't send you the files.*
  *There'**s been** an earthquake in Nepal.*
- repeated actions using a specific number, e.g.
  *I'**ve drunk** six cups of coffee today.*
  *She'**s read** 25 pages so far.*

We often use certain time expressions with the present perfect: *today*, *this week*, *this month*, *this year*, *this decade*, *this century*, *already*, *for*, *since*.

We form positive and negative statements in the present perfect with:

- the present simple form of the verb *to have*
- the past participle form of the main verb.

I/You/We/They	**have / 've** **have not / haven't**	**finished** the homework.
He/She/It	**has / 's** **has not / hasn't**	

We form *yes/no* questions and answers in the present perfect as shown in the table below.

Have	I/you/we/they	**finished** the homework?	**Yes,**	I/you/we/they	**have.**
				he/she/it	**has.**
Has	he/she/it		**No,**	I/you/we/they	**have not / haven't.**
				he/she/it	**has not / hasn't.**

WATCH OUT!

It is easy to confuse contractions in the present continuous and present perfect, e.g.

He's ***playing*** *football at the park.* (He is playing football.)

He's ***played*** *football for 6 years.* (He has played football.)

PRESENT PERFECT CONTINUOUS

We use the **present perfect continuous** to talk about:

- periods of activity which are ongoing, emphasising that they have taken place in the past and the present, e.g.

  I've been working *here a long time.*

  *Eva**'s been reading** since two o'clock.*

- recently finished actions, e.g.

  That smells wonderful. ***Have*** *you* ***been baking****?*

  *He's very tired. He**'s been playing** football.*

- repeated actions, e.g.

  That dog ***has been barking*** *all afternoon.*

  I've been phoning *her for 30 minutes but she's not answering.*

WATCH OUT!

We use the **present perfect continuous** when the activity is not finished. We use the **present perfect** when the activity is clearly finished.

Martin ***has been cooking*** *for an hour.* (He has not finished cooking.)

Martin ***has cooked*** *dinner for us.* (He has already finished cooking.)

We often use certain time expressions with the present perfect continuous: *lately*, *recently*, *all day*, *since*, *for*.

We form positive and negative statements in the present perfect continuous with:

- the present simple form of the verb *to have*
- the past participle form of the verb *to be* (*been*)
- the *-ing* form of the main verb.

I/You/We/They	**have / 've** **have not / haven't**	**been**	**reading** all afternoon. **playing** football.
He/She/It	**has / 's** **has not / hasn't**		

We form *yes/no* questions and answers in the present perfect continuous as shown in the table below.

Have	I/you/we/they	**been**	**reading** all afternoon? **playing** football?	**Yes,**	I/you/we/they	**have.**
					he/she/it	**has.**
Has	he/she/it			**No,**	I/you/we/they	**have not / haven't.**
					he/she/it	**has not / hasn't.**

PAST SIMPLE

We use the **past simple** to talk about:

- completed actions that are no longer relevant to the current situation, e.g.

  I ***grew up*** *in York.*

  Elena ***lived*** *in Madrid for 3 years.*

- actions that take place in a period of time that have finished, e.g.

  I ***met*** *him last week.*

  Pedro just ***left*** *a minute ago.*

- talk about (recount) events or tell stories, e.g.

  I ***went*** *to a concert and it* ***was*** *very exciting.*

  The wizard ***reached*** *into his bag and* ***took out*** *a mouse.*

- talk about the shorter of two actions in the past, e.g.

  I was eating dinner when the phone ***rang****.*

*It **started** raining while they were playing football.*

We often use certain time expressions with the past simple: *yesterday*, *ago*, *last week/month/year*, *in March.*

We form positive and negative statements in the past simple as shown in the table below.

Main verbs	I/You/He/She/It	**worked**	at the hospital.
	We/They	**did not / didn't work**	
Verb *to be*	I/You/He/She/It	**was** **was not / wasn't**	at the concert.
	We/They	**were** **were not / weren't**	

We form *yes/no* questions and answers in the past simple as shown in the table below.

Main verbs	Did	I/you/he/she/it/we/they	work at the hospital?	Yes,	I/you/he/she/it/we/they	**did.**
				No,		**did not / didn't.**
Verb *to be*	Was	I/he/she/it	kind?	Yes,	I/he/she/it	**was.**
	Were	you/we/they			you/we/they	**were.**
				No,	I/he/she/it	**was not / wasn't.**
					you/we/they	**were not / weren't.**

In the past simple, we form regular verbs in different ways.

Verbs	We …	Examples
For most verbs	add *-ed*	*miss* → *missed* *relax* → *relaxed* *wash* → *washed* *buzz* → *buzzed*
For verbs ending in *-e*	remove *e* and add *-ed*	*agree* → *agreed* *close* → *closed* *dance* → *danced* *hope* → *hoped*
For verbs ending in a consonant and *-y*	remove the *-y* and add *-ied*	*carry* → *carried* *cry* → *cried* *study* → *studied* *worry* → *worried*
For verbs ending in a vowel + a consonant when there is a stressed vowel before the consonant (except for *w* and *y*)	double the consonant and add *-ed*	*rub* → *rubbed* *pin* → *pinned* *prefer* → *preferred* *stop* → *stopped* *travel* → *travelled*

PAST CONTINUOUS

We use the **past continuous** to:

- talk about events that continued for a period of time in the past, e.g.

  *My stomach **was hurting** all night long.*

  *I **was reading** all afternoon.*

- talk about the longer of two actions in the past, e.g.

  *I **was eating dinner** when the phone rang.*

  *She cut her finger while she **was preparing** dinner.*

- talk about two actions in the past that were happening at the same time, e.g.

  *I **was watching** television and the children **were playing**.*

  *While I **was cooking** dinner, my wife **was folding** the clothes.*

- talk about (recount) events or tell stories, e.g.

  *I **was sitting** on the grass and **listening** to the music.*

  *The rain **was pouring** down and the two travellers **were walking** through the forest.*

- make polite requests, usually with *wonder* or *hope*, e.g.

  *I **was wondering** if you might be able to help me.*

  *I **was hoping** you would be kind enough to open the door.*

We often use certain time expressions with the past continuous: *while*, *last week/month/year*, *in March.*

We form positive and negative statements in the past continuous with:

- the past simple form of the verb *to be*
- the *-ing* form of the main verb.

I/He/She/It	**was** **was not / wasn't**	**reading** a book.
You/We/They	**were** **were not / weren't**	

We form *yes/no* questions and answers in the past continuous as shown in the table below.

Was	I/he/she/it	**reading** a book?	Yes,	I/he/she/it	**was.**
Were	you/we/they			you/we/they	**were.**
			No,	I/he/she/it	**was not / wasn't.**
				you/we/they	**were not / weren't.**

PAST PERFECT

We use the **past perfect** to talk about:

- the first of two actions in the past, e.g.
  *I **had slept** for 8 hours when they woke me.*
  *Anna didn't go to the cinema with us because she **had** already **seen** the film.*
- actions that occur before a point in the past, e.g.
  ***I'd collected** more than 1000 stamps by last November.*
  *She**'d finished** her homework by 11.*
- states that are true until a moment in the past, e.g.
  *I was so happy. I **had** never **been** to Paris before.*
  *Alex **had had** that phone for 2 years before he lost it.*

We often use certain time expressions with the past perfect: *until*, *before*, *when*, *by*, *by the time*.

We form positive and negative statements in the past perfect with:

- the past simple form of the verb *to have*
- the past participle form of the main verb.

I/You/He/She/ It/We/They	**had / 'd / had not / hadn't**	**finished** the homework.

We form *yes/no* questions and answers in the past perfect as shown in the table below.

Had	I/you/he/she/ it/we/they	**finished** the homework?	**Yes,**	I/you/he/ she/it/ we/they	**had.**
			No,		**had not / hadn't.**

PAST PERFECT CONTINUOUS

We use the **past perfect continuous** to talk about:

- periods of activity that began in the past and continued up to and including another point in the past, e.g.
  *I **had been learning** English for 3 years before I finally passed my exam.*
  *When I first met Mateo, he**'d been taking** painting classes for 3 years.*
- the cause of a past state, e.g.
  *I was full because **I'd been eating** all morning.*
  *She**'d been working** all day and was very tired.*

WATCH OUT!

We use the **past perfect continuous** when the activity is not finished. We use the **past perfect** when the activity is clearly finished, e.g.

*When I got home, I found that Martin **had been cooking** dinner.* (He had not finished cooking at that time.)

*When I got home, I found that Martin **had cooked** dinner.* (He had already finished cooking at that time.)

We often use certain time expressions with the past perfect continuous: *until*, *before*, *when*, *by*, *by the time*.

We form positive and negative statements in the past perfect continuous with:

- the past simple form of the verb *to have*
- the past participle form of the verb *to be* (*been*)
- the *-ing* form of the main verb.

I/You/He/She/ It/We/They	**had / 'd** **had not / hadn't**	**been**	**reading** all afternoon. **playing** football.

We form *yes/no* questions in the past perfect continuous as shown in the table below.

Had	I/you/he/ she/it/ we/they	**been**	**reading** all afternoon? **playing** football?	**Yes,**	I/you/he/ she/it/ we/they	**had.**
				No,		**had not / hadn't.**

FUTURE SIMPLE

We use the **future simple** to:

- make predictions, e.g.
  *I think Spain **will win** on Monday.*
  ***Will** the test **be** next week?*
- make promises, e.g.
  ***I'll take** the rubbish out tomorrow morning.*
  ***I'll buy** you a new phone for your birthday.*
- make offers, e.g.
  ***I'll take care of** your dog while you're away.*
  ***Shall** I **take** your coat?*
- make suggestions, e.g.
  ***Shall** we **go** to the lake tomorrow?*
  ***Shall** we **have** pizza for dinner?*
- express willingness, e.g.
  ***I'll do** the dishes.*
  *She**'ll be** happy to help you with your homework.*

- make decisions at the time of speaking, e.g.
  *I'll **have** lunch at 12, not 1.*
  *Don't worry. **I'll pay** for dinner.*
- give orders, e.g.
  *You **will do** exactly as I say.*
  *You **will finish** your vegetables.*

WATCH OUT!

We can use *will* with the first, second and third person, but we can only use *shall* with *I* and *we*. We especially use *shall* to make offers and suggestions.

We often use the future simple after certain verbs and verb phrases, such as *be afraid*, *be sure*, *believe*, *expect* and *think*, e.g.

***I'm afraid** I **won't** be able to come.*
***I'm sure** he**'ll be** late for the party.*
*I **believe** Elena **will get** the job.*
*We **expect** they**'ll arrive** soon.*
*I **think** I**'ll go** to bed early.*

We form positive and negative statements in the future simple with:
- the auxiliary verb *will*
- the simple form of the main verb.

I/You/He/She/ It/We/They	**will/ 'll/will not/ won't**	**play** football this weekend. **wash** the dishes.

We form *yes/no* questions and answers in the future simple as shown in the table below.

Will	I/you/he/ she/it/ we/they	**play** football this weekend?	**Yes,**	I/you/he/ she/it/ we/they	**will.**
		clean my room?	**No,**		**will not / won't.**

FUTURE CONTINUOUS

We use the **future continuous** to:
- talk about actions in progress in the future, e.g.
  *We**'ll be skiing** in Japan this time next week.*
  ***I'll be preparing** for exams next year.*
- make predictions about a current event, e.g.
  *Rose **will be leaving** her house about now.*
  ***I'll be missing** the warm weather once I'm back in England.*
- make predictions about future trends, e.g.
  *Most people **will be living** in urban areas by 2050.*
  *I think lots of people **will be switching** to solar energy in the next decade.*
- talk about the longer of two simultaneous actions in the future, e.g.
  ***I'll be cooking** dinner when my friends arrive.*
  *The baby **will be sleeping** when we get home.*
- talk about what we believe at the moment of speaking, e.g.
  *Don't call him now. He**'ll be doing** his homework.*
  *It's almost noon. I'm sure she **won't be sleeping**.*

We form positive and negative statements in the future continuous with:
- the auxiliary verb *will*
- the simple form of the verb *to be*
- the *-ing* form of the main verb.

I/You/He/She/ It/We/They	**will / 'll** **will not / won't**	**be**	**skiing** in Japan next week. **studying** all afternoon.

We form *yes/no* questions and answers in the future continuous as shown in the table below.

Will	I/you/he/ she/it/ we/they	**be**	**skiing** in Japan next week? **studying** all afternoon?	**Yes,**	I/you/he/ she/it/ we/they	**will.**
				No,		**will not / won't.**

FUTURE PERFECT

We use the **future perfect** to:
- talk about actions that will be completed by a certain time in the future, e.g.
  ***I'll have finished** the homework by 10 o'clock tonight.*
  *My father **will have retired** by the year 2030.*
- talk about actions that continue up to the time mentioned, e.g.
  *By this time next year, I **will have known** you for 10 years.*
  *Marta **will have lived** in Shanghai for 20 years by 2021.*
- express beliefs about the near past, e.g.
  *The train **will have left** by now, so how will we get there?*
  *My parents **will have landed** by now. Let's go and wait at the gate.*

We form positive and negative statements in the future perfect with:
- the auxiliary verb *will*
- the simple form of the auxiliary verb *to have*
- the past participle form of the main verb.

I/You/He/She/ It/We/They	will / 'll will not / won't	have	**lived** in Shanghai for 20 years by 2021. **eaten** dinner by that time.

We form *yes/no* questions and answers in the future perfect as shown in the table below.

Will	I/you/ he/ she/ it/we/ they	have	**lived** in Shanghai for 20 years by 2021? **eaten** dinner by that time?	Yes,	I/you/ he/ she/ it/we/ they	will.
				No,		will not / won't.

FUTURE PERFECT CONTINUOUS

We use the **future perfect continuous** to talk about:

- periods of activity that will begin in the future and continue up to and including another point in the future, e.g.

  *By 11 a.m. tomorrow, **I'll have been playing** football for two and a half hours.*

  *When we meet my parents in Madrid, we**'ll have been travelling** for 10 days.*

- periods of activity that began in the past and continue up to and including a point in the future, e.g.

  *Next month **I'll have been living** in Thailand for exactly 5 years.*

  *By 1st November, **I'll have been travelling** for 3 weeks.*

We form positive and negative statements in the future perfect continuous with:

- the auxiliary verb *will*
- the simple form of the auxiliary verb *to have*
- the past participle form of the verb *to be* (*been*)
- the *-ing* form of the action verb.

I/You/He/She/ It/We/They	will / 'll will not / won't	have been	**travelling** for 3 weeks.

We form *yes/no* questions and answers in the future perfect continuous as shown in the table below.

Will	I/you/he/ she/it/ we/they	have been	**travelling** for 3 weeks?	Yes,	I/you/he/ she/it/ we/they	will.
				No,		will not / won't.

OTHER WAYS TO TALK ABOUT THE PAST

We can also use the auxiliary verbs *would* and *used to* to talk about the past.

USED TO AND *WOULD*

We can use *used to* and *would* to talk about past habits and repeated past actions, e.g.

*When I was a child, I **used to** / **would** go to sleep very late.*

*When Eva was a child, she **didn't use to** / **wouldn't** eat her vegetables.*

*When my parents were young, they **used to** / **would** go hiking every weekend.*

With *would*, we need to use a time phrase or clause at the beginning of the sentence, e.g.

*I **would go** to sleep very late.* ✘

*When I was a child, I **would go** to sleep very late.* ✔

We use *used to* (not *would*) to talk about past states. We use *used to* with *be*, *have* (possession) and other stative verbs, e.g.

*In primary school, Joel **used to be** very talkative.* ✔

*In primary school, Joel **would be** very talkative.* ✘

*When I was a young girl, I **used to have** very long hair.* ✔

*When I was a young girl, I **would have** very long hair.* ✘

*We **used to live** in Spain.* ✔

*We **would live** in Spain.* ✘

WATCH OUT!

We do not use *used to* with *for* and *since*, e.g.

I used to live in Cairo for 3 years. ✘

I lived in Cairo for 3 years. ✔

She used to play the violin since she was five. ✘

She has played the violin since she was five. ✔

OTHER WAYS TO TALK ABOUT THE FUTURE

We can use *going to*, *be about to* and *be due to* to talk about the future.

GOING TO

We use *be* + *going to* + simple form of the verb. We can use *going to* for:

- predictions, especially when we are talking about the immediate future, e.g.

  *Look at those clouds. It**'s going to rain**.*

- definite plans in the future, e.g.

  ***I'm going to watch** a film tomorrow.*

BE ABOUT TO

We can use *be about to* to talk about actions that are going to happen very soon, e.g.

*The train **is about to leave**. Hurry up!*

BE DUE TO

We can use *be due to* to talk about actions that are planned or expected to happen at a certain time, e.g.

*The plane **is due to arrive** at 10.15.*

BE LIKELY TO

We can use *be likely to* to talk about actions that are probably going to happen, e.g.

*If you keep studying you**'re likely to** pass the exam.*

SHOULD / MODALS

We can use different modals to talk about the possible future, e.g.

*I **should** be at the station at 10 o'clock.*

PHRASAL VERBS

Phrasal verbs are verbs with two or more words (e.g. *make up*, *turn off*). There are two types of phrasal verbs: separable and non-separable.

SEPARABLE PHRASAL VERBS

We can separate some phrasal verbs by putting an object between the verb and the other word(s), e.g.

*She made up **the story**.*

*She made **the story** up.*

*She made **it** up.*

*He turned off **the lights**.*

*He turned **the lights** off.*

*He turned **them** off.*

*Dwayne cheered up **the boy**.*

*Dwayne cheered **the boy** up.*

*Dwayne cheered **him** up.*

When the object of the phrasal verb is a pronoun, we must separate the phrasal verb. We cannot put the pronoun at the end, e.g.

She made it up. ✔

She made up it. ✘

He turned them off. ✔

He turned off them. ✘

Dwayne cheered up him. ✘

Dwayne cheered him up. ✔

NON-SEPARABLE PHRASAL VERBS

We cannot separate some phrasal verbs. We must put the object (if there is one) after the phrasal verb, e.g.

He came into the room. ✔

He came the room into. ✘

I get along with him. ✔

I get him along with. ✘

She came across him in the street. ✔

She came him across in the street. ✘

MULTI-MEANING PHRASAL VERBS

There are several phrasal verbs which have more than one meaning. Some phrasal verbs are separable in one meaning, but non-separable in another meaning. Here is a list of some of the more common multi-meaning phrasal verbs.

BACK UP

- (separable): make a copy of computer data, e.g. *He's backed **all his files** up.*
- (separable): move backwards, e.g. *They're backing **the car** up.*

MAKE UP

- (separable): invent a story, lie about something, e.g. *He made **an excuse** up to explain why he was late.*
- (non-separable): forgive each other, e.g. *They made up **after the fight**.*

PICK UP

- (separable): collect somebody to take them somewhere, e.g. *Can you pick **me** up from the train station?*
- (separable): learn a new skill, e.g. *He picked **Chinese** up very quickly.*
- (non-separable): improve after a bad period, e.g. *I hope your exam results pick up soon.*

TAKE UP

- (separable): occupy space, e.g. *The sofa takes **a lot of space** up in the living room.*
- (separable): begin a hobby, e.g. *I'm taking **skiing** up. It's really fun!*

WORK OUT

- (separable): solve a problem, e.g. *I can't work* ***this Maths problem*** *out.*
- (non-separable): do exercise, e.g. *He works out quite often.*
- (non-separable): have a happy resolution, e.g. *Everything worked out well in the end.*

IMPERATIVES

The imperative form is the same as the simple form of the verb (e.g. *be*, *go*, *stop*). With the imperative, gesture, facial expressions, stress and intonation and, most importantly, situation and context show whether the use of the imperative is friendly, angry or impatient, e.g.

- friendly: ***Be*** *quiet. The baby is sleeping.* (a wife talking to her husband)
- angry: ***Be*** *quiet! This is a classroom, not a playground!* (a teacher to her class)

We use the **imperative** to:

- give orders to somebody e.g.
  Sit up *straight!*
  Be *quiet!*
- give direct commands, e.g.
  Mum, ***pass*** *the salt please.*
  Follow *me!*
- make requests, e.g.
  Shut *the door please.*
  Help *me move this table.*
- make suggestions or give advice, e.g.
  Don't worry *about that!*
  Try *restarting the computer.*
- give warnings, e.g.
  Look out*! There's a bus.*
  Don't do *that!*
- give directions, e.g.
  Take *the second turning on the right.*
  Go *straight for two blocks.*
- give instructions, e.g.
  Bake *for 20 minutes.*
  Roll *the dice to move.*
- state prohibitions, e.g.
  Please ***keep off*** *the grass.*
  Don't roller-blade *in the park.*
- offer invitations, e.g.
  Come *and* ***have*** *dinner with us.*
  Join *us at the party this weekend.*
- make offers, e.g.
  Have *a biscuit.*
  Take *one of the chocolate cakes.*

We can use *do* before the imperative for emphasis in a formal context, e.g.

Do have *another cup or tea.*

Do stop *talking.*

We often use the **imperative** with *nobody*, *everybody* and *somebody*, e.g.

Nobody move*!*

Everybody, come *with me.*

Somebody answer *the phone, please.*

MODAL VERBS

Modal verbs are a type of **auxiliary verb** that we can use to express ability, permission, obligation, advice, probability, possibility, speculation and deduction, and offers.

ABILITY

We can use the modal verb *can* to talk about ability in the present, e.g.

I ***can speak*** *Arabic but I* ***can't speak*** *Italian.*

I ***can't play*** *piano.*

Can *you* ***swim****?*

We can use *could* or *be able to* to talk about ability in the past, e.g.

I ***could*** */* ***was able to play*** *football well before I broke my leg.*

I ***couldn't*** */* ***wasn't able to ride*** *a bicycle until I was five.*

When we need to express ability in other tenses, we can use *be able to* and *managed to*, e.g.

I'll be able to run *a marathon after a bit more training.*

She ***hasn't managed to finish*** *her essay yet.*

When we talk about a specific success or failure in the past, we need to use *be able to*, e.g.

The exam was very difficult so no one ***was able to pass*** *it.* ✔

The exam was very difficult so no one ***could pass*** *it.* ✘

We ***were able to reach*** *the campsite before it got dark.* ✔

We ***could reach*** *the campsite before it got dark.* ✘

PERMISSION

We can also use the modal verb *can* to talk about permission, e.g.

My parents say I ***can go*** *to see a film with you on Saturday.*

He ***can't play*** *cricket because he needs to do his homework.*

Can *I* ***go*** *to the party?*

When we request permission, we can use the modal verbs *might*, *may*, *could* and *can*.

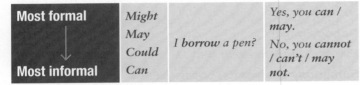

Most formal ↓ **Most informal**	*Might* *May* *Could* *Can*	*I borrow a pen?*	*Yes, you can / may.* *No, you cannot / can't / may not.*

Note that we cannot use *could* or *might* when we answer requests for permission.

OBLIGATION AND ADVICE

We can use *must*, *have to*, *had better*, *ought to* and *should* to talk about obligation.

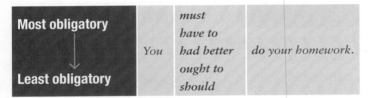

Most obligatory ↓ **Least obligatory**	*You*	*must* *have to* *had better* *ought to* *should*	*do your homework.*

We use *should*, *ought to*, *had better* and *don't have to* to give advice and make suggestions, e.g.

You ***should work*** *hard.*

You ***shouldn't be*** *so late.*

You ***ought to eat*** *a good breakfast.*

You ***had better*** *clean your room.*

You ***don't have to*** *speak English at break time.*

WATCH OUT!

It is a very common mistake to think that *don't have to* means the same as *must not*, e.g.

You ***mustn't forget*** *to do your homework.* (You have no choice.)

We ***don't have to*** *do homework during break time* (You have a choice.)

PROBABILITY

We can use *will*, *must*, *should*, *might*, *may*, and *could* to talk about probability.

Most probable ↓ **Least probable**	*I* ***will pass*** *the Maths exam for sure.* *They* ***must be*** *at school. There's no one at home.* *He* ***should be*** *awake by now. It's almost 8.* *He* ***might bring*** *some dessert to the party.* *She* ***may bring*** *some friends to the party.* *She* ***could be*** *at the market.*

We can use *will*, *must have* and *should have* to talk about certainty and probability in the past, e.g.

They ***must have gone*** *to school already. There's no one home.*

Joel ***should have woken up*** *by now. His alarm went off an hour ago.*

We often combine these modal verbs with *probably*, *definitely* etc., especially with *will* and *won't*, e.g.

Amir ***will probably have finished*** *the work by now.*

She ***definitely won't be*** *on time.*

POSSIBILITY

We can use *may*, *might* and *could* to talk about possibility in the present and future, e.g.

She ***may be*** *at the supermarket.*

Marco and Eva ***may come*** *to the party tonight.*

They ***might be*** *at home.*

Anna ***might go*** *to school early tomorrow.*

He ***could leave*** *at 10 and still arrive on time.*

Sunil ***could be*** *late for dinner tonight.*

We can use *may have*, *might have* and *could have* to talk about possibility in the past, e.g.

She ***may have*** *finished her homework.*

Anna ***might have*** *already gone to school.*

Sunil ***could have*** *arrived already.*

We can use *cannot/can't* to show that something is impossible, e.g.

That ***cannot be*** *Maria. She's got long hair.*

That answer ***can't be*** *right.*

SPECULATION AND DEDUCTION

We can use *will*, *must*, *can't*, *might*, *may* and *could* to talk about deduction.

Most certain ↓ Least certain	
	*She'll **be late** for the bus; she only woke up 5 minutes ago.*
	*He passed his exams. He **must be** happy.*
	*Diego **can't be** in the office. I just saw him at the supermarket.*
	*What's that noise? There **might be** a dog in the rubbish.*
	*There's lots of traffic, so they **may be** late.*
	*She **could be** at the mall. She said she needed new shoes.*

We use *must*, *can't*, *might*, *may*, *could* + perfect infinitive to talk about deduction in the past, e.g.

*He **must have been** happy when he saw his marks.*

*That **can't have been** Diego in the office. He's on holiday this week.*

*The dog **might have crawled** under the fence.*

*He **may have been caught** in a traffic jam.*

*She **could have gone** to the shopping centre.*

OFFERS

We can use modal verbs to make different kinds of offers. We can use *can*, *could*, *will/won't* and *would/wouldn't* to offer things to others, e.g.

***Can** I **offer** you something to drink?*

***Could** I **get** you a chair?*

***Will/Won't** you please **stay** for dinner?*

***Would/Wouldn't** you **like** to have a rest?*

We can also make offers with *what*, e.g.

*What **will** you **have**?*

*What **would** you **like** to drink?*

We can also use *shall*, *can*, *might*, *could* and *would* to offer to do things for others, e.g.

***Shall** I **help** you with your shopping?*

*What **shall/can** I **get** for you?*

***Can** I **help** you with the door?*

***Might** I **carry** your bag for you?*

***Could** we **give** you a lift to school?*

***Would** you **like** me to open the window?*

WATCH OUT!

We can use some modal verbs in more than one way. Pay attention to the context, e.g.

*I **can't go** to the party on Thursday. My parents won't let me.* (permission)

*I **can't go** to the party on Thursday. I have a football match that night.* (possibility)

PASSIVE

We use the **passive** to emphasise the object of the sentence, e.g.

Amir fixed my computer. (active)

*<u>My computer</u> **was fixed**.* (passive)

My mum is cooking dinner. (active)

*<u>Dinner</u> **is being cooked**.* (passive)

We form the passive with *be* + past participle. The object becomes the subject of the sentence. We often use the passive when:

- we are not sure who the subject is, e.g.

  *The assembly **was cancelled**.*

  *The packages **were delivered** earlier today.*
- the subject of the sentence is less important than the object of the sentence, e.g.

  *Hamlet **was written** around 1600.*

  *These buildings **were built** in 1920.*
- we prefer not to say who the subject is, e.g.

  *Mistakes **were made**.*

  *The window **has been broken**.*
- we are writing a legal or scientific text, e.g.

  *The victim **was approached** by the thief.*

  *Water **should be added** to the mixture.*

We can use the **passive** with verb tenses and with modal verbs, e.g.

*China **is known** for its food.*

*My car **is being fixed**.*

*My homework **has been checked**.*

*Our house **was damaged** in the flood.*

*We **were being helped** by the clerk.*

*My hometown **has been visited** by many tourists.*

*The room **had been painted** by Joel.*

*The dress **will be designed** by my sister.*

*The tree **will have died** by then.*

*The car **can** easily **be fixed**.*

*The music **could be heard** from far away.*

*I **might be sent** to Cairo for work.*

We do not usually use the passive with these tenses:

- present perfect continuous
- future continuous
- future perfect continuous
- past perfect continuous

PASSIVE WITH *BY*

When we want to say who or what did something, we can use *by*, e.g.

'Romeo and Juliet' was written ***by William Shakespeare****.*
This house was built ***by my grandfather****.*

QUESTIONS

Question forms are covered in the tenses sections (pages 260–268). For other types of question, see below.

WH- QUESTIONS

We use ***wh-* questions** to ask for different types of information. We use:

- *who* to ask for people's names, e.g.
  Who *is that girl over there?*
  Who *is going to clean up this mess?*
- *what* to ask for specific information about something, e.g.
  What*'s your name?*
  What *did you buy at the shops?*
  What *do you do?*
- *when* to ask about time, e.g.
  When *is the next holiday?*
  When *are you moving to China?*
- *which* to ask about things or people, e.g.
  Which *book do you prefer?*
  Which *trainers are yours?*
- *why* to ask about reasons, e.g.
  Why *are you late?*
  Why *is Eva angry?*
- *where* to ask about place, e.g.
  Where *do you live?*
  Where *have you been?*
- *whose* to ask about possession, e.g.
  Whose *pen is this?*
  Whose *shoes are those?*
- *how* to ask about manner or quality, e.g.
  How *do you get to school?*
  How *good is the course?*

QUESTION TAGS

Question tags are short questions at the end of statements. We usually use question tags to ask for agreement or confirmation, e.g.

She ***doesn't look*** *well,* ***does she****?* (agreement)

You ***are*** *from Spain,* ***aren't you****?* (confirmation)

When the sentence is positive, the question tag is negative, e.g.

*He****'s*** *going to the party,* ***isn't he****?* (positive – negative)

When the sentence is negative, the question tag is positive, e.g.

You ***haven't*** *been to Qatar,* ***have you****?* (negative – positive)

With **auxiliary verbs**, we use the same auxiliary verb from the sentence to form the question tag, e.g.

*You****'re*** *going to the class on Friday,* ***aren't*** *you?*
You ***haven't*** *seen the film,* ***have*** *you?*
*We****'ve*** *been working hard lately,* ***haven't*** *we?*
She ***was*** *watching television,* ***wasn't*** *she?*
We ***were*** *cooking dinner together,* ***weren't*** *we?*
He ***hadn't*** *practised the speech,* ***had*** *he?*

With **main verbs**, we form the question tag with the appropriate form of *do*, e.g.

He ***lives*** *in Scotland,* ***doesn't*** *he?*
You ***don't*** *go to school there,* ***do*** *you?*
They ***went*** *to the concert,* ***didn't*** *they?*
I ***didn't*** *say hello this morning,* ***did*** *I?*

With **modal verbs**, we form the question tag with the same modal verb, e.g.

*They****'ll*** *be home for the weekend,* ***won't*** *they?*
I ***can*** *tell him,* ***can't*** *I?*
She ***could*** *play piano when she was five,* ***couldn't*** *she?*
We ***must*** *speak English in class,* ***mustn't*** *we?*
They ***shouldn't*** *walk on the grass,* ***should*** *they?*
We ***ought*** *to talk to them,* ***oughtn't*** *we?*

CONDITIONALS

We use **conditional sentences** to talk about possible or imaginary situations. Conditional sentences usually have an *if-* clause (cause) and a main clause (effect). When we put the *if-* clause first, we use a comma to separate the clauses.

(cause)	(effect)
if- clause	main clause
If it rains,	*we'll cancel the picnic.*
(effect)	(cause)
main clause	*if-* clause
We'll cancel the picnic	*if it rains.*

There are four basic types of conditional sentence:

- **zero conditional**, e.g.

if + present simple	+ present simple
*If you **drop** something,*	*it **falls** to the ground.*

- **first conditional**, e.g.

if + present simple	+ *will* + base form
*If we **invite** them to the party,*	*they **will come**.*

- **second conditional**, e.g.

if + past simple	+ *would* + base form
*If we **invited** them to the party,*	*they **would come**.*

- **third conditional**, e.g.

if + past perfect	+ *would have* + past participle
*If we **had invited** them to the party,*	*they **would have come**.*

WATCH OUT!

We never use *will* or *would* in the *if-* clause, e.g.

*If it **will** rain, we'll cancel the picnic.* ✘

ZERO CONDITIONAL

We use the **zero conditional** to talk about causes that always produce a certain effect. We use the present simple in both the *if-* clause and main clause.

We use the **zero conditional** to talk about:

- universal laws, e.g.
  *If you **heat** ice, it **melts**.*
  *If you **mix** blue and yellow, you **get** green.*
- causes which always result in the given effect, e.g.
  *If I **see** food, I **eat** it.*
  *If babies **are** hungry, they **cry**.*

We can also use the zero conditional with the imperative in the main clause to give instructions, e.g.

*If Lila calls, **tell** her I'm on the way.*

***Meet** me at the bookshop if we get separated.*

We can use *unless* with the zero conditional, e.g.

*You can't vote **unless** you are eighteen or older.*

***Unless** you water plants, they will die.*

UNREAL TENSES

When we talk about imaginary situations, we use **unreal tenses**. We can use unreal tenses to talk about the present and the past, e.g.

*We wish we **could come** to your party.*
(present: They cannot come to the party.)

*We wish we **could have come** to your party.*
(past: They were not able to come to the party.)

We often use these phrases with unreal tenses:

- *I wish*, e.g.
  ***I wish** I **were** a doctor.*
  ***I wish** I **had gone** to university.*
- *if only*, e.g.
  ***If only** I **were** taller.*
  ***If only** I **had studied** more.*
- *as if*, e.g.
  *It seems **as if** they **haven't eaten** for days.*
  *It looked **as if** he **hadn't showered** yet.*
- *I would rather*, e.g.
  ***I'd rather** you **went** to the party.*
  ***I'd rather** you **hadn't stayed** up all night.*

FIRST CONDITIONAL

We use the **first conditional** to talk about situations where the causes are quite possible, e.g.

*If my bus **is** late, **I'll call** you.*

***I'll move** back home if I **lose** my job.*

*If it **rains**, we**'ll go** to the cinema.*

With the first conditional, we can also use different present tenses and modal verbs in the *if-* clause and modal verbs in the main clause.

	If- clause			Main clause
Present simple	If Marta **comes** home early,	we	can could might should	go to see a film tonight.
Present continuous	If Marta **is arriving** today,			
Present perfect	If Marta **has arrived**,			
Modal verb	If Marta **can arrive** early,			

SECOND CONDITIONAL

We use the **second conditional** to:

- talk about unlikely or impossible future situations, e.g.
  *If I **were** invisible, I **would help** the police catch criminals.*
  *If I **won** the lottery, **I'd buy** a boat.*
  *If I **were** rich, **I'd buy** a house for everyone in my family.*

- talk about imaginary situations in the present, e.g.

  *We **would go** swimming if it **were** warmer.* (It's not warm.)

  *If I **knew** her phone number, I **would call** her.* (I don't know her number.)

  *We **would get** there faster if we **took** the train.* (We didn't take the train.)
- give advice, e.g.

  *If I **were/was** you, **I'd see** the doctor.*

  ***I'd spend** less time playing computer games if I **were/ was** you.*

We can use *were/was* in the *if-* clause, but *was* is less formal, e.g.

*If I **was** invisible, I would help the police catch criminals.*

*If I **was** rich, I'd buy a house for everyone in my family.*

We can also use *could* or *might* in the main clause, e.g.

*If I were invisible, I **could** help the police catch criminals.* (ability)

*If I knew her phone number, I **might** call her.* (possibility)

THIRD CONDITIONAL

We use the **third conditional** to talk about imaginary situations in the past, e.g.

*If Mike **had joined** the team earlier, we **would have had** a winning season.*

*I **would have got** better marks if I **had studied** harder for the exam.*

*If we **had** never **met**, I **would not have gone** to Paris.*

We can also use *could* in the main clause in some situations to express possibility, e.g.

*If Mike had joined the team earlier, we **could have had** a winning season.*

*I **could have got** better marks if I had studied harder for the exam.*

MIXED CONDITIONALS

We can sometimes combine the cause from one type of conditional with the effect from another type of conditional.

PAST CAUSE → PRESENT RESULT

We use this **mixed conditional** when a past cause would have led to a different present result, e.g.

past cause +	present result
*If you **hadn't caught** the bus,*	*you **would be** late.*
*If you **had brought** the map,*	*we **wouldn't be** lost.*

PRESENT CAUSE → PAST RESULT

We use this **mixed conditional** when a past and present (continuing) cause would have led to a different past result, e.g.

present cause +	past result
*If I **felt** happy with my French,*	*I **would have taken** the exam last year.*
*If I **knew** how to cook,*	*I **would have cooked** dinner for you.*

INVERSION

We sometimes change the order of a sentence to put the **verb** or **auxiliary verb** in front of the **subject**. We call this **inversion**.

Inversion occurs most frequently in questions, e.g.

***He likes** to play basketball.*	***Does he like** to play basketball?*
***She's** never **been** to Cairo.*	***Has she** ever **been** to Cairo?*
***They went** to the cinema last night.*	***Did they go** to the cinema last night?*
***We'll go** camping next month.*	***Will we go** camping next month?*
***She can ski** very well.*	***Can she ski** very well?*

We can also use **inversion** with **negative adverbs** and **adverbial expressions**:

- *scarcely*, e.g.

  ***Scarcely had I arrived** when he asked me where I'd been.*

  ***Scarcely did I** make it in time.*
- *rarely*, e.g.

  ***Rarely had** I **seen** a lazier team.*

  ***Rarely will** you **see** such beautiful paintings.*
- *under no circumstances*, e.g.

  ***Under no circumstances** will I shop here again.*

  ***Under no circumstances** would he ever admit defeat.*
- *never*, e.g.

  ***Never have I heard** of anything like this.*

  ***Never had she tasted** anything so delicious.*
- *little*, e.g.

  ***Little did I realise** we would soon be under attack.*

  ***Little did they know** the restaurant was so expensive.*
- *hardly*, e.g.

  ***Hardly had I recognised** her when she spoke.*

  ***Hardly had he closed** his eyes when the phone rang.*

- *no sooner*, e.g.

  No sooner had I left *than my phone rang.*

  No sooner had they started *swimming when it began to rain.*
- *not only*, e.g.

  Not only did he make *dinner, but he cleaned the kitchen too.*

  Not only does she paint*, but she also writes.*
- *not until later*, e.g.

  Not until later did I realise *what she meant.*

  Not until later did I find out *my mistake.*

We also sometimes use **inversion** to construct the **third conditional**, but this is very formal, e.g.

If Mike had joined *the team earlier, we could have had a winning season.*

Had Mike joined *the team earlier, we could have had a winning season.*

I could have got better marks if ***I had studied*** *harder for the exam.*

I could have got better marks ***had I studied*** *harder for the exam.*

We sometimes use **inversion** after **adverbs of place**, especially in literary texts. We rarely use this form of **inversion** in spoken English, e.g.

Under the bridge ***sat the troll****.* (The troll sat under the bridge.)

At the end of the street ***is a bookshop****.* (There's a bookshop at the end of the street.)

We can also use inversion with statements that begin with *here* and *there*, e.g.

Here ***comes the train*** *now.*

There ***goes the dog****.*

Here ***is my email address****.*

REPORTED SPEECH

We use **reported speech** to tell someone what somebody else has said.

Direct speech	**Reported speech**
'I'm tired today,' said Alex.	*Alex said (that) he was tired today.*

When we report statements, we use a reporting verb (e.g. *said*) and change the verbs as shown in the table opposite (above).

Direct speech	Reported speech
Present simple *'I like History,' said Eva.*	→ Past simple *Eva said (that) she* ***liked*** *History.*
Present continuous *'I am living in France,' said Jinhai.*	→ Past continuous *Jinhai said (that) he* ***was living*** *in France.*
Present perfect *'I have not finished,' said Solomon.*	→ Past perfect *Solomon said (that) he* ***had not finished****.*
Present perfect continuous *'I have been playing golf,' said Lara.*	→ Past perfect continuous *Lara said (that) she* ***had been playing*** *golf.*
Past simple *'I studied until 10 p.m.,' said Mateo.*	→ Past perfect *Mateo said (that) she* ***had studied*** *until 10 p.m.*
Past continuous *'I was living in France,' said Jinhai.*	→ Past perfect continuous *Jinhai said (that) he* ***had been living*** *in France.*
Future simple *'I will go camping,' said Eva.*	→ ***would*** *Eva said (that) she* ***would go*** *camping.*

We do not change the tense when we report the past perfect and the past perfect continuous.

Past perfect *'I had not finished,' said Solomon.*	→ Past perfect *Solomon said (that) he* ***had not finished****.*
Past perfect continuous *'I had been playing golf,' said Eva.*	→ Past perfect continuous *Eva said (that) she* ***had been playing*** *golf.*

We can also change modal verbs as shown in the table below.

Can *'I can play piano,' said Daniel.*	→ Could *Daniel said (that) he* ***could play*** *piano.*
May *'I may go with Paul,' said Ling.*	→ Might *Ling said (that) he* ***might go*** *with Paul.*
Must *'I must finish my project soon,' said Diego.*	→ Had to *Diego said (that) he* ***had to finish*** *his project soon.*
Will *'I will be living in France,' said Jinhai.* *'I will have finished,' said Solomon.* *'I will have been playing golf,' said Eva.*	→ Would *Jinhai said (that) he* ***would be living*** *in France.* *Solomon said (that) she* ***would have finished****.* *Eva said (that) she* ***would have been playing*** *golf.*

We do not change the modal verbs *could* and *should* in reported speech.

We change **pronouns** and **possessive adjectives** as shown in the table below.

	Direct speech	Reported speech
Subject pronouns	I/you we/you	→ he/she → they
Object pronouns	me/you us/you	→ him/her → them
Possessive adjectives	my/your our/your	→ his/her → their
Possessive pronouns	mine/yours ours/yours	→ his/hers → theirs

We change **time** and **place** words as shown in the table below.

	Direct speech	Reported speech
Time words	now today tonight tomorrow next yesterday last week last year this morning, etc.	→ then → that day → that night → the next day → the following → the day before → the week before/the previous week → the year before/the previous year → that morning, etc.
Place words	here this place (e.g. street) these places (e.g. streets)	→ there → that place → those places

REPORTED QUESTIONS

When we report yes/no questions, we:

- use *if*
- change the tense
- remove *do*, *does* and *did* (if necessary)
- use subject-object order
- use the reporting verb *asked*.

Direct *yes/no* questions	Reported *yes/no* questions
'Is he ready?' asked Marco.	*Marco asked **if he was** ready.*
'Are they hungry?' asked Eva.	*Eva asked **if they were** hungry*
'Do you study here?' asked Ling.	*Ling asked **if I studied** there.*
'Does Alex live here?' asked Joel.	*Joel asked **if Alex lived** here.*
'Did you see the film?' Diego asked Ling.	*Diego asked **if Ling had seen** the film.*
'Did she pass the exam?' asked Mateo.	*Mateo asked **if she had passed** the exam.*
'Was she eating dinner?' asked Jinhai.	*Jinhai asked **if she had been eating** dinner.*
'Have you ever been to Spain?' asked Ling.	*Ling asked **if I had ever been** to Spain.*
'Can you speak Chinese?' Lila asked Diego.	*Lila asked **if Diego could speak** Chinese.*

When we report *wh-* questions, we:

- change the tense
- remove *do*, *does* and *did* (if necessary)
- place the *wh-* word after the question word or object pronoun
- use subject-object order
- use the reporting verb *asked*.

Direct *wh-* questions	Reported *wh-* questions
'Why is she angry?' asked Marco.	*Marco asked (me) **why she was** angry.*
'Which shirt do you want?' asked Eva.	*Eva asked (me) **which shirt I wanted.***
'What are you doing?' asked Ling.	*Ling asked (me) **what I was doing.***
'Where have you been?' asked Joel.	*Joel asked (me) **where I had been.***
'When did you go to Cairo?' asked Diego.	*Diego asked (me) **when I had gone** to Cairo.*
'Who was at the party?' asked Mateo.	*Mateo asked (me) **who had been** at the party.*
'How can I get to the library?' asked Jinhai.	*Jinhai asked (me) **how she could get** to the library.*

REPORTED COMMANDS AND REQUESTS

When we report commands and requests, we change the verb to the infinitive form.
(negative) commands and requests: (*not*) + *to* + infinitive

Direct commands and requests	Reported commands and requests
'Give me the pen,' said Marco.	*Marco said **to give** him the pen.*
'Don't worry,' said Eva.	*Eva told me **not to worry**.*
'Have a seat,' said Ling.	*Ling asked me **to have** a seat.*
'Come at seven,' said Joel.	*Joel told me **to come** at seven.*
'Relax,' said Diego.	*Diego said **to relax**.*
'Hold on,' said Mateo.	*Mateo told me **to hold on**.*
'Don't talk,' said Jinhai.	*Jinhai asked me **not to talk**.*

REPORTING VERBS

Here is a list of common reporting verbs:

Verb	Reported sentence
add*	*Hannah **added** that it was late.*
admit*	*Alya **admitted** that she was wrong.*
agree*	*Adam **agreed** that the weather was nice.*
announce	*The boss **announced** he was leaving.*
answer*	*Zara **answered** that she would love to go.*
argue*	*The boy **argued** that he should go first.*
ask	*Omar **asked** if I had shut the window.*
boast*	*Fatima **boasted** that she had got good marks.*
claim*	*Sofia **claimed** she didn't know the answer.*
comment*	*Rui **commented** that the food was too spicy.*
complain*	*Daniel **complained** that there was too much noise.*
confirm*	*Ibrahim **confirmed** he had been sick for the past week.*
consider*	*Carmen **considered** that her friend had been helpful.*
decide	*Katja **decided** she would not to go to the meeting.*
explain*	*The student **explained** that his dog had eaten his homework.*
fear*	*Omar **feared** that he would not succeed.*
feel*	*Basil **felt** that he had studied enough.*
guarantee*	*Akira **guaranteed** that they would arrive soon.*
hope*	*Mia **hoped** that she would find a new job.*

Verb	Reported sentence
insist*	*Erik **insisted** that he would pay for the bill.*
know	*Tamika **knew** she would pass the exam.*
mention*	*Ben **mentioned** that he had allergies.*
observe*	*The girl **observed** that they had missed the last date of registration.*
promise*	*Stella **promised** that she would do her homework.*
propose*	*Leon **proposed** that they went home.*
remember*	*Rocco **remembered** that he had left his keys.*
repeat*	*Ichiro **repeated** that he had forgotten his essay.*
reply*	*Sonya **replied** that she had not seen him.*
report*	*Carlos **reported** that he had had a problem.*
say	*Li **said** it was fun.*
state*	*Felicia **stated** that she didn't know.*
suggest*	*Mike **suggested** that I went.*
suppose*	*Jeff **supposed** that it was true.*
swear*	*Rachel **swore** that she had locked the door.*
tell	*Amy **told** me she knew him.*
think	*Sandeep **thought** he had won.*
understand	*Andrew **understood** what I meant.*
warn	*David **warned** me not to come to the party.*

*In formal English, we do not usually omit *that* with these verbs.

ADJECTIVES

We use **adjectives** to describe nouns (e.g. people, things). We normally place them before the noun, e.g.

*What a **beautiful** day!*

*Is that a **new** handbag?*

*I love **Japanese** food.*

We can also place them after verbs, e.g.

*I am **cold**.*

*He remains **quiet**.*

When we use several adjectives to describe a noun, we usually follow a set order for the adjectives, e.g.

-ED AND *-ING* ADJECTIVES

In English, we can use some *-ed* and *-ing* forms as adjectives.

We usually use *-ed* adjectives to talk about how somebody feels, e.g.

*She's very **interested** in art.*

We usually use *-ing* adjectives to talk about the cause of the feeling, e.g.

*She's reading an **interesting** book about art.*

Number	Opinion	Size	Age	Condition	Shape	Colour	Origin	Material	Purpose	Noun
	handsome		young				Egyptian			man
two		large			square			wooden		tables
			old	dirty		red			running	shoes

*He wore an **ugly green** tie.* ✔

*He wore a **green ugly** tie* ✘

*I like the **big square** painting.* ✔

*I like the **square big** painting.* ✘

Here are some common *-ed* and *-ing* adjectives:

amused	*amusing*	*interested*	*interesting*
annoyed	*annoying*	*irritated*	*irritating*
bored	*boring*	*relaxed*	*relaxing*
confused	*confusing*	*satisfied*	*satisfying*
embarrassed	*embarrassing*	*shocked*	*shocking*
excited	*exciting*	*surprised*	*surprising*
exhausted	*exhausting*	*terrified*	*terrifying*
fascinated	*fascinating*	*thrilled*	*thrilling*
frightened	*frightening*	*tired*	*tiring*
frustrated	*frustrating*		

LINKING VERBS WITH ADJECTIVES

We use linking verbs to show a relationship between the subject of the sentence and the adjective. The most common linking verb is *be*, e.g.

*My parents **are** happy with my marks.*

*Maths **has been** easy this year.*

Other common linking verbs are: *appear, become, feel, get, grow, look, remain, seem, smell, sound, stay, taste, turn*, e.g.

***I'm feeling** very tired.*

*The children **are getting** hungry.*

*The coach **doesn't look** happy.*

*Dinner **smells** good.*

*The milk **has turned** sour.*

COMPARATIVE AND SUPERLATIVE ADJECTIVES

We use **comparative adjectives** to compare two nouns. We need to use *than* with comparative adjectives, e.g.

*Alex is **taller than** Marco.*

*My bag is **heavier than** your bag.*

*History is **more interesting than** Science.*

We use **superlatives adjectives** to compare three or more things. We use *the* before a superlative adjective, e.g.

*Alex is **the tallest** student in the class.*

*Marco's bag is **the heaviest**.*

*History is **the most interesting** subject.*

	Adjectives	Comparative	Superlative
For most one-syllable adjectives, add *-er/-est*	*clean* *hard* *neat* *short*	*cleaner* *harder* *neater* *shorter*	*cleanest* *shortest* *hardest* *neatest*
For one-syllable adjectives that end with a single consonant (not *w* or *y*) after a single vowel, double the consonant and add *-er/-est*	*big* *hot* *slim* *sad*	*bigger* *hotter* *slimmer* *sadder*	*biggest* *hottest* *slimmest* *saddest*
For one-syllable adjectives that end in *-e*, add *-r/-st*	*cute* *large* *nice* *wide*	*cuter* *larger* *nicer* *wider*	*cutest* *largest* *nicest* *widest*
For two-syllable adjectives that end in *-y*, remove *-y* and add *-ier/-iest*	*crazy* *dirty* *happy* *tidy*	*crazier* *dirtier* *happier* *tidier*	*craziest* *dirtiest* *happiest* *tidiest*
For most other adjectives with two syllables or more, add *more/most* in front of the adjective	*beautiful* *careful* *expensive* *important*	***more** beautiful* ***more** careful* ***more** expensive* ***more** important*	***most** beautiful* ***most** careful* ***most** expensive* ***most** important*
For some two-syllable adjectives, we can use *-(i)er/-(i)est* or *more/most*	*clever* *common* *friendly* *quiet* *simple*	***cleverer** / **more** clever* ***commoner** / **more** common* ***friendlier** / **more** friendly* ***quieter** / **more** quiet* ***simpler** / **more** simple*	***cleverest** / **most** clever* ***commonest** / **most** common* ***friendliest** / **most** friendly* ***quietest** / **most** quiet* ***simplest** / **most** simple*
Some adjectives have irregular forms	*bad* *far* *good* *well* *old* *real* *right* *fun*	*worse* *farther / further* *better* *better* *older / elder* *more real* *more right* *more fun*	*worst* *farthest / furthest* *best* *best** *oldest / eldest^* *most real* *most right* *most fun*

*We can use *well/better/best* to talk about health, e.g.

Lara was sick, but she's ***better*** *today.* (health)

Lara is ***better*** *at Maths than Sunil.* (general use)

^We use *elder/eldest* to talk about people in our family, e.g. *Sunil is* ***the eldest*** *child in my family.*

For general use, we use *older/oldest*, e.g.

Sunil is ***the oldest*** *boy in the class.*

COMPARING EQUAL OR SIMILAR THINGS

We can also use *as* + adjective + *as* to make comparisons when the things are equal or similar in some way, e.g.

Some hippos are ***as big as*** *small elephants.*

This winter is just ***as bad as*** *last winter.*

Paris is ***as beautiful as*** *London.*

Simon is just ***as intelligent as*** *Paul.*

Spanish food is ***as tasty as*** *Italian.*

NEGATIVE COMPARATIVES AND SUPERLATIVES

For most adjectives with two syllables or more, we can use *less/least* to form negative comparative and superlative adjectives, e.g.

This painting is ***less beautiful than*** *that one.*

Eva bought ***the least expensive*** *phone at the shop.*

We can also use *less/least* to form negative comparative and superlative adjectives with one-syllable and two-syllable adjectives that end in *-y*, e.g.

This is ***the least happy*** *she's been.*

We can also use *not as* + adjective + *as* to form negative comparative and superlative adjectives, e.g.

This exam was ***not as hard as*** *the last one.*

She's ***not as happy as*** *she was yesterday.*

My phone is ***not as expensive as*** *your phone.*

That film was ***not as bad as*** *people said.*

RELATIVE PRONOUNS AND RELATIVE CLAUSES

We use **relative clauses** to put two pieces of information into one sentence, using **relative pronouns** (*who(m)*, *whose*, *which* and *that*) or **relative adverbs** (*when* and *where*), e.g.

The waiter served us. He was very nice.

The waiter ***who served us*** *was very nice.*

I had pasta for lunch. It was very salty.

The pasta ***which/that I had for lunch*** *was very salty.*

I've only had my laptop for 2 years. It isn't working.

My laptop, ***which I've only had for 2 years****, isn't working.*

The film won an Oscar. The director of the film was happy.

The director ***whose*** *film won an Oscar was very happy.*

This is a house. I used to live in this house.

This is the house ***where*** *I used to live.*

I remember that day. I met Lucy that day.

I remember the day ***when*** *I met Lucy.*

There are two types of relative clauses: **defining** and **non-defining**.

Defining relative clauses give us information that we need to complete the sentence. We do not use a comma with these relative clauses, e.g.

The man ***who lives next door to me*** *is a pilot.*

(Now we know which man is the pilot.)

The boy ***who(m) I met at the park*** *is very friendly.*

(Now we know which boy is very friendly.)

We bought a house ***which/that is near the ocean****.*

(Now we know which house they bought.)

The computer ***which/that I bought*** *is very fast.*

(Now we know which computer is fast.)

With defining relative clauses, we can omit the relative pronoun when it is an object.

The boy ***I met at the park*** *is very friendly.*

The computer ***I bought*** *is very fast.*

Non-defining relative clauses give us extra information. We do not need this information to complete the sentence. We use a comma with these relative clauses, e.g.

My English teacher, ***who is from the UK****, knows how to speak four languages.*

(We can omit 'who is from the UK', so this is extra information.)

Diego, ***who(m) I think is very funny****, is always getting into trouble.*

(We can omit 'who(m) I think is very funny', so this is extra information.)

I'm from Qatar, ***which is known for its pearl diving****.*

(Everybody knows that Qatar is a country, so the information about pearl diving is extra.)

With non-defining relative clauses, note that we cannot:

- use *that*
- omit the relative pronoun.

ADVERBS

We use adverbs to describe verbs and adjectives, e.g.

*He runs **quickly**.* (*quickly* describes *run*)

*She is **utterly** amazing.* (*utterly* describes *amazing*)

There are several types of adverb: **adverbs of manner**, **adverbs of degree** and **adverbs of time**.

ADVERBS OF MANNER

We use **adverbs of manner** to talk about how we do something. We can form adverbs of manner with some adjectives by adding *-ly*.

ADJECTIVES	WE …	EXAMPLES
For some adjectives	add *-ly*	*close* → *closely** *quick* → *quickly* *slow* → *slowly* *sudden* → *suddenly*
For adjectives ending in a consonant and -*y*	remove the -*y* and add -*ily*	*angry* → *angrily* *busy* → *busily* *funny* → *funnily* *happy* → *happily*
For adjectives ending in -*le*	remove the -*e* and add -*y*	*horrible* → *horribly* *possible* → *possibly* *terrible* → *terribly* *simple* → *simply*
For adjectives ending in -*ic*	add -*ally*	*basic* → *basically* *enthusiastic* → *enthusiastically* *fantastic* → *fantastically*

*For adjectives ending in -*e*, note the exception: *truly*.

WELL

The adverb form of *good* is *well*, e.g.

*Hope plays the piano **well**.*

*Anna speaks English very **well**.*

WATCH OUT!

- *Lately* means the same as *recently*. It is not the adverb for *late*.
- *Hardly* means the same as *not very much*. It is not the adverb for *hard*.
- The adjectives *friendly*, *lively*, *lovely*, and *lonely* have no adverb form.

ADVERBS OF DEGREE / INTENSIFIERS

We can use **adverbs of degree** to change the meaning of adjectives. Adverbs of degree can change the intensity or strength of the adjective, e.g.

*The book is **quite** interesting.* (The book was not very interesting.)

*The book is **very** interesting.* (The book is more than just interesting.)

Some common adverbs of degree include:

- almost, e.g. *My homework was **almost** perfect.*
- completely, e.g. *She was **completely** horrified.*
- extremely, e.g. *Paul is **extremely** competitive.*
- nearly, e.g. *We are **nearly** frozen.*
- quite, e.g. *He's **quite** intelligent.*
- very, e.g. *I'm **very** sad.*

We can also use many adverbs of degree before verbs:

- almost, e.g. *Danny **almost** ran.*
- hardly, e.g. *I **hardly** know what to think.*
- just, e.g. *We were **just** leaving.*
- nearly, e.g. *He has **nearly** finished.*
- quite, e.g. *I haven't **quite** worked it out.*
- scarcely, e.g. *Richard **scarcely** survived.*

TOO AND *ENOUGH*

We use *too* and *enough* to talk about degree. When we have more than we need of something, we can use *too* before an adjective or an adverb, e.g.

*That cheese is **too old** to eat.*

*Does he have **too much** free time?*

*I am not **too old** to enjoy video games.*

*He is swimming **too slowly**.*

When we have as much as we need, we can use *enough* after an adjective or adverb, e.g.

*He is **rich enough** to buy a car.*

*Is your food **salty enough**?*

*This room is not **warm enough**.*

*She's not doing her exam **quickly enough**.*

ADVERBS OF TIME

We can use adverbs of time to talk about when something happened. We usually use them with past tenses or to refer to the future. They usually go at the end of a sentence, e.g.

*Paola went to the cinema **yesterday afternoon**.*

*Bo needed a ride **today**.*

*Safiya's going to a party **tomorrow**.*

*Jan will be sixteen **next month**.*

Some adverbs of time can go at the beginning of a sentence, e.g.

Today *I'm going to Hong Kong.*

This morning *I cooked breakfast for my sister.*

On Monday*, I was late for school.*

Last night*, there was a terrible storm.*

ADVERBS OF FREQUENCY

We can use **adverbs of frequency** to talk about how often something happened. They usually go after the verb *to be* and before the main verb.

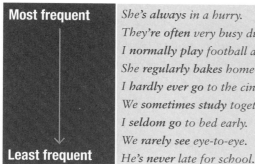

Most frequent	*She's **always** in a hurry.*
↓	*They're **often** very busy during the week.*
	*I **normally play** football at weekends.*
	*She **regularly bakes** home-made pizza.*
	*I **hardly ever go** to the cinema.*
	*We **sometimes study** together.*
	*I **seldom go** to bed early.*
	*We **rarely see** eye-to-eye.*
Least frequent	*He's **never** late for school.*

PREPOSITIONS

We can use **prepositions** to describe the relationship between nouns, e.g.

*I'm going hiking **at** the weekend.*

*My birthday is **in** June.*

*The pen is **on** the table.*

PREPOSITIONS OF TIME

We can use *at*, *in* and *on* to refer to times.

We can use *at* with:

- times, e.g. ***at*** *8p.m.*, ***at*** *10.30a.m.*
- meal times, e.g. ***at*** *breakfast*, ***at*** *lunch*
- times of day (or night), e.g. ***at*** *night*, ***at*** *midnight*
- festivals, e.g. ***at*** *Christmas*, ***at*** *Diwali*
- other points of time, e.g. ***at*** *the weekend*, ***at*** *noon*
- age, e.g. ***at*** *14*, ***at*** *the age of 26*
- + *time*, e.g. ***at*** *this time*

We can use *in* with:

- months, e.g. ***in*** *July*, ***in*** *September*
- seasons, e.g. ***in*** *Winter*, ***in*** *Spring*
- years, e.g. ***in*** *1745*, ***in*** *1992*
- decades, e.g. ***in*** *the nineties*, ***in*** *the 1860s*
- centuries, e.g. ***in*** *the 1700s*, ***in*** *the 19th century*
- times of day (except *night*), e.g. ***in*** *the morning*, ***in*** *the evening*
- times of year, e.g. ***in*** *the summer*, ***in*** *the holidays*
- periods of time, e.g. ***in*** *5 minutes' time*, ***in*** *a week from now*

We can use *on* with:

- days of the week, e.g. ***on*** *Monday*, ***on*** *Saturdays*
- parts of the day, e.g. ***on*** *Tuesday morning*, ***on*** *Sunday night*
- dates, e.g. ***on*** *June 1st*, ***on*** *28th March*
- day and date, e.g. ***on*** *Friday, June 1st*
- particular occasions, e.g. ***on*** *that day*, ***on*** *that morning*
- birthdays, weddings etc., e.g. ***on*** *your birthday*, ***on*** *your anniversary*
- specific days, e.g. ***on*** *Christmas day*, ***on*** *New Year's Day*

WATCH OUT!

We often omit *at* when we ask questions and give short answers about time.

A: *(At) What time shall we meet to watch the film?*

B: *(At) Nine o'clock.*

PREPOSITIONS OF PLACE AND MOVEMENT

We can also use *at*, *in* and *on* to refer to places.

We can use *at* with:

- points (places a person can stand), e.g. ***at*** *the front*, ***at*** *the top*, ***at*** *the corner*, ***at*** *the bus stop*
- points in a room or building, e.g. ***at*** *the door*, ***at*** *the window*, ***at*** *the front desk*
- buildings, e.g. ***at*** *home*, ***at*** *the hospital*, ***at*** *the school*, ***at*** *the restaurant*
- points on a surface, e.g. ***at*** *the top*, ***at*** *the side*

We can use *in* with:

- contained objects, e.g. ***in*** *a box*, ***in*** *a cup*, ***in*** *a drawer*, ***in*** *a house*, ***in*** *a flat*, ***in*** *a car*, ***in*** *a book*, ***in*** *a bottle*, ***in*** *a bag*, ***in*** *my stomach*, ***in*** *the bed*, ***in*** *the snow*
- buildings, e.g. ***in*** *my house*, ***in*** *a supermarket*, ***in*** *a hospital*, ***in*** *the city centre*
- wide, flat spaces, e.g. ***in*** *a desert*, ***in*** *a field*, ***in*** *a garden*
- bodies of water, e.g. ***in*** *a river*, ***in*** *the sea*
- places that we walk into, e.g. ***in*** *the mountains*, ***in*** *a forest*
- cities, e.g. ***in*** *Madrid*, ***in*** *Shanghai*

- counties, e.g. ***in*** *Berkshire county*, ***in*** *Essex*
- regions, e.g. ***in*** *the Amazon*, ***in*** *Andalusia*
- countries, e.g. ***in*** *China*, ***in*** *Ecuador*
- continents, e.g. ***in*** *Africa*, ***in*** *Asia*

We can use *on* with:

- surfaces, e.g. ***on*** *a table*, ***on*** *a wall*, ***on*** *the floor*, ***on*** *the first floor*, ***on*** *the screen*, ***on*** *her face*, ***on*** *a plate*
- names of streets, roads etc., e.g. ***on*** *North Street*, ***on*** *Mountain Road*, ***on*** *the highway*
- kinds of transport, e.g. ***on*** *a bike*, ***on*** *a horse*, ***on*** *a bus*, ***on*** *a plane*, ***on*** *a ferry*
- directions, e.g. ***on*** *the left*, ***on*** *the corner*
- electronic locations, e.g. ***on*** *the screen*, ***on*** *the internet*, ***on*** *the radio*, ***on*** *TV*, ***on*** *radar*

WATCH OUT!

It is possible to use both *in* and *at* for buildings. We use *in* when we are thinking of the building and *at* when we are thinking of the concept, e.g.

There are fourteen classrooms ***in*** *the school.*
I don't have a kitchen ***in*** *my house.*
I can't find Michael. Are you sure he is ***in*** *the office?*

I won't be ***at*** *home this weekend.*
I'm ***at*** *school until four.*
Doctors and nurses work ***at*** *the hospital.*

As well as *at*, *in* and *on*, there are also many prepositions of place, e.g.

It's ***above/over*** *the door.*
He's ***behind*** *you.*
The plant is ***beside*** *the elevator.*
The book you want is ***between*** *the two red ones.*
My bank is ***in front of*** *the train station.*
Is it ***near*** *here?*
It's ***towards*** *the bus stop.*
There is a nice picnic area ***below/under*** *the bridge.*

We can also use some prepositions with movement, e.g.

They're walking ***across*** *the river.*
He's coming ***into*** *the room.*
The dog is jumping ***out of*** *the box.*
The train is coming ***through*** *the tunnel now.*
He's running ***towards*** *us.*
She's climbing ***up*** *the ladder.*

ADJECTIVES + PREPOSITIONS

We often use prepositions to connect adjectives to a noun. The preposition that we use depends on the adjective.

OF

- afraid, e.g. *She's* ***afraid of*** *the dark.*
- ashamed, e.g. *He's* ***ashamed of*** *his car.*
- capable, e.g. *I never would have thought him* ***capable of*** *murder.*
- fond, e.g. *I'm* ***fond of*** *Natalia.*
- frightened, e.g. *He's* ***frightened of*** *clowns.*
- good, e.g. *It's* ***good of*** *you to help.*
- guilty, e.g. *She's* ***guilty of*** *four counts of theft.*
- hopeful, e.g. *I'm still* ***hopeful of*** *making the deadline.*
- proud, e.g. *I am* ***proud of*** *our results.*
- terrified, e.g. *I'm* ***terrified of*** *sharks.*
- tired, e.g. *I'm* ***tired of*** *English food.*
- scared, e.g. *We're not* ***scared of*** *a challenge.*

TO

- accustomed, e.g. *They're* ***accustomed to*** *eating dinner very late.*
- committed, e.g. *He's* ***committed to*** *moving forward.*
- cruel, e.g. *It's not nice to be* ***cruel to*** *others.*
- devoted, e.g. *They're* ***devoted to*** *each other.*
- good, e.g. *My parents are very* ***good to*** *me.*
- kind, e.g. *Let's do our best to be* ***kind to*** *others.*
- married, e.g. *She's been* ***married to*** *him for 10 years now.*
- opposed, e.g. *He's* ***opposed to*** *the plan.*
- reasonable, e.g. *That seems* ***reasonable to*** *me.*
- similar, e.g. *Coffee isn't* ***similar to*** *tea.*
- used, e.g. *I'm* ***used to*** *waking up early.*

WITH

- bored, e.g. *I'm* ***bored with*** *football.*
- disappointed, e.g. *She's very* ***disappointed with*** *her new computer.*
- fed up, e.g. *They're* ***fed up with*** *this book.*
- good, e.g. *You're* ***good with*** *animals.*
- happy, e.g. *Mike's* ***unhappy with*** *his new boss.*
- satisfied, e.g. *He is very* ***satisfied with*** *the service.*

ABOUT

- anxious, e.g. *I'm* ***anxious about*** *my exams.*
- concerned, e.g. *We're* ***concerned about*** *your marks.*
- excited, e.g. *He's very* ***excited about*** *this opportunity.*
- happy, e.g. *She's* ***happy about*** *the news.*
- nervous, e.g. *They're* ***nervous about*** *swimming in deep water.*
- worried, e.g. *Many people are* ***worried about*** *global warming.*

FOR

- famous, e.g. *France is* ***famous for*** *its cheese.*
- known, e.g. *Chinese is* ***known for*** *its delicious noodles.*
- recognised, e.g. *Milan is* ***recognised for*** *being the fashion capital of Europe.*
- remembered, e.g. *Shakespeare is mostly* ***remembered for*** *his plays and sonnets.*

IN

- disappointed, e.g. *I'm very* ***disappointed in*** *you, young man.*
- interested, e.g. *I heard you're quite* ***interested in*** *football.*
- involved, e.g. *They're very* ***involved in*** *the community.*

AT

- good, e.g. *He's* ***good at*** *cooking.*
- bad, e.g. *They're* ***bad at*** *singing.*

FROM

- different, e.g. *She's not very* ***different from*** *me.*

ON

- keen, e.g. *I'm quite* ***keen on*** *the idea.*

IRREGULAR PAST VERB FORMS

These are the most common **irregular verbs**, with their **past simple** and **past participle forms**.

Simple form	Past simple	Past participle
be	was, were	been
beat	beat	beaten / beat
become	became	become
begin	began	begun
bend	bent	bent
bet	bet	bet
bind	bound	bound
bite	bit	bitten
bleed	bled	bled
blow	blew	blown
break	broke	broken
bring	brought	brought
build	built	built
burn	burned / burnt	burned / burnt
buy	bought	bought
catch	caught	caught
choose	chose	chosen
come	came	come
cost	cost	cost
creep	crept	crept
cut	cut	cut
deal	dealt	dealt
dig	dug	dug
dive	dove / dived	dived
do	did	done
draw	drew	drawn
dream	dreamed / dreamt	dreamed / dreamt
drink	drank	drunk
drive	drove	driven
eat	ate	eaten
fall	fell	fallen
feed	fed	fed
feel	felt	felt
fight	fought	fought
find	found	found

Simple form	Past simple	Past participle
fit	fitted / fit	fitted / fit
flee	fled	fled
fly	flew	flown
forget	forgot	forgotten
forgive	forgave	forgiven
freeze	froze	frozen
get	got	got
give	gave	given
go	went	gone
grow	grew	grown
hang	hung	hung
have	had	had
hear	heard	heard
hide	hid	hidden
hit	hit	hit
hold	held	held
hurt	hurt	hurt
keep	kept	kept
know	knew	known
lay	laid	laid
lead	led	led
learn	learned / learnt	learned / learnt
leave	left	left
lend	lent	lent
let	let	let
lie	lied	lied
lie (down)	lay (down)	lain (down)
light	lit	lit
lose	lost	lost
make	made	made
mean	meant	meant
meet	met	met
mistake	mistook	mistaken
pay	paid	paid
prove	proved	proven / proved

Simple form	Past simple	Past participle
put	put	put
quit	quit	quit
read	read	read
reset	reset	reset
ride	rode	ridden
ring	rang	rung
rise	rose	risen
run	ran	run
say	said	said
see	saw	seen
seek	sought	sought
sell	sold	sold
send	sent	sent
set	set	set
sew	sewed	sewn / sewed
shake	shook	shaken
shine	shined / shone	shined / shone
shoot	shot	shot
show	showed	shown / showed
shrink	shrank / shrunk	shrunk
shut	shut	shut
sing	sang	sung
sink	sank / sunk	sunk
sit	sat	sat
sleep	slept	slept
slide	slid	slid
smell	smelled / smelt	smelled / smelt
sow	sowed	sown / sowed
speak	spoke	spoken
spell	spelled / spelt	spelled / spelt
spend	spent	spent
spill	spilled / spilt	spilled / spilt
spin	spun	spun
split	split	split
spoil	spoiled / spoilt	spoiled / spoilt

Simple form	Past simple	Past participle
spread	spread	spread
spring	sprang / sprung	sprung
stand	stood	stood
steal	stole	stolen
stick	stuck	stuck
sting	stung	stung
stink	stunk / stank	stunk
strike	struck	struck / stricken
swear	swore	sworn
sweep	swept	swept
swim	swam	swum
swing	swung	swung
take	took	taken
teach	taught	taught
tear	tore	torn
tell	told	told
think	thought	thought
throw	threw	thrown
understand	understood	understood
upset	upset	upset
wake	woke	woken
wear	wore	worn
win	won	won
wind	wound	wound
write	wrote	written

AUDIOSCRIPTS

UNIT 1: READING PREPARATION PART 2

p.15, Activity 1

Announcer: Welcome to the Ridgefield United Press Conference. The manager can now take questions.

Reporter: José, congratulations on your team's victory.

José: Thank you. We are playing very well at the moment and we are getting the results that we deserve.

Reporter: There was some controversy about the penalty kick in the first half.

José: Yes, the referee, unfortunately, is not performing as well as we are. The important thing is the other team didn't score any goals and we have three points, so we are feeling pretty pleased with ourselves.

Reporter: Fred Sandilands doesn't seem to be playing for the team at the moment. Lucas Harger was in goal today.

José: That's right, Freddie isn't on the team at the moment. Maybe next week. Right now, Lucas is playing and he is doing a great job.

Reporter: Can you tell me why Freddie is not playing for the team?

José: I am sure you know there are lots of stories about him in the newspapers at the moment. He's a little distracted by all the media attention. So, he isn't playing for us right now.

Reporter: All right. Now, let's talk about the future. Especially the club's transfer policy.

José: Journalists always want to know which players are coming in the future. They never want to talk about the players we already have! We have some excellent players. We are working and we are improving ...

Reporter: Yes, but people are talking about a transfer which …

José: I do not want to talk about transfers. I know the player you are talking about. At the moment, he is playing for another club. I have nothing more to say.

Reporter: All right, but is it true that you are offering over 100 million euros …

José: I do not want to talk about transfers. Next question, please.

p.21, Vocabulary and Grammar, Activity 1

Jeremy: Hello and welcome to Celeb Chat. I'm your host Jeremy Miles. Today we're chatting with overnight reality TV sensation and singer, Rachel Ritz. Rachel, please, tell us a little bit about the last six months and your experience with stardom.

Rachel: Hello, Jeremy. Well, it's amazing, really. All the fans are incredible and I'm really enjoying all the publicity. It's like a fairy tale.

Jeremy: So, everything's going well? You're not finding it difficult to deal with the lack of privacy?

Rachel: Oh, no. I'm an extrovert. And the paparazzi don't really disturb me; they go after the bigger celebrities.

Jeremy: Well, you're getting there, aren't you? I heard a piece of gossip about you, actually.

Rachel: Oh?

Jeremy: Yes, I heard this week on social media that you're signing for a major record deal, is that true?

Rachel: Oh, yes!

Jeremy: So, you're going to make the leap from reality TV star to singer? What amazing career opportunities you've had!

Rachel: I'm going to try! It's something I think I have a lot of talent for, so if people like it – that's brilliant.

Jeremy: Great, good luck with that and thanks for coming on the show. Can we have a huge round of applause for Rachel Ritz?

UNIT 1: READING PREPARATION PART 3

p.27, Activity 1

Gallery guide: This is an image of King Canute. King Canute was the ruler of Denmark, Norway and England more than 1000 years ago. He is a ruler with a very interesting story and people have given many different versions of it over the years. His date of birth is thought to be around the year 995 and he died in 1035, aged about 40. As you can see, the picture shows him standing at the edge of the sea surrounded by his servants and advisors. You will notice in the picture that he's wearing very rich and brightly-coloured robes. This, of course, is because he was a king and therefore had high wealth and status. There have been many paintings of King Canute over the centuries. This picture dates from around 1850. It is a well-known representation of Canute, even though it was painted so long after his life.

A legend about King Canute says that he once tried to command the waves. Here the sea is rising around his feet and he is getting wet. The legend says he did this to show that, even though he was the king, he could not control the forces of nature. This is why some people remember him as a humble ruler.

Unfortunately, there are not many records about the event, so it is difficult to know whether or not this story about King Canute is actually true. We don't know if he really did try to stop the tide. However, people still use the legend to talk about trying to stop the unstoppable. The tale is still popular, even now, because it is a good illustration of a fact: there are some things that we cannot change.

UNIT 2: WRITING PREPARATION PART 4

p.43, Vocabulary and Grammar, Activity 1

Jane: I'm glad we've already booked a table! It's pretty crowded for a weekday, isn't it?

Hassan: I agree. I've heard several times that it's the best place for fine dining in this area! No wonder it's popular.

Jane: You're right there. I've eaten here twice. The food was delicious both times – so mouth-watering!

Hassan: Even the cutlery is stylish – look at this knife and fork! And the way they've decorated the dining room … They must have hired an interior designer!

Jane: Probably! And the service is excellent, don't you think?

Hassan: I certainly do. Right, let's see what's on the menu.

Jane: Ooh! I've just seen what I'd like to order …

Hassan: Well, you're right; this does look good, but it feels as if there's something a bit strange about the fish.

Jane: I was just going to say that!

Hassan: It's got a sort of metallic taste to it.

Jane: Yes. Almost as if it's past its expiry date ...

Hassan: I'm not sure I want to keep eating it. I don't want to get food poisoning.

Jane: Me neither. Should we ask them to take it back, do you think?

Hassan: The head chef would be really upset if we did that. I've heard that he takes a lot of pride in his work.

Jane: But we can't make ourselves ill just to avoid upsetting him! And the fish is definitely odd. I think we should ask for a full refund. If that's not possible, they should at least bring us a different main course.

UNIT 3: LISTENING PREPARATION PART 1

p.72, Activity 4

1 The training for this job is long, but I think it's worth it. I help people every day. The most rewarding thing for me is treating young children and helping them to get well again.

2 My company has built bridges all across Portugal. We are well-known for using environmentally-friendly materials. My personal responsibilities include technical planning and working on site.

3 Sometimes I'm really busy, sometimes not so much. For example, last week I played in four concerts in three different cities, but next week I have none. I do practise for several hours a day, though, and I occasionally give lessons – on three different instruments!

4 I'm working on a case about gender discrimination. It's about an employee. She was unfairly treated because she is a woman. That's not right, is it? I help people fight for their rights and that's rewarding.

5 I get a lot of inspiration from my travels. I look carefully at the very different styles of dress, the variety of fabric, the different use of colour. I think people like my clothes because they're original.

6 My training is intensive. I work out in the gym for 3 hours every day. I also work with my trainer every day for at least 3 hours – normally on the tracks. I also have to be very careful with my diet.

UNIT 3: LISTENING PREPARATION PART 2

p.79, Activity 2

1 First up in the arena, we have one fine creature! He can fly high above the jungle treetops and there's no way you could miss his amazing bright colours …

2 And next! Please welcome one of nature's most elegant animals. Ancient Egyptians worshipped them as a god and a black one might bring you bad luck if you're superstitious! This beauty is only three months old, but she's already outshining all others in her category …

3 OK, now here's one fluffy friend that will have you 'jumping' with excitement! Those long ears and strong legs are just perfect for this little guy to hear you from a mile away and run off at any sign of danger! And who says that this one only eats carrots? This fine specimen eats a whole lot more …

4 If you're a water fan, you'll love this next contender! This golden female just loves to shake her tail and show off her colour. Some people say that these creatures don't have much memory, but this lady is an exception, I can tell you …

p.80, Activity 4

Dog trainer: Dogs enjoy activity and most dogs need several walks a day. That's good news for dog owners like me who love hiking. Older dogs may need shorter walks but they will still enjoy a change of scene. It is important that you exercise your dog in a safe place and that you always know where it is. Even if your dog behaves well off-lead, other dogs might not!

Walking your dog at night will bring its own challenges. Some dogs may not be seen very easily so it is important to make them visible to others in some way.

UNIT 4: SPEAKING PREPARATION

p.109, Activity 2

1 Well first down the runway we can see this rather stunning outfit that would be very suitable for office wear. The checked pattern looks really smart and if you pair it with the right shirt, this is a look that could be a real winner.

2 Checks are popular this year but so are spots, as you can see from these amazing shoes. Wear these to stand out in any crowd! They're guaranteed to turn heads on any occasion.

3 Next, turn your attention to the necklace this model is wearing. It's a heart-shaped delight and will go well with any look.

4 This trendy jacket is a real favourite of mine. Stylish and comfortable – it's a real winner and is the ultimate in looking cool.

5 This collection has a real emphasis on elegance – look at this fantastic hat – it doesn't get much more sophisticated than that!

6 Everyone needs to carry their belongings round with them – this model gives us an example of a perfect and stylish way to do it!

UNIT 5: READING PRACTICE PART 1

p.122, Activity 1

Oscar: So, Zelda, what's it like being a tour guide?

Zelda: Well, I must say it's a fantastic job. I've travelled all around the world, for a start.

Oscar: Really? Which countries have you visited?

Zelda: I was in Japan last week and China just before that. I've also been to Egypt and to India, as well as lots of countries in Europe.

Oscar: I would guess that you've seen lots of well-known tourist spots then?

Zelda: Yes, I have, although my favourite places are often the places that aren't quite so well-known.

Oscar: Oh?

Zelda: Mm. Some of the most awe-inspiring sights are the natural ones, like waterfalls, rather than buildings, although of course there are some 'must-see' buildings too!

Oscar: Yes. I guess you've seen all the world-famous ones?

Zelda: Most, yes. Although I haven't see the Taj Mahal yet and I'd really like to. Apparently, it's absolutely amazing. And I'd love to go up the Oriental Pearl Tower and enjoy the all-round, 360-degree view.

Oscar: So, what's it like actually working as a tour guide? Don't you get fed up, feeling that you're on call for 24 hours a day if something goes wrong for the travellers you're looking after?

Zelda: I can see how you might think that and I suppose it could be a problem. But usually things are fine. It's quite rare for there to be any big problems and if anything does go wrong, I can usually sort it out quite quickly.

Oscar: What sort of things go wrong?

Zelda: Well, sometimes people don't like the view they have from their hotel, for example. They may expect to be looking out at forest-covered mountains and instead their room overlooks a car park. That doesn't make them happy.

Oscar: No, I can understand that. So, what can you do about it? You can't build a mountain for them!

Zelda: Well, no. But if the hotel has any available rooms with a better view, they can arrange for the guests to be moved. Mainly, I think it's about people having full and accurate information when they book, so that their expectations are realistic.

Oscar: Definitely.

Zelda: After all, if they've paid for a three-star hotel, they can't expect a five-star experience!

Oscar: That's very true ...

UNIT 5: READING PRACTICE PART 2

p.133, Activity 1

Farah: Morning, everyone. I'm delighted to be joined today by one of my favourite science fiction writers, Abdu Karim. Great to have you here, Abdu.

Abdu: Great to be here!

Farah: Thank you so much for coming to talk to our group. First question: What got you interested in science fiction in the first place?

Abdu: Well, as a child I loved reading and I also loved science, so ...

Farah: Sounds like science fiction was perfect for you!

Abdu: It was. As as child, I just loved escaping to another world through reading. Reading science fiction was a perfect escape, with so many stories about what could happen in the future.

Farah: And what is it about science that interested you most strongly? What particular area were you most drawn to?

Abdu: I'm really interested in the theory of relativity and in nuclear physics and atom-splitting, but what interests me most is the concept of time and time travel.

Farah: So, I'm assuming that, like me, you're a huge fan of *Doctor Who*, then?

Abdu: Definitely!

Farah: So, what is it about time travel that appeals to you?

Abdu: I think we can learn from the past. If we went back to see earlier times, we could get inspiration from ideas that we may have abandoned before and maybe rethink if they could actually be useful in the present! And there are definitely some historical figures I'd like to track down and talk to! Science fiction lets us imagine a world where all of that is possible.

Farah: It's certainly an interesting idea ... If we met them, we might find that certain people would go up in our estimation!

Abdu: Or down!

Farah: Yes, indeed! And is this the basis of your new book, the one that's coming out this week?

Abdu: That's right. I'm going to upload the first chapter to my website on Monday at midnight and then people will have to buy the book if they want to find out what happens next.

Farah: Great. And can they post feedback on your website too?

Abdu: Of course.

Farah: Sounds good. And just before you leave us, Abdu, what, for you, is the main reason we should keep reading and writing science fiction? What makes it important?

Abdu: Ah, that's a good question. For me, it gives us an insight into where technology may be heading. Once the ideas are in place, it's only a matter of time before the science catches up.

Farah: Fascinating. Thank you so much for your time, Abdu. Good luck with the new book!

UNIT 5: READING PRACTICE PART 3

p.147, Activity 2

Piers: Hello Gabriela, it's good to have you in the studio. You've worked as an architect for over 20 years and have had a fascinating career. I'd love to start by asking you: if a young person came to you asking for advice about how to get into the business, what would you say to them?

Gabriela: Hello. I think it's important that they get in the habit of observing the buildings around them carefully. Try to notice the detail. People see the buildings in their area but they often take them for granted – try to look at how they work as buildings and whether they're successful.

Piers: You mean, when people see a building every day, they might not pay so much attention to it?

Gabriela: Yes, exactly. If you go abroad and look at a building like the Taj Mahal or the Leaning Tower of Pisa, you will tend to study it, because it's new; it's different. Try to look at the buildings in your own area with that same sense of freshness.

Piers: I see. And what about originality? Should architects all be trying to design the next Angkor Thom?

Gabriela: Well, originality is certainly important. But a building needs to be functional too. And it also needs to blend in with the landscape. If it can't do those two things, then it's not a success.

Piers: You mean they should match what is already there?

Gabriela: Well, not necessarily. But you wouldn't want to build a steel and concrete tower in a village that's made of brick and wood. You need to have a sense of place and not to impose something that doesn't fit.

Piers: I see. And finally, as an architect, what's the most important item to carry with you at all times?

Gabriela: That's easy – my drawing pad – I'd never be without it! I don't know what I'd do if I lost it!

Piers: Brilliant! Thank you, Gabriela, for joining us in the studio today.

Gabriela: Thank you for inviting me.

UNIT 6: WRITING PRACTICE PART 4

p.163, Activity 1

Steven: Breaking into the job market isn't easy for anyone, whatever their age. Getting your first job, though, can be particularly difficult. Unlike older applicants, you have no previous work experience and you may have a smaller range of skills to offer. As a younger person, you are likely to have less life experience. For example, you may have travelled less than someone who is 10 years older.

So far, the picture doesn't look too positive for the would-be employee. However, it's not all bad news! Younger workers are often a very appealing option for employers. For one thing, they are often keen to learn and to get a job. This can mean they are very well-motivated. It may also cost less to employ them.

If you are a young person looking for a part-time job, there are several things you can do. First of all, watch out for job adverts in the local papers and on the internet. Many shops and restaurants put cards up in their windows and recruit staff that way. Friends and family members may also know of job openings. If you are very lucky, they might even own a business where you can work! It is also important to look out for training schemes and work experience opportunities. Who knows, they may be the pathway to your ideal job!

UNIT 6: WRITING PRACTICE PART 5

p.173, Activity 1

Frank: Hi Nina, have you seen my new car? It's parked just here.

Nina: Oh, is that car yours, Frank? It's very big.

Frank: Yes. It's not just big, though. It's also very advanced in terms of technology.

Nina: Really?

Frank: Absolutely. Look at this! Power steering!

Nina: Hmm. Don't most cars have that nowadays? Mine does.

Frank: Ah, but that's not all it's got. I really love the seat warmers too.

Nina: Yes, but lots of people's cars have those. Mine does. So does Raul's. So does Michael's.

Frank: Michael's doesn't! I travelled to Manchester with him last week and the seats were freezing. I'd have been warmer as a pedestrian! I was seriously thinking it would be better to get out and hitch-hike my way to Manchester. Or to use public transport. I nearly froze.

Nina: Well he doesn't always use the seat warmers, but his car definitely has them. He mentioned it to me the other day.

Frank: If you say so.

Nina: And Michael's car has a really great navigation system too,

Frank: Well, we got stuck in lots of really bad traffic on the way to Manchester. Some of the time we were travelling at walking pace. And the sun was in our eyes for most of the journey too. Luckily, my own car's windows are tinted, so I don't have that problem.

Nina: Hmm. OK.

UNIT 6: WRITING PRACTICE PART 6

p.182, Activity 1

Michael: Today we have a very special guest on the show. Dr Janaki Gupta has just written a book on a fascinating area of science: how it can play a role in keeping us healthy in the future. Interestingly, Janaki has been looking into people's emotional health, as well as their physical health. Welcome to the show, Janaki.

Dr Gupta: Thank you.

Michael: So, I've tried to give our viewers a brief outline, but can you tell us a bit more about your book and the research that you did for it?

Dr Gupta: Certainly. As you say, the book isn't just about science and the body – I was also very interested in looking at issues such as emotional development, particularly in teenagers, and also at health conditions where emotional problems might lead to physical problems, such as a weakened immune system, for example. We all know that we are more likely to catch colds and other illnesses when we're feeling stressed. Some scientists are trying to develop technology that enables us to identify those times, so that we can do something about it.

Michael: Interesting. Although I suppose people already know when they're feeling stressed…

Dr Gupta: Well, yes. But this would be a more scientific way of measuring it.

Michael: Right. And are scientists also suggesting changes in the way we approach diet in the future?

Dr Gupta: Definitely. Experts are looking at ways of identifying really nutritious food and they are designing devices that analyse meals accordingly. So you sit down to dinner, type in what you're having and a score will appear on your screen based on how nutritious the meal is.

Michael: Hmm. That sounds … well … It might make people a bit less sociable at mealtimes.

Dr Gupta: Ah, funny you should say that. Social interaction was another big topic that we looked at. A lot of young people nowadays have difficulties with their sense of self. They don't really have a very clear idea of who they are and that is another area that scientists are looking into.

Michael: And what causes people to have these problems?

Dr Gupta: Well, it's a mix of things. A lot of it is to do with peer pressure – social pressure created by people in the same age group.

Michael: I suppose that whereas peer pressure used to come from people in your immediate environment, nowadays it comes from people you meet online too.

Dr Gupta: Absolutely. Scientists are trying to develop the technology to deal with that and to give people a more positive outlook.

Michael: Although you could argue that it's technology that's caused the problem in the first place.

Dr Gupta: Well, yes.

UNIT 7: LISTENING PRACTICE PART 2

p.205, Activity 2

Speaker 1: My branch of science is Geology. Geology is known as an earth science. It looks at the way that rocks are formed and the history of the Earth itself, so it's very exciting. We look at how gems like diamonds form and at the chemicals that make up the Earth itself. We're used to looking at natural landscapes. Geology is the study of how these are formed and much more. It's fascinating!

Speaker 2: Like my Geologist colleague, my interest is also in the materials that make up the Earth, but I approach them from a slightly different perspective. Chemistry is the science I have chosen to specialise in and it is interesting – in my opinion, at least – because it looks in detail at the chemical formation of, potentially, every single substance on the planet. It also examines the reactions between different chemicals and explores what happens to them at different temperatures. Why the lava inside volcanoes, for example, is liquid and how and why it hardens as its temperature cools. To me, Chemistry is vital, as it looks at the building blocks of the world we live in. Where would we be without it?

Speaker 3: Rather than studying the Earth, I study Natural History, so that means looking at the creatures and plants that live on our planet. There is an amazing range of creatures and vegetation on this planet. Even a single species can vary tremendously. Natural History also looks at the way that animals have evolved over centuries to live in specific environments. Take moles as an example. They spend almost all of their lives underground, in almost total darkness, and their bodies are really well adapted to this.

UNIT 7: LISTENING PRACTICE PART 3

p.215, Activity 1

Speaker 1: This is a language which is used by the navy. It's a way of sending messages using flags. Normally, a signalman holds two flags in different positions to show different letters.

Speaker 2: This system was invented in 1824 by a 15-year-old boy. It is a tactile alphabet which helps the visually impaired to read and write and is now commonly used internationally.

Speaker 3: This is the fourth most widely spoken language in the world. It is one of the six official languages of the United Nations. Its many varieties are spoken by over 420 million people, mainly in the Middle East and North Africa.

Speaker 4: This is a system of movements and gestures that people use in everyday life to show their feelings. Sometimes these movements are conscious (we are aware of them), for example, gestures like bowing or waving, and some are sub-conscious (we are not aware of them), like when someone is shy and folds their arms.

UNIT 8: SPEAKING PRACTICE

p.237, Activity 1

1 The first house I'd like to show you is a peaceful retreat on a mountainside. The roof is obviously organic, so this is definitely the perfect choice for a nature lover.

2 Next is another house that's pleasantly secluded, but this one is set deep in the heart of the forest. Lovers of fairy tales will be enchanted by it!

3 If you prefer a more tropical setting, how about this intriguing home built out of bamboo? The views of the palm-covered island are spectacular.

4 If you want to get really close to the water, how about this house? It's actually standing in the sea – property doesn't get much more picturesque than that!

5 Of course, if you're looking for picturesque, this flower-covered gem might be for you. It's a real feast for the eyes and smells delectable too.

6 Finally, for those of you who enjoy something quirky, how about this upside-down cottage, whose foundations point to the skies?

p.239, Vocabulary and Grammar, Activity 1

Jane: Well, for me the perfect kitchen is all about convenience. The design doesn't have to be completely empty and minimalist, but it shouldn't be over-full or cluttered. It should be clear where everything is and only gadgets and appliances that have real value deserve a place in it. For example, if your kitchen is nice and spacious, you'll have lots of room for items such as a dishwasher. If the room is a bit on the small side, though, adding a dishwasher may make it feel cramped, so you need to think carefully about whether it's really necessary.

Of course, the problem with some appliances is that they have very specific uses so they're highly functional but not designed to be decorative. Washing machines are a great example of this. They're essentially just large metal cubes, so they don't really look that attractive – although they can transform our dirty washing back into gleaming clean clothes again, all in less than an hour, so we definitely wouldn't want to be without them!

Given that a lot of the appliances you want in your kitchen, like washing machines and fridges, are often white, black and silver, they do lend themselves to a look that's quite striking, especially if you add a feature wall in a bright, bold colour like red, rather than a colour scheme that's more understated. Of course, the problem with kitchens is that they tend to look rather characterless – they're not really the place to hang pictures, or have candles, or photos, or vases, or anything else that may make a room look interesting and atmospheric. The emphasis has to be on hygiene and shining, empty surfaces are best for that – it's quite a challenge to balance that with making the kitchen warm and welcoming, though!

NOTES